# Marketing Kit For Dummies®

Cheat Sheet

## Close More Sales

If you are having trouble getting someone to sign on the dotted line, try using a different closing technique from your usual one. Here are some of the options:

- **Direct close:** Ask them if they are ready to place their order.
- **Trial close:** Ask them to make small decisions that may eventually add up to a completed order.
- **Wrap-up close:** Summarize your presentation and their needs to set the stage for order-taking.
- **Process close:** Take them to the next steps as if they are going to order (for example, write down specifics of what they need).
- **Analytical close:** Examine the pros and cons of different options or otherwise analyze the prospect's decision, leading them to a logical purchase option.
- **Sales promotion close:** Offer a discount, time-sensitive extra, or other incentive to make the purchase.

## Newsletter Dos and Don'ts

- Do lay out your newsletter with plenty of headers, subheads, boxes and figures or illustrations.
- Don't invest in expensive four-color printing; desktop publishing or photocopying are best unless you have a large, paid circulation.
- Do build your own in-house list of customers, leads, and referrals.
- Don't buy an expensive mailing list; response rates will probably be low and it is costly to mail a newsletter.
- Do send your newsletter to a media list to generate publicity.
- Don't charge money for your newsletter.
- Do provide useful information, tips, and news about your industry.
- Don't go into your own products in detail or readers won't value the newsletter as an objective source of information.

## Does Your Business Card Bring You Business?

Most business cards are a yawn. They don't do any active image-building or lead generation. Why not upgrade this most basic of marketing materials into something that really works for your bottom line?

- Print custom business cards for specific events (your local copy shop can do short runs for you on the cheap).
- Design a two-fold, triple-sized business card. On the face it looks like a normal card, but open it up and you get a mini-catalog or brochure.
- Include customer quotes or testimonials on the back of your card.
- Design a contest (such as a lucky number drawing) and use your business card to distribute entry forms or numbers.
- Put a beautiful landscape photo on your card to make it appealing and memorable.
- Use unusual, high-quality paper to give your card a unique feel in the hand.
- Update your logo and layout to make your card look more sophisticated than the competitors' cards.

W9-AKV-724

*For Dummies: Bestselling Book Series for Beginners*

# Marketing Kit For Dummies®

Cheat Sheet

## Grow with the Four Ps

When in doubt as to how to improve sales and marketing performance, stop and think about whether you can take some action in one of the "P" areas:

- **Product:** Improve quality? Add new products or upgrades? Provide better service and support? Add a warrantee? Bundle products?
- **Price:** Cut costs? Reduce prices? Offer discounts for quantity? Offer discounts for loyalty? Offer discounts for timely purchases? Offer better terms? Guarantee a refund for dissatisfied customers?
- **Placement:** Increase the availability of your product(s) by adding more distributors, retailers, or sales-people? Expand your target market to new geographic areas? To new groups of customers? Sell product over the World Wide Web?
- **Promotion:** Improve the quantity or quality of sales leads through direct response ads, trade shows, a Web site or e-newsletter, direct mail, better brochures and letters, or a catalog? Polish your visual image by upgrading your business card, letterhead, Web brochure or other materials? Raise the stopping power of your ads or marketing materials? Write letters that create high involvement? Close more sales by diagnosing style issues behind tough customers? Use promotions more effectively?

## Generate More Sales Leads

To get more people to come forward and ask about your offerings, make sure you have plenty of lead-generating communications out in the market at all times. Here are some of the best all-around options:

- Toll-free telephone numbers
- Directory listings
- Web site address (in all your materials and ads)
- Reader service cards (in trade magazines, along with your ad or insert)
- Fax numbers (on all your catalogs, brochures and ads)
- Offers of free catalogs (through ads, brochures, directories, Web site)
- Coupons
- Publicity (any media coverage tends to generate leads)

If you turn one in three leads into a sale, then all you need to do to get 50 more sales is to generate 150 new leads. Not so hard when you look at it that way, is it!

The Hungry Minds logo is a trademark of Hungry Minds, Inc. The ...For Dummies logo and For Dummies are trademarks of Hungry Minds, Inc. All other trademarks are the property of their respective owners.

Copyright © 2000 Hungry Minds, Inc.
All rights reserved.
Cheat Sheet $2.95 value. Item 5238-4.
For more information about Hungry Minds, call 1-800-762-2974.

Hungry Minds™

## For Dummies: Bestselling Book Series for Beginners

TM

# ...FOR DUMMIES

# References for the Rest of Us!®

## BESTSELLING BOOK SERIES

Do you find that traditional reference books are overloaded with technical details and advice you'll never use? Do you postpone important life decisions because you just don't want to deal with them? Then our *For Dummies*® business and general reference book series is for you.

For Dummies business and general reference books are written for those frustrated and hard-working souls who know they aren't dumb, but find that the myriad of personal and business issues and the accompanying horror stories make them feel helpless. *For Dummies* books use a lighthearted approach, a down-to-earth style, and even cartoons and humorous icons to dispel fears and build confidence. Lighthearted but not lightweight, these books are perfect survival guides to solve your everyday personal and business problems.

> *"More than a publishing phenomenon, 'Dummies' is a sign of the times."*
>
> — The New York Times

> *"A world of detailed and authoritative information is packed into them..."*
>
> — U.S. News and World Report

> *"...you won't go wrong buying them."*
>
> — Walter Mossberg, Wall Street Journal, on For Dummies books

Already, millions of satisfied readers agree. They have made For Dummies the #1 introductory level computer book series and a best-selling business book series. They have written asking for more. So, if you're looking for the best and easiest way to learn about business and other general reference topics, look to *For Dummies* to give you a helping hand.

Hungry Minds™

1/01

# Marketing Kit

## FOR

# DUMMIES®

# Marketing Kit
## FOR
# DUMMIES®

## by Alexander Hiam

Hungry Minds™

Best-Selling Books • Digital Downloads • e-Books • Answer Networks • e-Newsletters • Branded Web Sites • e-Learning

New York, NY ◆ Cleveland, OH ◆ Indianapolis, IN

**Marketing Kit For Dummies®**

Published by
**Hungry Minds, Inc.**
909 Third Avenue
New York, NY 10022
www.hungryminds.com
www.dummies.com

Copyright © 2000 Hungry Minds Inc. All rights reserved. No part of this book, including interior design, cover design, and icons, may be reproduced or transmitted in any form, by any means (electronic, photocopying, recording, or otherwise) without the prior written permission of the publisher.

Library of Congress Catalog Card No.: 99-69723

ISBN: 0-7645-5238-4

Printed in the United States of America

10 9 8 7 6 5 4 3 2

1B/RW/QR/QS/IN

Distributed in the United States by Hungry Minds, Inc.

Distributed by CDG Books Canada Inc. for Canada; by Transworld Publishers Limited in the United Kingdom; by IDG Norge Books for Norway; by IDG Sweden Books for Sweden; by IDG Books Australia Publishing Corporation Pty. Ltd. for Australia and New Zealand; by TransQuest Publishers Pte Ltd. for Singapore, Malaysia, Thailand, Indonesia, and Hong Kong; by Gotop Information Inc. for Taiwan; by ICG Muse, Inc. for Japan; by Intersoft for South Africa; by Eyrolles for France; by International Thomson Publishing for Germany, Austria and Switzerland; by Distribuidora Cuspide for Argentina; by LR International for Brazil; by Galileo Libros for Chile; by Ediciones ZETA S.C.R. Ltda. for Peru; by WS Computer Publishing Corporation, Inc., for the Philippines; by Contemporanea de Ediciones for Venezuela; by Express Computer Distributors for the Caribbean and West Indies; by Micronesia Media Distributor, Inc. for Micronesia; by Chips Computadoras S.A. de C.V. for Mexico; by Editorial Norma de Panama S.A. for Panama; by American Bookshops for Finland.

For general information on Hungry Minds' products and services please contact our Customer Care Department within the U.S. at 800-762-2974, outside the U.S. at 317-572-3993 or fax 317-572-4002.

For sales inquiries and reseller information, including discounts, premium and bulk quantity sales, and foreign-language translations, please contact our Customer Care Department at 800-434-3422, fax 317-572-4002, or write to Hungry Minds, Inc., Attn: Customer Care Department, 10475 Crosspoint Boulevard, Indianapolis, IN 46256.

For information on licensing foreign or domestic rights, please contact our Sub-Rights Customer Care Department at 212-884-5000.

For information on using Hungry Minds' products and services in the classroom or for ordering examination copies, please contact our Educational Sales Department at 800-434-2086 or fax 317-572-4005.

Please contact our Public Relations Department at 212-884-5163 for press review copies or 212-884-5000 for author interviews and other publicity information or fax 212-884-5400.

For authorization to photocopy items for corporate, personal, or educational use, please contact Copyright Clearance Center, 222 Rosewood Drive, Danvers, MA 01923, or fax 978-750-4470.

**LIMIT OF LIABILITY/DISCLAIMER OF WARRANTY:** THE PUBLISHER AND AUTHOR HAVE USED THEIR BEST EFFORTS IN PREPARING THIS BOOK. THE PUBLISHER AND AUTHOR MAKE NO REPRESENTATIONS OR WARRANTIES WITH RESPECT TO THE ACCURACY OR COMPLETENESS OF THE CONTENTS OF THIS BOOK AND SPECIFICALLY DISCLAIM ANY IMPLIED WARRANTIES OF MERCHANTABILITY OR FITNESS FOR A PARTICULAR PURPOSE. THERE ARE NO WARRANTIES WHICH EXTEND BEYOND THE DESCRIPTIONS CONTAINED IN THIS PARAGRAPH. NO WARRANTY MAY BE CREATED OR EXTENDED BY SALES REPRESENTATIVES OR WRITTEN SALES MATERIALS. THE ACCURACY AND COMPLETENESS OF THE INFORMATION PROVIDED HEREIN AND THE OPINIONS STATED HEREIN ARE NOT GUARANTEED OR WARRANTED TO PRODUCE ANY PARTICULAR RESULTS, AND THE ADVICE AND STRATEGIES CONTAINED HEREIN MAY NOT BE SUITABLE FOR EVERY INDIVIDUAL. NEITHER THE PUBLISHER NOR AUTHOR SHALL BE LIABLE FOR ANY LOSS OF PROFIT OR ANY OTHER COMMERCIAL DAMAGES, INCLUDING BUT NOT LIMITED TO SPECIAL, INCIDENTAL, CONSEQUENTIAL, OR OTHER DAMAGES.

**Trademarks:** For Dummies, Dummies Man, A Reference for the Rest of Us!, The Dummies Way, Dummies Daily, and related trade dress are registered trademarks or trademarks of Hungry Minds, Inc. in the United States and other countries, and may not be used without written permission. All other trademarks are the property of their respective owners. Hungry Minds, Inc. is not associated with any product or vendor mentioned in this book.

Hungry Minds™  is a trademark of Hungry Minds, Inc.

# About the Author

Alex Hiam's consulting and training firm, Alexander Hiam & Associates, is active in a variety of sales and marketing areas, including the following:

- ✔ Facilitating creative new product and customer development sessions for companies such as Coca Cola and Kellogg's.
- ✔ Consulting on motivation and rewards for sales and service people.
- ✔ Providing training events or materials for use in sales, sales management, customer relationship, negotiation, conflict-handling, customer service, creativity, and other marketing-related topics.

Hiam has authored several popular books on marketing, including *The Portable MBA in Marketing, Marketing For Dummies,* and *The Vest-Pocket Marketer.* His *Motivating & Rewarding Employees* book addresses issues related to the motivation and supervision of sales and service personnel, among other topics. He has also authored a variety of training and assessment products and programs in the sales, service, and marketing areas, including the Creativity by Design workshop, the Personal Creativity Assessment, The Manager's Pocket Guide to Creativity, Creative Roles Analysis, the Managing Critical Incidents course, Dealing with Difficult Customers, Profiling New Customers to Plan Your Interpersonal Style, and the Attitudes of Success Profile. (See AlexHiam.com for details.)

Hiam received degrees from Harvard and U.C. Berkeley's Haas School of business, and was on the faculty of the marketing department at the University of Massachusetts, Amherst, for five years. You may reach his office at 413-253-3658 or hiam@javanet.com with inquires about training materials, consultations, presentations or workshops, or to request additional information.

# Author's Acknowledgments

This book includes contributions from dozens and dozens of marketers — too many even to list them all here! Many thanks to all of you who shared your methods, materials, tips and techniques. Your marketing materials and ideas are to be found throughout this book and accompanying CD, and I know readers will be as grateful as I am for your generosity.

I also wish to acknowledge the many clients of my consulting and training firm who have often served as test subjects in the development of my own marketing methods. You've helped me refine many of the tools included in this book and CD, from sales training to marketing communications, from Web strategies to creativity, and from the endless details of winning tactics to the fundamentals of great strategies and plans.

And thanks finally to the great team that makes it possible for me to produce great products, including Stephanie Sousbies-Forgette, Celia Rocks, Dottie DeHart, and Happi Cramer.

## Publisher's Acknowledgments

We're proud of this book; please send us your comments through our Online Registration Form located at www.dummies.com.

Some of the people who helped bring this book to market include the following:

### Acquisitions, Editorial, and Media Development

**Project Editor:** Colleen Totz

**Acquisitions Editor:** Karen Hanson

**Copy Editor:** Janet Withers

**Acquisitions Coordinator:** Jill Alexander

**Technical Editor:** Celia Rocks

**Editorial Manager:** Pam Mourouzis

**Editorial Assistant:** Carol Strickland

**Media Development Manager:**
Heather Heath Dismore

**Permissions Editor:** Carmen Krikorian

**Associate Media Development Specialist:**
Megan Decraene

**Media Development Assistant:** Marisa Pearman

### Production

**Project Coordinator:** Regina Snyder

**Layout and Graphics:** Amy Amrian, Karl Brandt, Barry Offringa, Tracy K. Oliver, Jill Piscitelli, Jacque Schneider, Janet Seib, Brian Torwelle

**Proofreaders:** Vickie Broyles, Christine Pingleton, Toni Settle, Charles Spencer

**Indexer:** Liz Cunningham

### General and Administrative

**Hungry Minds, Inc.:** John Kilcullen, CEO; Bill Barry, President and COO; John Ball, Executive VP, Operations & Administration; John Harris, Executive VP and CFO

**Hungry Minds Consumer Reference Group**

**Business:** Kathleen A. Welton, Vice President and Publisher; Kevin Thornton, Acquisitions Manager

**Cooking/Gardening:** Jennifer Feldman, Associate Vice President and Publisher

**Education/Reference:** Diane Graves Steele, Vice President and Publisher

**Lifestyles/Pets:** Kathleen Nebenhaus, Vice President and Publisher; Tracy Boggier, Managing Editor

**Travel:** Michael Spring, Vice President and Publisher; Suzanne Jannetta, Editorial Director; Brice Gosnell, Publishing Director

**Hungry Minds Consumer Editorial Services:** Kathleen Nebenhaus, Vice President and Publisher; Kristin A. Cocks, Editorial Director; Cindy Kitchel, Editorial Director

**Hungry Minds Consumer Production:** Debbie Stailey, Production Director

# Contents at a Glance

# Cartoons at a Glance

### By Rich Tennant

page 181

page 5

page 323

page 79

page 271

*Fax:* 978-546-7747

*E-mail:* richtennant@the5thwave.com

*World Wide Web:* www.the5thwave.com

# Table of Contents

# Part 3: Creating Great Marketing Communications ......181

# Introduction

**·······································································**

*N*o matter what you do in business, you are dependent upon the smooth, successful functioning of sales and marketing. Every business exists because and only because customers are willing to enter into business with it.

Where do these mysterious and wonderful customers come from? What makes them pick you over any of their multitudinous alternatives? Where do they go when they desert you? How can you get more? People have an understandable curiosity about such questions. And people who succeed in business, no matter the business, take their interest in customers much further than mere curiosity. To be successful means to attract and retain customers better. There is no other path to business success. That's what all business strategies must boil down to if they are to succeed.

But how? What can you do, today, to boost sales, attract new customers, retain old customers? In my first book for the *For Dummies* series, *Marketing For Dummies,* I addressed many of the practical concerns related to this urgent question. Now, in this new kit, I have been able to complement that coverage with entirely new information, resources and tools for the active salesperson or manager.

## Who Should Read This Book

*Marketing Kit For Dummies* has been written for all those who wish to take responsibility for any aspect of sales or marketing in their organizations — whether those organizations be as small as a one-person operation or as large as a multinational corporation.

It is certainly written for the hundreds of thousands of readers of my earlier marketing books, many of whom have called, e-mailed or written to share their interesting challenges and achievements in the past. They will find exciting new resources in this book to take them further than ever before. But this kit was also developed with a new generation of marketers in mind — from dot-com entrepreneurs to newly appointed marketing managers, from big-company executives to owners of family businesses, from front-line service and sales people to managers of customer-oriented functions.

It is also focused on helping readers communicate better with customers. Whether person-to-person, through a letter, the telephone, a brochure, a Web site or any other medium, your customer communications play a vital role in the success of your business. I've cued up an immense amount of information, resources and templates to help you improve your customer communications and your overall business image. Have a peek at the contents of the CD to see what I mean!

# What You'll Gain from This Book

The book covers a wide range of subjects and offers much to help anyone in business, including:

- Insights into how to successfully close the sale through improved sales or marketing techniques.

- Lots and lots and lots of tools you can use, right on your computer or even in the pages of the book, to perform useful sales and marketing activities with greater ease.

- Plenty of ideas, examples, tips, and templates to make your sales and marketing materials look great — and function well, too.

- Neat marketing software we've collected, with functional demo copies right on the CD.

- A library of original stock photos for use in your advertising, brochures, catalog covers, Web pages, or wherever.

- A collection of advertising templates, brochure templates, even templates for letterhead and business cards.

- Marketing plans and audits — with templates and forms as well as instructions.

- Plenty of hands-on tools and activities to help you boost your own personal performance in sales and marketing, many of them borrowed from high-level corporate training events and workshops.

- Your own Web page. Yup, here it is, a simple template you can use to create a "virtual" catalog for your business if you don't have one already, along with tips for improving and promoting existing sites.

# How This Book Is Organized

*Marketing Kit For Dummies* consists of 20 chapters and a CD-ROM with examples, templates, forms, and software organized to support and extend each chapter's coverage.

# Part I: Sales and Marketing Success

The opening chapter covers the gist of an introductory course in marketing in a few pages (I don't like to spend too much time on that stuff!) and then sets up a more action-oriented approach you can use to pursue rapid results. The next few chapters focus on the essential core of marketing, the individual sale and how to bring it about. Salespeople, service personnel and managers, entrepreneurs, and anyone else who depends on good personal relationships for their business success will find many new and useful techniques and tools in these chapters. Part I wraps up with a provocative chapter on how to make better use of referrals and quotes from customers — and how this underutilized strategy can work wonders for you.

# Part II: Research, Audits, and Plans

The first two chapters address the need to "know thy customer" as the old saying goes. They cover standard customer surveys and rapid forms of research. And you'll find an interesting diagnostic tool you can use to learn how to deal with that difficult customer who just doesn't seem to respond to your efforts. Also included in this part are the tough but necessary chores of performing a marketing audit or writing marketing plans. The CD permits me to include helpful tools to make diagnosis, planning, and budgeting far easier and more structured than it usually is, so take advantage of these helpful tools next time you need to role up your sleeves and do some serious analysis or planning.

# Part III: Creating Great Marketing Communications

Whether you want coverage in the press, an effective mailing, a new look for your logo and business cards, a newsletter that generates good sales leads, or a great advertisement, you'll find much to assist you in this section. Along with detailed chapters on all these and more, you'll find templates, inspirational examples, and lots and lots of advice on how to do it right. Marketing communications is a difficult art. Most efforts to communicate with and woo customers are actually unsuccessful! So please take the time to utilize the resources in this part before you communicate with your customers.

# Part IV: Web Marketing Techniques

In these three chapters, I cover the essentials of representing any business on the Web. Whether your strategy involves an appealing Web site, the use of advertising on other sites, or the use of an electronic newsletter, you'll find plenty of ideas and hands-on techniques to help you execute the strategy quickly and successfully. The Internet provides many new opportunities in sales and marketing that this part can help you take advantage of.

## Part V: The Part of Tens

Some readers might want to start here, with this part's useful information on how to be a more creative marketer (creativity does drive marketing success, after all!) and the collection of hot marketing ideas you can try.

And don't overlook the appendix on how to use the CD that's attached to the inside back cover of this book.

# Icons Used in This Book

I occasionally use little pictures, called *icons,* to flag certain passages. Here's what the icons mean:

A generally good idea.

An example of the method or approach in successful use.

Ideas or methods for Web marketing.

An area of concern or a tip to avoid trouble.

An example, form, or illustration on the CD.

Specific techniques or methods to achieve your goal.

# Part I
# Sales and Marketing Success

The 5th Wave

By Rich Tennant

@RICHTENNANT

Art's AUTO PARTS

GIFT BASKETS

Gasket Greetings

Valentine Tune Up

Spark plug Sampler

SALE
1/3 OFF
1/2 OFF

"I don't know, Art. I think you're just ahead of your time."

# In this part . . .

1 help you frame your approach to marketing by giving you an overview of the profession and its variety of tools and approaches. Then I take you into a close-up look at ways of improving sales performance. Why sales? Because the point of all marketing is to generate profitable sales — lots of them!

All marketing programs need to affect the individual's purchase decision, either directly or indirectly. Often, that's through a one-on-one sales situation. Other times, the individual makes a purchase or repurchase decision aided only by arms-length marketing tools like a catalog, letter, or Web site. Either way, the more sophisticated your understanding of how to bring about that sale, the more successful your marketing can be.

Oh, and one more thing. Wouldn't it be nice to get your customers to do some of your marketing for you? This part ends with ideas for how to do just that.

# Chapter 1

# Getting Started in Marketing

- - - - - - - - - - - - - - - - - - - - - - - - - - - - - - - - - - - - -

*In This Chapter*

▶ Dispelling common myths

▶ Examining the Four Ps

▶ Getting in touch with your imagination

▶ The importance of people

▶ The five-minute marketing plan

- - - - - - - - - - - - - - - - - - - - - - - - - - - - - - - - - - - - -

The whole point of this book is to help you see your way more clearly to increased revenues and profits. To do so, you need to think clearly about the subject of marketing. That means understanding what marketing is — and what it isn't. I'm going to start this chapter with what marketing is not — just to make sure you don't go down any wrong roads at the outset. Then, I take you through a quick tour of what marketing can realistically offer you and your business.

## Dispelling Common Myths

Let me start by dispelling some common myths.

First myth: Marketing and selling are different things. In truth, all great marketing is about selling and often includes face-to-face sales as well as advertising and any other means needed to bring in the business. In many traditional companies, the marketing department is separate from the sales department, and so it seems that sales and marketing are not always one. But when they don't act as one, the company's revenues and profits suffer.

This kit reflects an integrated view of sales and marketing so as to help you use the best techniques and tools for the situation, regardless of what they are conventionally termed. In fact, I start by focusing on tools and techniques for effective face-to-face selling and then move on to approaches that operate more at arms' length. In great marketing, the same principles apply no matter how you choose to inform and persuade your prospective customers. And you need to be ready to use whatever means best fit the moment.

That's what an old-fashioned gourmet and specialty foods store discovered when its building was destroyed in a fire. The store is located near the sea in a quiet New England town, which might just explain why it's called Duck Soup, but then again it might not. Duck Soup's customers were loyal, and the atmosphere was personal and friendly. You could count on them to keep your favorite oddities in stock, and to make sure that you left the store in a better mood than when you came in.

But then came the fire. And the owners faced a minimum delay of six months before they could reopen. How to keep in touch with their customers and keep Duck Soup's spirit alive in the interim? The tale is picked up by *Inc. Technology* magazine, which featured a story on the business that opened with these lines: "Duck Soup's banner ad differs from other banner ads in three ways. First, it is seven feet long by three feet high and made of vinyl. Second, it is pinned to a chain-link fence along Route 20, the sole commercial thoroughfare in the country-quiet town of Sudbury, Mass. And third, it is actually driving people to Duck Soup's Web site." (*Inc. Tech* 1999, No. 4.)

The site's purpose was "to keep a beloved store alive in its customers' thoughts" according to Leigh Buchanan, *Inc. Tech's* editor and one of many customers who needed that lifeline when her favorite store burned down. And that so-called banner ad she joked about in her magazine is not a rectangle of purchased space on some popular Web site, but actually a traditional sign stuck on the fence surrounding the construction site which will house the store when completed. It said simply, "What's Up at Duck Soup? Find out at www.quackquackquack.com."

This story illustrates the flexibility and ingenuity needed to nurture customer relationships and build a strong presence in any market. If you fall prey to the myth that marketing and sales don't mix, you'll have a hard time being as adaptable as this marketer was.

But that's not the only myth to beware of. Second, it is a widespread but dangerous myth to see marketing as a set of formulas and rules that, when learned, deliver successful sales. In truth, marketing doesn't really have any rules. Each new marketing success makes its *own* rules. And only when you're willing to enter upon the adventure of invention will you discover what marketing is truly about. Certainly there is much to be learned about marketing, and many useful tools and techniques to add to your repertoire. But you must put them to work in your own way, and no one can tell you exactly what that should be.

And third, I'm afraid it's a myth that marketing can be learned by studying it in school. I've taught thousands of business students in introductory marketing and advertising classes, but I'm afraid that none of them were ready to go forth and do great marketing upon graduation. That academic knowledge base, while valuable in principle, is of no consequence until you add to it a practical education in the trenches of marketing. Because success in marketing is as much about getting things done as it is about thinking or planning what to do.

Often the things you need to get done are difficult things like designing a great ad or letter, making a great sales pitch, or developing and positioning a new product offering. There's a great deal of craft in the field of marketing, and little of that craft can be learned in school.

Some people are amazingly skilled at getting a company's name or product in the media. Others have a remarkable facility for designing Web sites. Still others create logos, letterheads, and business cards that help you stand out from the pack. There's really no end to the many specialized crafts within the field of marketing. Yet to be a good all-around marketer, you need to be able to use all of these specialists' tools yourself in a pinch, and, when funding permits, you must know enough of their craft to select and manage the experts well.

There's a lot to know about marketing if you want to do it really well. Yet many of the people I meet and work with in business seem to know remarkably little about marketing. I'm often startled by how little knowledge executives and business owners seem to have. Similarly, I meet many people who have been assigned a staff position in marketing for the first time and must do something incredibly difficult like run an ad campaign or write the next marketing plan — and in truth, they know almost nothing of the field. It's a little scary. But that's the sort of problem the *For Dummies* books were invented to solve!

# Starting Point: The Four Ps

When people think of marketing, more often than not they think of the *Four Ps*. I've encountered this phenomenon many a time when someone has asked me what I write books about and I've mentioned a title on marketing. "Oh, you mean the Four Ps and stuff like that, right?" is a common answer.

The Four Ps stand for four broad areas where you can look to find ways to boost sales or accomplish other marketing goals. The following sections cover the Four Ps in detail.

Of course, the Four Ps are not all there is to marketing. Of course, the Four Ps are just one of many ways of thinking about what marketing's focus ought to be. The Four Ps are a good organizing concept — a good place to start — but really it's worth, oh, maybe a hundredth of the time we have to spend on your marketing efforts. So I'm going to give you a good look at the model and then move on to a great many other approaches that build upon and extend the Four Ps.

# Product

To marketers, *product* is what you sell, whether it be a service, product, idea, or even another person (as in politics) or yourself (as when you search for a new job). When you think about ways of changing your product offering to boost sales, you can look at anything from new or upgraded products to different packaging to added extras like services or warranties. And you can also think about ways of improving the quality of your product. After all, people want the best quality they can get, so any improvements in quality generally translate into gains in sales as well.

# Price

To marketers, *price* is not only the list price or sticker price of a product, but also any adjustments to that price, such as discounts, and any price-oriented inducements to buy including coupons, frequency rewards, quantity discounts, and free samples. Any such offers adjust the price the customer must pay to acquire the product, and their main influence over purchase is usually through these effects on what the customer pays. Price-based inducements to buy are generally termed sales promotions by marketers, just to confuse the issue hopelessly. (You'll see why this confuses things when you get to the fourth P, which is promotion, not to be confused with sales promotion. Bet you wish you never asked!)

# Placement

*Placement* is where and when the product is presented to customers. You have many options as to how you place the product in both time and space. Whether you're dealing with retail stores, catalogs, sales calls, Web pages, or 24-hour-a-day telephone call centers that can process customer orders, you're dealing with that placement P.

Oh, by the way, marketers stretch a point by calling this third P placement, because it's more conventional to call it distribution. But that starts with a D, so it won't work when teaching introductory marketing classes where memory aids are of the essence. However, just remember that when people talk about distribution they are talking about placement, and vice versa. Which makes it simple. Except that. . . .

There is one other term you'll hear that relates to placement. Logistics is the physical distribution of products — their shipping and inventorying, and all the fancy transportation and information technologies that can be harnessed to improve the efficiency and effectiveness of your distribution processes. So logistics is another useful path to go down when you want to think about where products should be placed for easy purchase.

Distribution concerns where and when products are offered for sale, whereas logistics addresses how they get there. These are related concerns, of course, and so they both fall under the list of options when you want to think hard about placement.

# Promotion

Promotion is all the sales, advertising, publicity, displays, signs, and other activities designed to inform and persuade people about your product. (Remember, please, that "product" simply means whatever you have to sell, be it an actual product, a service, or even an idea or candidate.) I like to think of promotion as the face of marketing. It's the part that reaches out to ask customers for their business. It ought to be a visible face, and it ought to be a friendly face, because you can't just tell people what to do and expect them to obey. Instead, promotion must find ways to attract prospective customers' attention long enough to communicate something appealing about the product.

The goal of all promotions is to stimulate people to want to buy. Promotions need to be motivational. They need to move people closer to purchase.

Sometimes a promotion's goal is to move people all the way to purchase. That's what a so-called direct response ad is supposed to do. It invites people to call, e-mail, fax, or mail their order in right away. That's what many catalogs attempt to do, also. Readers are supposed to select some items, fill in the order form, and mail it with their credit card number, for example. And many salespeople have as their goal to convince prospects to commit to orders.

Other promotions do less. A 30-second television spot may be designed only to make people remember and like a brand, so that they'll be a little more likely to buy it when they are next in a store where it's sold. But all promotions work toward that ultimate sale in some way, and when you think about all the creative options for communicating with prospective customers, you should always be clear about what part of the customer's movement toward purchase your promotion is supposed to accomplish.

# Profiting from the Four Ps

So there you have it — the most famous model in the field of marketing: the Four Ps. You'll never forget them now. But will you ever profit from them? Not unless you use these Four Ps as a mental tool to think about ways of growing your business and boosting your sales. The Four Ps are just a starting point, the street signs at an intersection, and to benefit from them you have to explore the paths they mark.

The way to profit from your knowledge of the Four Ps is to do some creative thinking about each of the Four Ps every day. Stop and ask yourself these four simple, powerful questions, and see if you can find ways to build your sales by doing something new and creative in at least one of the Four Ps:

- ✔ What could we be doing to make our product more appealing?
- ✔ What could we be doing to make our product more accessible?
- ✔ What could we be doing to make our prices more appealing?
- ✔ What could we be doing to make our promotions more visible and persuasive?

Notice that these questions are open-ended. They don't have "right" answers. Instead, they invite exploration and experimentation. They tease the imagination. That's because it takes considerable imagination to grow any business or boost the sales of any product. You won't find any pat formulas that are guaranteed to work.

Marketing is not like chemistry or algebra or bookkeeping. There are no right answers. Only the answers you invent, test, and develop. After much thinking and trying, you will develop new and better formulas for yourself and your business, formulas that will give you pretty good results at least for a time and then will have to be updated or replaced in order to keep sales flowing and growing.

# Exercising Your Marketing Imagination

What's marketing imagination? It's the one term I wish everyone would associate with marketing if they only remembered one thing because it's a great deal more important than the Four Ps. In fact, it's the most important thing in marketing. Marketing imagination is creative questioning about everything and anything that might help boost sales and make for more satisfied customers. And marketing imagination is what drives growth and development in any business and in economies as a whole.

Look at any successful business, and you find that it has done innovative things and tried many new ideas. Business leaders are imaginative and willing, even eager, to try out new ideas and approaches. They have active marketing imaginations. That's why good marketing is creative marketing. It's always seeking new and better ways. It's always perfecting all four of those Ps.

# Breaking the rules in car sales

What can you do to increase the number of shoppers visiting a car dealership? This simple marketing question gets a lot of attention every day because there are so many dealerships competing for business. In the U.S., the usual answer involves local television commercials featuring attractive shots of the latest car models. Sometimes human models are added to the scene. An attractive woman may smile or wink from the driver's seat of a sports car. Or perhaps the owner of the dealership (usually a balding fast-talker) will stand stiffly on his car lot and deliver some wooden lines to the camera.

Sounds like an opportunity for marketing imagination.

C&S Motor Cars, a Connecticut-based marketer of new Pontiac and Nissan automobiles and used vehicles of all makes, wanted to try something different. They wanted to get away from the slick salesman image that characterizes so many companies in their industry. They wanted to emphasize customer relationships. They wanted to be seen as friendly and helpful, not pushy and sneaky.

But how?

First, they decided not to hire trained salespeople. They decided to hire nice people instead, people who are polite and friendly and good listeners. People who naturally want to help customers find what they're looking for. People who aren't cutthroat by nature. People who don't make other people nervous.

So they hired a woman who had raised four children. And another woman who had worked in ski resorts. You get the idea. Not the sort of people who have "super salesperson" written all over them. In fact, they hired the sort of people you'd feel comfortable dropping by to chat with.

*(continued)*

*(continued)*

And then they hired a regional ad agency, Darby O'Brien, to help them communicate their unique point of difference to prospective customers. The goal was to come up with an inexpensive ad campaign that would quickly let the community know there was a new, friendlier, more helpful option in town when it came time to shop for automobiles.

Now, this is a dream assignment for a good creative agency, because there really *is* a point of difference to talk about. The client didn't leave the creativity entirely to the advertising stage. C&S Motor Cars had already done some imagineering of their own.

All they needed was a great ad or two — and maybe a fly swatter, although they didn't know they needed that until Darby O'Brien had done some imagineering of its own. Here's what they came up with: an ad featuring a stereotypical car salesman along with "other pests" such as a mosquito, tick, and fly. The headline is definitely designed to get a laugh — but also to make the key point clearly and memorably.

Then the small print of the ad (the body copy, as it is called in marketing) goes on to tell the story of what makes this dealership different — a less-pressured environment in which it is comfortable to shop, along with good selection and service. As the tag line at the end sums it up, "Same cars. Different people."

Oh, and then there was that fly swatter. They bought a bunch of them and had a local screen printer put their name and tag line on the handles. And in their print ad, at the end of the body copy, it says, "Stop in and see us — you'll see why this dealership is different from the moment you walk in. We won't bug you, but we will give you a fly swatter, just for walking through the door. That way, if you do want to shop around someplace else, you'll be able to defend yourself."

Point made. And they make a good case for the power of marketing imagination, too.

By the way, did I mention that this campaign was not only inexpensive — ads ran just a few times in local newspapers — but also highly effective? The dealership's store traffic increased dramatically as a result, boosting sales significantly and making a lot of customers and marketers very happy.

# To Plan or to Imagine?

Oddly, creativity is often left out of books and courses on marketing. People tend to think of advertising as creative, but they overlook the importance of creativity in other aspects of marketing. Yet a creative approach to distribution can be very powerful. Think about the success of Amazon.com, the first company to distribute a large selection of books over the Internet instead of through stores or catalogs. I guarantee that you can innovate in your distribution and logistics in order to win more sales through placement if you are willing to be open-minded and inquisitive about your options.

Similarly, plenty of examples of creativity exist in pricing and product offerings. How many times does a business succeed by offering a new or different
product selection? Here's a simple example from the town where my offices
are located. Quite a few gyms in the area compete for customers, and one of
them recently made two simple changes:

- ✔ **Product innovation.** They introduced a new course on kickboxing,
  something that had not been offered locally before, featuring a high-
  energy workout that appeals to people who are looking for something
  new and exciting to do.

- ✔ **Pricing.** They advertised a first-class-free policy for the new kickboxing
  course, because they felt that people would really like it if they just tried
  it. The price promotion worked. It attracted a whole bunch of curious
  people, many of whom liked the free course so much that they signed up
  for ten more courses at full price. And some of them went on to become
  full members of the athletic club, using the weight machines and other
  services, too.

This example illustrates two important points about the exercise of marketing imagination. The first point is that you don't have to come up with something dramatically new. Sure, a patentable new invention might be a great
product innovation. But in general, you can make plenty of progress simply
by coming up with many small ideas. We're not talking rocket science here.
Anyone in business has enough intelligence, imagination, and funding to be a
great marketer.

And the second point is that you have to go out and try your ideas, try them
in simple, easy ways that don't expose you to excessive risks of failure.

Great marketing arises from frequent cycles of thinking and trying. You have
an insight or idea. You think of ways to try it out. You test it in the real world
and see what happens. You learn from how customers respond. This fuels
more imagining and planning, which then leads to more testing and trying.
And so the process goes on, in an endless loop driven by your marketing
imagination but firmly rooted in the real world of customer opinion and
action.

So the thing to remember about marketing imagination is that it's not only
creative but also experimental. Great marketers alternately wear two hats —
the hat of the artist and the hat of the scientist. They might have an "Ah ha!"
experience in the shower one morning and show up at work thinking,
"Wouldn't it be cool to do such-and-such." By lunch time, they've changed
hats, and are carefully reviewing their options for trying the idea out. By the
time they go home, they've already said to themselves, "I think I've figured
out how to safely test my cool new idea."

# Product, Price, Place, Promotion . . . and People?

Before I move on from basic concepts to all the neat tools and techniques of this marketing kit, I want to discuss briefly those infamous Four Ps and ask you a provocative question. (Provocative questions are a powerful stimulus for the marketing imagination.) My question is this: Should there be a fifth P, and should it stand for People?

My reasoning is this. The purpose of the Four Ps model is to help you apply your marketing imagination broadly to all the areas that can influence future sales. Well, if you can come up with even more areas to work on, then your marketing imagination has even more room to work. And in my experience, there's a great deal of room for improvement in the way we work with people.

In most businesses, people are responsible for many aspects of product or service quality. Help them work better, and you improve the product. And in most businesses, people are responsible for all the customer contacts, either directly through personal sales or service or indirectly when they create promotions aimed at prospects and customers.

And in all businesses, people are responsible for performing the many behind-the-scenes tasks and jobs that make it possible to offer products to customers.

Businesses and other organizations are simply groups of people. Sure, sometimes they use lots of fancy machinery or computer equipment. But there are no organizations without people. Not a one. And so when you're looking for ways to improve your offerings or otherwise boost your sales, it's often profitable to turn your attention to your own people.

There are many and often surprising connections between how employees feel and how customers feel. In my training and consulting work, I explore a variety of interesting techniques based on building the motivation of salespeople and employees in general, improving communications with customers, and handling service problems and customer frustrations.

The people side of marketing is certainly the least visible — that's why people are not traditionally included in that list of Four Ps. But it offers another powerful lever for achieving your sales and marketing goals. In this book, I include a bunch of people-oriented tools along with the many tools that help you apply your marketing imagination to successful experiments in the areas of product, pricing, placement, and promotions.

# The Five-Minute Marketing Plan

Here's a simple five-minute marketing plan (see Figure 1-1) you can prepare once a week to help you apply your marketing imagination and boost your sales. Or use it as the starting point for a longer, more careful annual planning process if you want.

The way to use this plan is to ask yourself each of the questions, and jot down quick answers to each. Then revisit your answers at least once a week to make sure that you are pursuing any ideas they brought up.

And yes, I really want you to time yourself and give each of the five sections just one minute. Because each section has two questions, you can spend only thirty seconds on each question, including both thinking and writing time. So this exercise requires almost instantaneous response. You'll have to scribble frantically to complete it in five minutes. And I want you to. As you'll see when you try it, attacking these questions at very high speed loosens up the marketing imagination. Fresh ideas may pop up, or you may find yourself bringing a long-standing assumption into question for the first time. So limber up that wrist, clear your head, take a deep breath of fresh air, and then glance at the clock and get started!

Come up with any useful ideas? Have a look at what you wrote and see whether any of the ideas are worth pursuing. In the majority of cases, people come up with at least one good idea in the five minutes it takes to do this creative-planning exercise.

And one good idea could be worth a lot of sales some day. That's the nice thing about using your marketing imagination.

You'll find a template for Five-Minute Marketing Plans on the CD (filename CD0101) so you can do this exercise regularly.

# On the CD

Check out the following item on the CD-ROM:

▪ ✔ Five-Minute Marketing Plan (CD0101)

**First Minute: Product**

What could we do right now to improve the quality of our product(s)/service(s) in the eyes of our customers?

What additional product or service would our customers most like us to offer?

**Second Minute: Price**

What could we do right away to cut costs without hurting our quality?

What offers could we afford to make to encourage new customers to try us or encourage current customers to be more loyal?

**Third Minute: Placement**

What could we do right now to make our current distribution process work more efficiently or effectively for our customers?

What new approach could we try to reach different customers or reach current customers in a different way?

**Fourth Minute: Promotion**

What could we do right now to make our customer communications more clear and compelling?

What new ways of communicating with customers could we try right away?

**Fifth Minute: People**

What could we do to increase our motivation and enthusiasm?

What could we do to make our customers feel more enthusiastic and thankful toward us?

**STOP! Your time is up.**

**Figure 1-1:**
The five-
minute mar-
keting plan.

# Chapter 2
# Mastering the Sales Process

- - - - - - - - - - - - - - - - - - - - - - - - - - - - - - - - - - - - - - - - -

- - - - - - - - - - - - - - - - - - - - - - - - - - - - - - - - - - - - - - - - -

*I*'ve chosen to start this book with two chapters that are largely about sales (based on sales trainings my firm puts on) because sales is really the essence of marketing.

Let me explain.

Salespeople and sales forces pursue sales on a one-to-one basis. So do many of the owners and managers of smaller businesses that cannot afford the luxury of dedicated sales staff or independent sales representatives. But sales also means something else, something more abstract and vague. In the marketing department of a big company, when people say *sales,* they don't really have in mind an actual transaction between a salesperson and a customer. They mean instead some vague, nebulous, abstract thing that goes on out there somewhere and is hopefully influenced by their marketing programs, and then produces, as if by magic, a bottom-line statistic they call sales.

That, to my mind, is really the difference between sales and marketing. It's just a different perspective. The sales perspective looks at the market one customer at a time. The marketing perspective looks at the market as a whole. Sales focuses on the trees, marketing on the forest. Marketers may not even know what kind of trees grow in the forest, but they know how many acres of trees there are and how fast they are growing. And salespeople may not know where the forest begins or ends, but they know some of those trees very, very well.

Put these two perspectives together and you get a pretty powerful thing. You get a whole view of the customer and the market that sees all the way from the individual sale to the big picture of trends and opportunities in the overall market. You get an integrated view of sales and marketing and an ability to influence sales one at a time, as well as on a mass scale, through the use of marketing media and programs.

# An Integrated View of Sales and Marketing

You always need to be selling, and you always need to be marketing. The point of marketing is to generate sales. The point of sales is to generate sales. The two fields are aligned in their purpose, and often in their practices, in spite of their differing perspectives. Yet each offers a fascinating and unique set of strategies and techniques. Combine them into an integrated approach, and you have a pragmatic, action-oriented set of tools for finding good prospects, converting them to customers, and retaining and growing those customers.

That's what I do throughout *The Marketing Kit For Dummies*. And so doing keeps the focus on the all-important goal of any integrated sales and marketing effort: generating profitable sales by finding and retaining customers.

You can generate sales in many ways. With the new options on the World Wide Web, some businesses conduct their sales and marketing without using any of the traditional means. No salespeople. No mailings. No ads. No stores. No service personnel. No brochures. Everything virtual.

Other businesses emphasize direct mail and use a toll-free number to make those sales. Still others advertise their products to consumers and let retailers or distributors worry about getting product out where people can actually see and buy it. There are really no limits to the options — only your imagination limits your choices in marketing!

But at its heart, marketing must come down to sales. People or businesses need to say yes, one at a time, because they have been approached and persuaded to buy. And in most cases, this process follows the basic rules that guide the age-old tradition of personal selling. The salesperson's focus on how each individual can be moved through a purchase process is very helpful to all marketers — although, of course, it is especially helpful when you are making a personal sale. So I'm going to cover the salesperson's perspective on marketing.

# The Sales Process

Every expert has a different model of the sales process. Some are simple, many are highly elaborate, and to be honest, few of them really give you much help in improving your sales success. That's because they're rarely realistic or prescriptive. I favor a model that reflects the reality that you need to do some work to figure out what the prospect needs and present your offerings to meet that need. And I also favor a model that suggests what to do and how and when to do it to optimize your sales efficiency. Sometimes that means abandoning a sales call and going on to another — something few sales models or trainings are willing to admit! Here is the model I generally prefer when I train salespeople or work on the sales and marketing process for consulting clients:

**Step 1. Contact.** This first step involves the identification of prospects through lead-generation systems, cold calling, referrals, and any and every other method you can think of to scare up potential buyers. As the name of this step implies, the whole point of it is to create the context for prolonged contact with them so that you can attempt to make the sale. Speak or write or e-mail or fax to them. Ask for a chance to see them. Set up appointments, get them on the phone, or find a way to drop by and catch them at an available moment. Plan and make that vital contact that opens the door to the sales process, permitting you into their busy lives for long enough to have a decent shot at a sale.

**Step 2. Need Discovery.** This second step focuses on gaining sufficient understanding of the prospect and his or her situation to be able to propose a purchase that makes sense to the prospect. Use brief interactions and the beginning of a longer sales meeting to ask both confirming and exploring questions in order to learn more about the prospect's requirements. The knowledge and insight you gain in this phase helps you present a proposal that is customized to their needs.

**Step 3. Proposal(s).** In this step, you present your offerings to the prospect. You show what you have to sell. But because you've done some discovery in the previous step, you adapt your presentation of your wares to the needs and wants of the prospect. You may describe certain services or products and not others. You may emphasize price to one prospect, quality to another, and speed to a third. And where possible, you can show specifically how your products and/or services can help the prospect overcome constraints and achieve goals.

**Step 4. Attempted Closes.** In this step, you ask the prospect for the business. You initiate the process of making an actual purchase and see how they react. If the prospect is reluctant, you may cycle back to Step 3 or even to Step 2, based on your judgment of the situation. Then you make another attempt to close the deal later on. In general, salespeople try at least three times to close before they conclude that the prospect is truly unwilling to make a purchase at the moment.

**Step 5. Follow-up.** In this step, you contact the prospect after the sales meeting to thank him or her for the time (and the order if you closed), to reinforce any key points, and to prepare the prospect for the next contact. If your attempts to close failed, then the follow-up may explore the reasons why and can certainly seek a future opportunity to recontact the prospect and initiate another sales effort. If the close succeeded, the follow-up confirms the purchase and prepares the prospect for the next step, service.

**Step 6. Service.** In this step, you build upon the initial sale. You seek future sales and you continue to explore needs and propose solutions in an ongoing effort to form a consultative selling partnership with the prospect. Excellent customer service and follow-through on all promises is vital to effective building. The building stage may go on long after the initial sales meeting has ended.

Figure 2-1 illustrates this process, showing the several options for moving through it depending upon how the prospect reacts. The sales process may not flow smoothly from step to step. Sometimes you need to revisit earlier steps. And sometimes you need to abandon all hope and write off the prospect, moving on to another prospect and sales attempt, at least for the time being. This flow chart of the sales process contains considerable insight about when and how to make the sale. I use it in my training business to improve the performance of salespeople in a wide variety of businesses and industries, so it will make a good framework for the next few sections of this chapter.

## Contact methods

You need to identify and then establish contact with any prospect before you can hope to make a sale to them. Contact may be made by an individual sales-person or may come through the use of a great many choices of marketing materials and techniques. Here are some of the ways of generating leads — names and contact information of likely prospects:

- ✔ Attend or display at a trade show, convention, or other event that attracts prospects. Make sure that you find ways to interact with them and collect information about them for later follow-up.

- ✔ Buy mailing lists (from list compilers, brokers, membership organizations, or subscription-based publications). Send letters, postcards, fliers, or other mail solicitations inviting them to return something by mail, visit your Web site, or call if they are interested in more information. Use telephone sales or personal sales calls to follow up with those who respond.

- ✔ Buy e-mail or fax lists (until these options are regulated out of existence) and use them just as you would a mailing list (see the preceding paragraph).

- ✔ Network through friends and customers to new prospects.

- ✔ Speak at industry or community events to let people know what you do and share your expertise — and collect leads after the event.

- ✔ Run a small display ad in an appropriate magazine or newspaper and include your number, Web site, and/or address. Use the ad to generate inquiries from interested prospects.

✔ Develop a telephone sales script and have an employee or temp worker or (for larger lists) a telemarketing firm make calls to generate leads or even try to close some sales for you.

✔ Send an e-mail newsletter to interested prospects, sharing useful information and positioning yourself or your business as a source of expertise. Include marketing messages in the newsletter designed to send prospects your way, either by phone or to a supporting Web site.

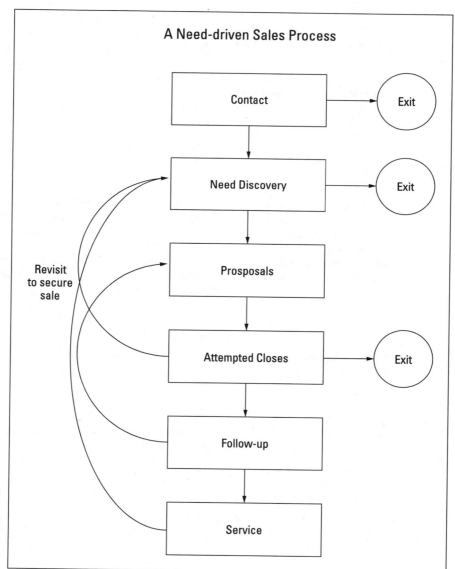

**Figure 2-1:**
A need-
driven sales
process.

These are just a few of the strategies you may use to reach out and identify prospects and cue them up for a sales contact. Throughout this book, you see these and many more methods illustrated over and over, and you also find details of how to implement many of these methods yourself. Sometimes it's feasible to let the marketing communications do all the selling, taking the prospect through a purchase process without the fuss of an interactive sales encounter. But often — in fact, in the majority of businesses — it is ultimately necessary to bring those contacts on to a personal sales process, a situation which means that the next step you need to take them to is need discovery.

## *Attracting customers to your call center*

Many businesses list a toll-free number in directories and in their marketing materials and ads, and then wait by the phone for calls. When calls come in, you know they are from prospects who have self-selected because they think you might be able to help them make a purchase. So the person answering the phone is in an enviable position for any salesperson. He or she simply needs to help callers figure out what they need and write up the orders.

Or do they?

If you have non-salespeople answering the phones and taking orders, you are missing a great chance to do some selling. Anyone who responds to a marketing communication and makes the effort to call you is a serious prospect and deserves serious sales attention. Whoever handles that call needs to be knowledgeable and skilled in soft-sell sales methods because, in addition to simply writing up whatever order the prospect gives, they can conceivably pursue a number of other marketing objectives:

- ✔ Gather useful information about the caller for your database (and for use in future marketing initiatives aimed at the caller)

- ✔ Cross-sell other products/services to the caller

- ✔ Help the caller make a tough decision

- ✔ Diagnose the caller's situation and suggest solutions (involving your products/services if possible, of course!)

- ✔ Project a positive, helpful, interested image for your business that will bring the prospect back again and stimulate positive word of mouth

- ✔ Handle any complaints or concerns with sensitivity, recovering the caller and preventing him or her from hanging up with a negative feeling toward your business

- ✔ Gather useful suggestions and ideas from the caller for use in refining the marketing program, product offerings, or other elements of your business process

## Don't get enough calls? Draw them from a Web site

Car Club is a San Francisco, California–based company with a host of services of value to people who are shopping for a car or car loan. It has links to many dealerships, it acts as a clearinghouse to match buyers and sellers of used cars, and much more. It used to generate calls from prospective customers by advertising its services and toll-free number (which is 1-800-car-club, a memorable number that works well for this purpose).

Then along came the Internet. Now there is carclub.com, an impressive Web site with lots of services available right there on your computer. The Web is a new way to interface with customers, and some customers interact with Car Club only over the Web. But many still want to talk to someone on the phone, so almost every page of the Web site includes the company's toll-free number. And a great many callers are now generated from this Web site.

In addition, the Car Club site gives people the option of requesting a phone call by simply clicking on a Call Me icon. Then an operator contacts them by phone as soon as possible to help them with their questions.

Buying a car is an involved process. Many people need the personal touch of a telephone call at some point in the process. And the Web site does a great job of sending those calls to the call center when they are needed.

I think these are valuable objectives and don't like to see them ignored. Yet many businesses put people to work at their reception phone or call center without giving them enough training and support to pursue such objectives. In fact, few operators or telephone salespeople are ever even given a list like this to think about. They don't even know that they can be doing these things, let alone how to do them!

## Need discovery techniques

In marketing and in business in general, it's vital to understand the customer's needs as fully as possible. The better you understand their needs and how they prefer to fulfill those needs, the better you can position yourself and your products or services to serve the customer. Large-company marketing programs use extensive marketing research to explore customer needs. In smaller organizations, individual, one-on-one discussions with customers and occasional do-it-yourself surveys are more commonly used. And in all organizations in which individuals interact in person with prospects and customers, a great deal of information can be gathered through the use of need discovery techniques.

Need discovery techniques were developed for use in consultative selling, where the salesperson plays a problem-solving role for the customer and tries to become part of the customer's business team. Like a business consultant, the salesperson uses a combination of research and exploratory questions to diagnose the client's situation. This need discovery process puts the salesperson in a position to generate and propose helpful solutions to the customer's problems. Often, those solutions involve the products and services of the salesperson's business.

Over time, the customer comes to trust and rely upon the consultative salesperson and will open up and share more details so that the salesperson can discover more needs and offer more solutions. The result of this process is a collaborative business partnership that is beneficial to both parties. Because collaboration provides many intangible benefits, consultative selling often shifts the focus away from price. Businesses that emphasize consultative selling are valued by customers for their superior service, flexibility, and willingness to help the customer succeed. The customer who enjoys such benefits is not as quick to give the business to some new competitor just because the competitor offers a minor price reduction or other incentive to switch.

The following sections look closely at some simple but powerful conversational techniques that help you uncover customer needs and concerns. Here is an approach you can use to uncover needs.

### Plan your questions

Start by reviewing what you know about your prospects. What are their needs? What are their constraints? What sorts of changes or trends in the news these days may be affecting them? If you're planning a call on a business, seek out information about the business on the Web, in the local newspapers, by reviewing their marketing communications, and by talking to others who work for or do business with them.

From these inquiries, you should find yourself asking questions and generating hypotheses about the prospect. Thinking about and researching a prospect tends to lead you to some theories about what turns them on and what their needs and concerns will be. If you have trouble clarifying your thoughts about the prospect, try filling in the form shown in Figure 2-2 (a template of which is on the CD with the filename CD0201 so you can print a stack of them and keep them in your customer files):

You may need ten minutes to fill in this form. If you are eager to see as many prospects as possible, you may be tempted to skip it. Why plan when you can just go there and give a canned presentation and trust to luck? Because the planning phase greatly increases the chances of building a consultative relationship and securing a sale. Most salespeople find that ten minutes of planning is well invested and well worthwhile.

Next, you need to preplan some questions for the prospect. Doing so takes another five minutes. Again, the temptation may be to skip this step, but the sales call will go much better if you do the preparation.

To preplan your questions, review your Prospect Analysis Sheet and simply generate confirming or exploring questions from it. Here's how.

## Prospect Analysis Sheet

| | |
|---|---|
| **Prospect name** | |
| | |
| Does prospect make purchase decision? (If not, who does?) | |
| Who else is involved in the decision? | |
| Past purchase history | |
| Known brand preferences | |
| **Suspected priorities** | |
| Any budget constraints? | |
| Any time constraints? | |
| Other constraints of relevance? | |
| **What is their most important challenge or goal right now?** | |

**Figure 2-2:**
Prospect
Analysis
Sheet.

### Confirming questions

A *confirming question* is one that checks facts or checks your understanding or interpretation of the situation. It's always wise to use confirming questions to check your assumptions and update your Prospect Profile. It's amazing how many things we think we know about prospects turn out not to be so!

Here are some examples of confirming questions:

> ✔ I recall that you said you needed to make a purchase decision by _____. Is that still the case?
>
> ✔ Is it true that Bob wants to stick with black-and-white labels for now?
>
> ✔ Are you definitely committed to buying only organic produce?
>
> ✔ Is this a good time to go into the details of what you need?
>
> ✔ Am I right that your top priority is service, followed by price?

### Exploring questions

Exploring questions probe to learn more about the situation. They fill in missing facts, they seek reasons for preferences or unusual requests, and they seek to reveal more about the prospect's preferences and needs. When you ask exploring questions, you very often learn something surprising and helpful about the prospect.

Here are some examples of typical exploring questions:

> ✔ Why is it so important for your organization to get same-day deliveries?
>
> ✔ Are you the one who is in charge of the final purchase decision?
>
> ✔ Does the color have to match your office color scheme?
>
> ✔ Do you have any other problems that we might be able to help you with?
>
> ✔ Why do you do it that way?
>
> ✔ Why haven't you updated this equipment in recent years?
>
> ✔ What goals do you hope to accomplish this season?
>
> ✔ Are you experiencing any service problems or frustrations right now?
>
> ✔ Are you looking for ways to cut costs?
>
> ✔ Are you looking for better quality?

Figure 2-3 shows a form you can use to preplan your questions.

Now that you've done all this planning , you are bound to have some good insights and questions as you approach the prospect. Basically, the idea is to use your insights from the need discovery stage to make your presentation interactive and consultative, instead of just forcing your information down the prospect's throat.

## Question Preplanning Form

| Prospect: _____ | |
|---|---|
| **Confirming Questions:** | **Exploring Questions:** |
| 1. | 1. |
| 2. | 2. |
| 3. | 3. |
| 4. | 4. |
| 5. | 5. |
| | |
| | |
| Other comments or notes: | |

**Figure 2-3:**
Question
Preplanning
Form.

# Making the presentation

I'm not going to give you much detail on this step because I find in sales trainings and marketing consultations that most people have already put a great deal of thought into it. The presentation of your offerings is what you really want to do. It's why you went to the trouble of finding a prospect and setting up an opportunity for contact. You probably already know what you want to say.

Or do you?

Before you present your products or services to the prospect, ask yourself what you learned during the need discovery process. Then focus on what you can do to help meet the prospect's needs. The idea is to adapt your presentation to fit the specific needs and wants of each prospect. Be flexible. Emphasize different things. Offer different approaches or select different items to present.

It will feel natural to take a flexible approach to presenting your offerings when you've used the sales process and asked enough questions to understand the prospect's position.

Then all you need to do is translate your extensive knowledge of the product or service into a clear, compelling presentation.

You did say you were an expert in the ins and outs of your product, didn't you? If not, you better work on it.

 One other thing needs saying here. In the end, everything and anything you do or show is part of your presentation. You need to have impeccable manners, clean and attractive clothing, a nice smile, a firm handshake, and you need to have good, attractive reference material about the product at your fingertips. All of the later chapters on writing and designing good marketing materials come to bear here in the presentation phase of the sales process.

And often, when you use the power of marketing media to reach out and make a sale remotely, without the need of a "warm body" to help close the sale, it is the marketing materials that do all the work of presenting your offering and asking for the business. So please give some attention and care to the later chapters and make sure that you are presenting yourself and your marketing materials in as effective a manner as possible.

## Don't forget to ask for the business

You've contacted the prospect, explored their needs, and presented your offerings as the most natural and appropriate solution. You think they like you and your product or service, and you believe the timing is right. Now what?

You've got to ask them to do business with you. You have to try to close the sale. Sure, some customers may volunteer their order and make it easy for you. In retail stores, it's especially easy to fall into a passive role and wait for people to step up with a desired purchase. But it's always a mistake. You need to manage the close, whether subtly or overtly. And in my mind, there's nothing as challenging and interesting in sales as the close.

## On the CD

Check out the following items on the CD-ROM:

- Prospect Analysis Sheet (CD0201)
- Question Preplanning Form (CD0202)

# Chapter 3

# How to Close the Sale

*Y*ou have your foot in the door. The prospect agreed to meet with you. You presented your products or services. You even answered some questions. The prospect seems interested, and you think you've got something he or she needs. Now what? How do you turn that interest into immediate action? Will it be possible to actually secure an order before you leave?

To find out, you've got to ask for some business. You've got to try to close the deal. In fact, in many cases you may have to try to close it more than once. Some salespeople say you can't accept a no until you've tried to close at least three times. Others say you should never accept a no when you sense there is a chance for a yes. I think the truth lies somewhere between — but that you will have to accept far fewer rejections if you make a careful study of closing techniques. Because *how* you ask for the business often determines whether you get the business or, if you do, how much business you get. This chapter discusses some strategies for closing the deal.

# Are Closes Only for Salespeople?

Few people realize that the challenges of personal selling and marketing are very much the same. Marketing simply sells from a distance. Its ultimate goal is to make the sale, just as in personal selling. So that means every marketing program needs to have some good closes built into it, whether they are delivered by salespeople or not.

Sometimes, it's at the point of purchase that your marketing program "asks for the business" by presenting a tempting product with a price tag and other indications that you expect the prospect to purchase it. And sometimes, the marketing materials themselves must incorporate the close. Many calls, letters, faxes, and e-mails to prospects are no more nor less than long-distance sales calls. And less personal forms of marketing communication, like a direct mail piece or catalog, also need to incorporate multiple efforts to close the deal.

Because every marketing program needs to include multiple efforts to close, you can often improve the effectiveness of marketing materials by using classic sales closing techniques in the materials instead of in a personal presentation. For instance, in a direct mail letter or mailed catalog, you can incorporate a number of trail closes that say something like:

- You'll find that our order form is detachable in case you want to check off possible purchases on it as you read the catalog.

- If you are serious about solving your problems, you'll no doubt be making regular use of our services. Which means you'll want to have our contact information handy. So why not get a head start by popping out the perforated Rolodex card on the bottom of this page and filing it under O for our name right now?

By raising hypotheticals relating to future use of your product or service, such *trial closes* help move the reader closer to a real close and a big fat order for your business. And they can be incorporated into any and all marketing materials with a little imagination — and some basic knowledge of the salesperson's lexicon of closing techniques.

# Closing Techniques

I've collected a variety of techniques from super salespeople I've met and interviewed over the years, and also from the sales training programs of a variety of companies. In an earlier book, *The Vest-Pocket Marketer*, I also presented a selection of closes that are used by the Dr. Pepper and Drackett Co. sales forces. Based on these various sources, I've compiled a master list of superior closes you can learn and try out in your own sales and marketing efforts. Here it is:

## 1. The direct close

This is the most basic technique, so I start with it. If you're lucky, it will work, and you won't have to try anything harder. The direct close simply involves asking the prospect to place an order or sign a contract now. You generally want to ask for the business in a specific manner by saying what you'd like them to do, how much you'd like them to buy, or when you'd like them to start accepting deliveries. (If you're designing a brochure, catalog, or ad, make sure that you incorporate direct close requests. For example, include an order form or a message such as, "To place your order, call. . . .")

The idea behind the direct close is to simply propose a business relationship and see what they say. They may just say, "Fine, let's get started. Can you draw up a contract?" or "Do you need a purchase order from me?" More often, they begin to negotiate the specifics of doing business, which is also a happy result because it means you are probably going to be able to do business after a little haggling. For instance, the prospect may say, "Not so fast, my friend. I'd like to hire you, but we'll need to find a way to do this project for less money than what you suggested, and I need to have some guarantees of performance." Great! The direct close has opened the door to a serious discussion of how to do business. If you negotiate in good faith, you should be able to walk away with a deal.

When you are selling products, the direct close should generally include the suggestion that the prospect purchase whatever amount of product is usual or appropriate. You can't expect a store buyer to commit to six months' inventory of your product. Asking them to put in a two-week supply might be just about right, if that's conventional in the category or industry in question.

Sometimes the direct close just doesn't work. The prospect ducks the question, refusing to give you an immediate yes or no. Often people avoid responding to a direct close by raising a question or objection that requires your detailed response. Respond to their question fully. Don't be put off by their unwillingness to close a deal. Nobody is going to say yes until he or she is ready. Customers don't care if you're ready. Bide your time, keep the conversation going if possible, and try another type of close in a few minutes or when they next give you a chance to talk to them.

Here are some examples of direct close scripts:

- Shall I write up an order for . . . now?
- Would an order for X amount be appropriate right now?
- It sounds like it might make sense for us to try working together. Would you be willing to sign a contract for, let's say, (X units) if I get one prepared for you and fax it over later today?
- Based on what you've told me, it sounds like you really could use the XYZ product right now. I can start processing your order tomorrow if you want to give me a purchase order number for it before I go.

## 2. The trial close

This technique is a good one to use casually throughout a sales presentation or discussion as a way of seeing how close to buying the prospect really is. It does not ask directly for the business, but it tests the water by asking hypothetical questions. To come up with appropriate hypotheticals, ask yourself what sorts of things the prospect would know or do if he or she were really going to order. Then ask questions about those things. If the answers are specific and well thought out, then the prospect is thinking the same way you are and may be ready for you to escalate to a real close by using the direct close technique.

For example, imagine you are selling leases on office equipment and you've just given an impressive presentation of a new Xerox copier that includes some new desktop publishing features. To test the waters with a trial close, you might ask hypothetical questions such as, "If you lease this machine, would you get rid of one or more of your older machines?" or "Do you think this machine would permit you to do some things in-house that you currently have to pay to have done by graphic artists or printers?"

If the prospect answers these questions with ease, then you know he or she is thinking detailed thoughts about what it would be like to lease your equipment. Your trial close tells you it's time to work around to a real closing effort. You might go on to say something like, "Well, it sounds like you've thought this through pretty carefully already. Are you ready to sign a contract right now?"

If, however, your trial closes don't generate the sort of responses you hoped for, well, no harm done. The prospect who answers a trial close question with an "I don't know" or "I haven't really had time to think about it" is not yet ready for a close. Go back to probing for insights into their needs and wants, and to communicating information about your offerings. Then try another trial close later on.

Here are some sample trial close scripts:

- If you start carrying our brand, will you drop another to make room for it?
- If you do decide to use our delivery service, what sort of volume would we need to be able to handle for you on a weekly basis?
- If you decide to switch to us, when do you think would be a good time to make the transition?
- Do you have a date in mind?
- Do you have a specific project in mind so we could develop a proposal for you?
- How much have you budgeted for this purchase, and what kind of payment schedule are you thinking of?

You can also use trial closes in sales letters, Web sites, brochures, or other arms-length marketing communications. Incorporate questions such as, "Are you in need of specific supplies right now?" When prospects read these questions, some may be spurred to action.

# 3. The wrap-up close

Also called the summary close or the scripted close by some salespeople, this close signals to the prospect that the time has come to make a decision. It works especially well if you have given some kind of presentation or reviewed information about your offering and/or their needs and wants. You perform the wrap-up close by summarizing the main points of the meeting or presentation. Use language that signals your feeling that a natural ending point has been reached and you are ready to move on to the next stage. Also use body language to signal that you are attempting to wrap up the proceedings. If you are sitting, sit up straight, put your hands on your knees, and look the prospect in the eye. These body movements traditionally signal an intention to get up and leave in many cultures, so they help set the stage for a wrap-up period. (In a brochure or letter, use a heading like "In Conclusion" to signal the start of a wrap-up close.)

In wrapping up the business, try to summarize the main points you've made, and also those the prospect has made. It's also appropriate in many cases to ask the prospect to clarify any points you didn't understand or to raise any "final questions." When you sense that the wrap-up is beginning to feel complete, then you can naturally move on to the question of whether and how much they will buy. Your closing technique at the end of the wrap-up should generally involve a direct close such as those described in technique #1.

Here are some sample wrap-up close scripts:

- ✔ Well, if I might just take a minute to summarize the main concerns I think you've raised, . . . .

- ✔ To wrap up my presentation, I'd like to reiterate our commitment to meeting or exceeding all of your specifications. Specifically, we can . . . and . . . and . . . .

- ✔ I appreciate all the time you've made for me today, but I'm sure you have other appointments, too. Would this be a good time to wrap up our discussion and see where we are?

- ✔ Well, I think I'm beginning to get a clear picture of what you're looking for. As I understand it, you need . . . . Does that sound about right?

# 4. The process close

Sometimes called an action close, a contract close, or an order form close, this close simply gets a process started and sees how far into it the prospect will go. To make it work, you need to have a multi-step purchase process in which the first few steps aren't very difficult to go along with. For example, you might start people off by completing a spec sheet with them, or by entering them into your database of national accounts so they qualify for a discount. Once you get them to take an initial step like one of these, then you move on to the next step of the close. Perhaps that step is to take down detailed information about their order or project in a notebook, then read it back to them as if you are checking a formal order. Finally, you move toward whatever the actual purchase is in your business.

In some businesses, the deal closes when money changes hands. In others, it's when a contract is signed or an order form initialed. Whatever that last step is for you, your process close should move you and the buyer inexorably nearer to it. And the nearer you get, the more committed the buyer must be to stick with your process.

The process close does secure some business quite quickly, but it also weeds out prospects who are just shopping around and aren't ready to close the deal. They will get more and more resistant and uncomfortable as you try to move them through the process. They may bail out by saying something like, "I'm just not ready to sign anything right now" or "I don't think we need to go into all this right now." In which case, keep them alive as prospects, keep trying to find out more about their needs and wants, tell them more about your offerings, and then try a different close on them next time.

Here are some sample process close scripts:

- ✔ Okay, let's get started on this order form. Do you use the same billing and shipping addresses?

- ✔ To qualify for credit terms, we need to make sure that your company is in our customer database. Can I go through what we've got in the computer right now and make sure that it's complete?

- ✔ Assuming you do end up making this purchase, we'll need to have a completed order form. I can get that process started now. What kind of quantities are you thinking about?

- ✔ The next step is usually for us to prepare a detailed proposal. To do that, I need to clarify a few points. Can we go over those now so I can send you a proposal in the next day or two?

## 5. The analytical close

This close is good for careful, thoughtful prospects when the purchase decision is fairly complicated and they are highly involved in the purchase decision. Use it when selling an expensive new car to someone who is shopping around to compare models. Use it when someone is trying to decide what sort of new camera to buy or which insurance policy makes the most sense. Also use it in many business-to-business sales situations, because when people make purchases on behalf of their businesses they generally take a fairly analytical approach.

The analytical close is a guided decision-making process in which you help the prospect compare options and weigh alternatives. You can frame the analysis however you think best fits the situation. Sometimes the key question in the prospect's mind is whether to buy or not. Other times it is which of the competing alternatives to try. More rarely, the prospect may be wrestling in his or her mind with which of your offerings to purchase or how much to buy. Whatever the decision, the analytical close helps the prospect think it through. Why? Because until the prospect thinks the decision through, he or she won't be ready to close.

Perhaps the easiest way to help someone think through the options and reach a comfortable decision is to present the pros and cons of each alternative. You can do this verbally or on paper or a flip chart or white board, depending on the physical environment and the prospect's openness to various alternatives. To present the pros and cons of making a purchase right now, you can divide a sheet of paper or flip chart into two columns, label the left one PROS and the right one CONS. But don't feel you have to complete it in that order. It isn't wise to end your analysis with the cons, or negatives, of the purchase. So start by skipping over the pros column and asking the prospect to help you identify any cons, anything that might be negative in his or her mind about the purchase. For example, you might suggest, the purchase will, of course, cost some money.

Then go on to the pros side, listing as many good things about the purchase and what is to be purchased as you can. Frame them all in terms of their effect on the buyer. Keep it personal and specific. You will, happily, find that the pros column naturally grows considerably longer than the cons column. It is far easier to list benefits of a purchase than negative consequences.

When the analysis is done, you can ask the prospect how it balances out in his or her mind. Something like, "So, what do you think? Do the benefits outweigh the costs to your eye?" Hopefully, you have a good enough offering, targeted to someone who really would benefit from it, so the analysis will clearly favor a decision to purchase. But if not, don't give up. Just keep the lines of communication open and try another close later on.

Another alternative for the analytical close is to offer multiple scenarios and work out in some detail how each would impact the prospect. One scenario might be to do nothing right now. Another might be to purchase from some alternative vendor that the prospect is obviously considering. And, of course, you have to include at least one alternative in which the prospect buys from you. Then you try to engage them through questions in your analysis of each of these alternatives. Work them through with the goal of seeing what happens over time and how each scenario affects the prospect. Hopefully, the scenario you construct around the purchase of your product or service is the most appealing one to the prospect, and your analysis helps him or her make the decision to buy.

Here are sample wrap-up close scripts:

- It sounds like you're having a little bit of trouble thinking this decision through in all its complexity. Why don't we analyze your options and see what really makes the most sense?

- We've explored quite a few different issues as we discussed the idea of a possible purchase. In fact, I'm feeling a little confused by all the details. Would you mind if I did a simple pro/con analysis of the decision you're facing right now so that I can see the issues more clearly?

- I gather you are seriously considering several alternatives right now. I'd like to help you analyze each of these alternatives, because it will help me see whether my offering makes sense. And it should help you make a better decision, too. Do you mind if we spend a few minutes thinking each of these options through to see how they'd affect you in the long run?

Printed marketing materials also lend themselves to analytical closes. Use tables, charts, diagrams, or statistics to prove the value of your offering.

# 6. The sales promotion close

This close uses some inducement to encourage immediate action. It could be a special discount offer that expires soon, it could be an offer to bundle additional product or service into the sale, or it could be any promotion you can dream up as long as it is likely to interest the prospect and not wipe out all of your profit margin.

A gift for new customers is often a great device for securing an immediate close. *Sports Illustrated* has used this technique for many years. They buy large numbers of inexpensive but reasonably nice gifts — a bag with their logo, a portable radio, or whatever — and offer to send you one for free if you subscribe by a certain deadline.

Gifts can work especially well for business-to-business sales, where the margins are often large enough that you can afford something nice. But remember not to make the gift overly expensive or you are entering the realm of bribery. A good rule is that you don't want to offer buyers any gift they would be embarrassed to display openly in their office or home.

If you are uncomfortable with personal gifts when selling to businesses, consider the idea of offering to make a modest donation in the individual's name to a charity of his or her choice. You can call it your Sales for Society program, or whatever you like. The prospect may find it quite exciting to select a charity and fill in a donor form (have some nice cards made up for this purpose). It's a novel inducement that feels good because it does some good for society — and also helps you accomplish your goal of getting the prospect in the right frame of mind to close the deal now instead of next week.

# Secrets of a Master Salesperson

Joe Arak is president of Professional Marketing Associates, a marketing agency that provides a range of services including telemarketing, direct mail programs, and Web site design and maintenance. The company's emphasis is generally on designing programs that produce leads or close sales for their clients, which range widely in both size and industrial category. Joe is therefore often in the position of generating sales for his clients, and as a result has a tremendous amount of experience in selling.

I asked him to share some secrets from his experience and client work. He emphasized the importance of good communications in selling, specifically by first connecting with the prospect to find out where they are at, and by "establishing rapport so people trust the situation, listen to what you say, and share information about themselves." Arak points out that when you've connected well with a prospect, the close is a lot easier. In fact, often failures to close are simply symptoms of an earlier failure to connect.

You may not really test the quality of your connection with the prospect until you try to close. And *if it's a poor quality connection, it is often too late to fix it* by the time your closing attempts fail.

So how do you make a good connection and maximize the chances of arriving at the end of your sales process prepared to close the deal? Arak offers four principles to guide you, principles which I think can be applied not only to person-to-person or telephone selling, but also to any client or prospect development process, even ones that are initiated at arm's length through advertising, direct mail, or the Internet. Here are his principles of connection:

✔ **Ride the horse in the direction it's already going.** According to Arak, "This works a lot like Jujitsu. Rather than trying to overcome the suspect's objections, you use their own momentum to achieve your purpose. You allow them plenty of room to express their feelings and you tame their negativity by going along with it." The key behaviors for using this technique are to listen actively, acknowledge what the prospect says, and give the prospect's feelings a name.

✔ **People would rather talk about their garden than hear about your seeds.** Arak explains that "The main idea is to listen and learn rather than jump in with a tell-and-sell approach. If you let them, people do like to talk about their business and tell you about their concerns." The key behaviors for using this technique are to ask questions that involve and engage, to focus on the prospect's concerns, and to show that you understand what's important to them.

✔ **Before you operate on the patient, find out where it hurts.** As Arak puts it, "The more dissatisfaction the prospect feels, the more likely he'll let you operate." This principle is intuitive, yet often we fail to explore a prospect's situation fully. You have to do some detective work to find out what their problems are. They may not see those problems clearly, and therefore may not be able to tell you when you first ask. Or even if they do know what their problems are, they may not see that you could offer solutions. So it takes some creative investigation to implement this principle fully. The key behaviors for using this technique are to probe for specific kinds of dissatisfaction, to zero in on the implications of the dissatisfaction, and to try to get the prospect to acknowledge the importance of their dissatisfaction.

✔ **Remove the boulders before you plow the field.** Arak explains that many things can get in the way of the prospect paying attention to what you have to say. You have to find out what those "boulders" are and help get them off the prospect's mind. "Perhaps they're still preoccupied with what they were doing before you called, or maybe their distrust of salespeople prevents them from giving you a fair moment of their time." To remove such barriers requires several key skills. You need to be alert to instances when there is a barrier between you and the prospect. You need to acknowledge the person's preoccupation or negative feelings. And if necessary, you should offer to postpone the sales call until a better time of their choosing.

Scripts illustrating the use of the preceding techniques are on the CD.

# On the CD

Check out the following items on the CD-ROM:

✔ Professional Marketing Associates' "Make the Connection" Telemarketing Scripts (CD0301)

✔ Closing Scripts (CD0302)

# Chapter 4

# Secrets of Sales and Marketing Success

In this chapter, I cover many techniques and topics that are helpful in achieving high performance in sales and in marketing in general. Much of the contents of this chapter comes from trainings my firm does with salespeople, sales managers, and marketing managers. These trainings focus on attitudes and learning strategies because these two topics are key to solving many sales problems and often explain the difference between top sales performers and ordinary ones. It sounds simple, and in some ways it is. To sell really well, you need a healthy attitude and you need to learn faster from your experiences than others do.

But plenty of leads also help. You need someone to sell to, after all. And although I address this stage of the sales process in Chapter 2, I want to revisit it briefly before going on to the subject of attitude.

## How Do You Get Leads to Identify Themselves?

The best lead is . . . ?

When you ask yourself this question, you are on the road to figuring out what sort of leads you most want. That should help you generate those leads. After all, it's easiest to find something when you know what it is you're looking for!

And when many people ask themselves what kind of leads they most want, the answer goes something like this:

"I want leads who are actively considering a purchase and who want to talk to me to learn more about my offerings."

Leads who are ready to explore purchase options and approach you for information are ideal. You know the timing is right. They want to hear your information. And if they approach you instead of the other way around, it's much more efficient and easier for you! So how do you generate these ideal leads?

Well, the long answer is that your entire marketing program should be focused on doing just that. As you explore other aspects of marketing, whether in this book, in *Marketing For Dummies,* or in other sources, keep in mind that you want your marketing activities to generate active leads and bring inquiries to you or your salespeople.

The quick answer to the question of how to generate great leads is to make sure that you do the things that customers say work. In a survey of buyers by Penton Research Service, people were asked what things made them most likely to request information from a marketer. The most effective stimulus by far was a toll-free number. The next most effective was a Web site address. Also good are reader service cards (postcards included in many magazines for requesting more information from advertisers), fax numbers, and offers of free catalogs. Coupons also helped bring in inquiries from customers, but at a lower rate than most marketers expected. Table 4-1 shows the results.

| Table 4-1 | What Prompts Buyers to Ask for Information |
|---|---|
| *Prompt* | *Percent Using* |
| Toll-free telephone numbers | 48% |
| Web site addresses | 40% |
| Reader service cards | 32% |
| Fax numbers | 30% |
| Offers of free catalogs | 25% |
| Coupons | 11% |

Many marketers and business owners I know grumble about the cost of offering toll-free telephone service to their customers and prospects. As this survey shows, the cost of toll-free service is the best investment you can make in sales. Even in the modern Internet era, more prospects prefer to talk to someone by phone than to contact you in any other way. So make sure that you publicize your phone number, and if you don't already offer it, seriously consider an investment in toll-free service.

Also make sure that you have well-trained, polite people (not machines, please!) ready to answer those calls. And give them a good form or computerized database to record information about each caller and training in how to use it. The telephone is still the most important source of leads and sales in most industries. Treat it with respect. It should be a cornerstone of your sales and marketing programs!

Web sites are a recent arrival on the lead-generating scene. The fact that customers rate them almost as high as toll-free telephone service means that you better take your Web site seriously, too. If it's not generating at least a quarter of your sales leads today, then it's probably not doing its job. Sorry, but you had better plan to spend some serious time with the two chapters in this book on Web-based marketing.

# The Importance of Great Sales Collateral

Sales and marketing departments or functions intersect in many places. Marketing activities, such as advertising and Web promotions, help generate good leads, for example. And nowhere is the connection closer than in the area of sales collateral. This umbrella term covers anything that can be designed and supplied to salespeople to help them in their work. That's a pretty broad description because it's a good idea to turn your marketing imagination loose and see whether you can come up with better sales collateral.

But first, make sure that you don't use (or provide) collateral that *hurts* sales. Any materials, such as brochures or product literature, that don't look really professional and appealing hurt sales. The sales collateral is a vital part of the "packaging" of the salesperson. If it doesn't look really good, it makes the salesperson look bad. The effects of poor collateral on the prospect are subtle and often unconscious, but they are *extremely* powerful.

So make sure that everything the salesperson carries and/or distributes is really polished and impressive. This is a good place to spend your design and printing budget — a very good place! And look out especially for:

- ✔ **Plastic.** Cheap plastic folders, clear plastic page protectors, or big, ugly plastic sample cases all say "tacky" and "cheap" to prospects. Use high quality papers and favor cloth or leather cases or bindings if at all possible.

- ✔ **Amateur designs and layouts.** Sure, anyone can design sales and marketing materials in this era of high quality laser printers, but most people shouldn't. They create poor-looking, confusing layouts. Their work just doesn't have that special look that characterizes fine design. And the better prospects will notice.

✔ **Errors.** An amazing number of factual and spelling errors exists in sales collateral. Salespeople are perpetually having to make corrections or explain errors in front of prospects. That's like saying, "Please use our business. Of course, we can't even type a spec sheet accurately, but I'm sure we'll muddle through your order somehow." Right.

✔ **Omissions.** Most salespeople go on calls without all the collateral materials and information they need to do a great job. They don't have a good brochure. Their business cards don't have the current address or the company's fax number and Web site. The price list is out-of-date. Their order form is a cheap pad bought at the local stationery store. Make a dream list of everything that might be needed throughout the sales process, such as:

- Impressive stationery and fax forms in multiple sizes for advance letters and other correspondence.

- Matching business cards, preferably with information about the company/product and all the correct contact options. (Consider special paper, unusual designs, even oversized or fold-out cards. If they are noticeably special and interesting, they will generate calls. If not, they'll be lost.)

- Clear, appealing specification sheets describing the facts of each and every product or service accurately so as to answer all possible factual questions for prospects.

- Samples, demos, and/or catalogs making it easy to show and tell.

- Cases, stories, testimonials, and other evidence from happy customers. (Only a few percent of salespeople have any collateral of this type. Yet it's the most powerful form of sales collateral! See Chapter 5 for more details and examples.)

- Attractive, valuable, premium items marked subtly with the company name and contact information. These leave-behinds are appreciated if they are nice. A really nice pen, mug, cap, box of candies, or whatever helps remind the prospect that you exist — and that you value their business. Need not be expensive, but should be seen as valuable enough to keep.

What's the difference between a nice and a cheap premium item? A box of truffles in gold foil stamped "We appreciate your business" and your company name is nice. A plastic mug with your company logo, filled with hard candies and wrapped in cellophane and a ribbon, is tacky. They probably cost the same, but they will be perceived quite differently.

For more on premiums and how to use them, see my coverage of this topic in *Marketing For Dummies*. And for details of how to design great business cards, letterhead, brochures, spec sheets, and so forth, check out Part III of this book. Many design principles, examples, and templates are included for your use.

# Learning from "No"

Sometimes people say no. Sometimes they refuse to purchase. Sometimes they just aren't ready, or just don't like the product, or just aren't in a good mood. This context means that in sales and marketing, there will always be rejections and failures.

In fact, the rate at which various sales and marketing initiatives fail is surprisingly high. Table 4-2 provides typical failure rates for various initiatives.

| Table 4-2 | Failure Rates for Various Sales and Marketing Initiatives |
|---|---|
| *Initiative* | *Percent of Targets Who Say No* |
| Sales cold calls to homes | 50-95% |
| Sales cold calls to businesses | 40-90% |
| Pre-arranged sales calls to individuals | 35-80% |
| Pre-arranged sales calls to businesses | 25-75% |
| Cold telemarketing calls | 90-99.5% |
| Pre-arranged telemarketing calls | 60-90% |
| Direct mail solicitations (letters, catalogs) | 90-99.5% |
| Printed direct response ads | 95-99.99% |
| Web pages | 95-99.999% |

As these average ranges indicate, most people reject most efforts to make the sale. Sales and marketing face a very high rate of rejection. In fact, the pessimist might look at statistics like that and say, "Why bother?"

But in sales and marketing, rejections are inevitable. You can't ever reach prospects who are ready to buy with 100 percent efficiency. A good sales or marketing program is more efficient and suffers fewer wasted calls than a poor one. You can improve your success rates and reduce your rejection rates significantly. There is always room for improvement through increased efficiency and effectiveness. But you will never achieve perfection. Marketing is not that precise of a science. In fact, if you ever do find yourself dealing with prospects who always say yes, it's a sign you need to push your program a bit. Try asking more people, or raising your prices. Unless you ask a few people who say no, you're not really stretching yourself. So failures are a natural and important part of healthy sales and marketing.

How you handle failures has a great deal to do with how successful you are:

- ✔ If you bounce back from each rejection with an optimistic outlook, it won't hold you back. You'll keep trying instead of giving up. In fact, you might even try harder.

- ✔ If you learn from each rejection, you can reduce the failure rate in the future. You'll improve your odds of success over time.

Oddly, both of those points are closely related. Your ability to bounce back, to stay positive and motivated, has everything to do with how you explain each failure to yourself. If you take a positive attitude, attributing failures to appropriate, accurate causes that you can exercise some control over, then you will be resilient. Failures won't upset you or slow you down. In fact, they'll give you renewed energy because you will learn something from each failure that should help you with the next try.

Why is your style of explaining a failure so important to your ability to achieve success next time? For two reasons. First, there is a psychological factor at work. Recent breakthroughs in behavioral research have shown that how you explain events in your life determines how optimistic and effective you will be. To be a successful marketer or salesperson — or to be successful at achieving your goals in general — you need to explain your successes and failures as follows:

- ✔ **Take credit for success.** You need to attribute successes to aspects of your own personality, talent, and behavior. Giving yourself at least a share of the credit for each success builds the essential positive attitude needed to maintain motivation and build momentum. People who explain away their successes as simply good luck are encouraging a feeling of helplessness.

  Oh, and one more thing. It's helpful to generalize from a success. You need to avoid narrow, meaningless ways of giving yourself credit. Don't say something demeaning to yourself like, "Oh, I guess I was responsible for closing that sale, but it was only because I happened to know that prospect personally." It's more productive to explain that success as follows: "I closed that sale easily with an old acquaintance, which proves that I am able to present this product effectively. I should be able to close sales with other people, too." Generalizing from one success to an ability to achieve other successes is important as you build the attitudes needed to pursue success.

- ✔ **Don't blame yourself for failure.** It's important to attribute failures to factors outside of your own personality and abilities. Many people question themselves when they receive a rejection or get a "no" answer. This happens in personal selling all the time, and it also happens throughout marketing. Someone who tries running an ad and gets no responses will not run a second one if he assumes the cause of failure was that he does not know how to do advertising. Many other factors are better to consider that are external to the individual and relatively easy to adjust.

External factors are within your control. It's not you. It's the wrong list of prospects, wrong closing technique, wrong timing, wrong way of presenting the product, or even the wrong product. When you look at specific, controllable factors, then you can take a philosophical attitude toward failure. Oh well, sometimes something goes wrong. But not all the time!

Oh, and one other thing. Notice that when you blame specific, controllable factors for your failures, you are avoiding generalizations. It's very easy to make sweeping generalizations when you encounter a sales rejection or marketing failure. Big mistake. Big, big mistake. Because when you allow yourself to generalize about failures, you will come to see them as unavoidable. It will look like the cards are stacked against you, which will discourage you from playing in the future. I've heard many managers and marketers say things like,

- We don't advertise. We tried it once or twice, and it just doesn't work for our business.

- We can't do direct mail. Our products don't have high enough prices to work, given the typical low response rates for mailings.

- Web sites are fine for communicating information about our business, but it doesn't work to try to close actual sales on the Web. We take a low-key approach to our site. It's really just an online brochure.

- I can't sell. I'm just no good at it. Believe me, I've tried! That's why I sub all our sales out to independent sales reps.

By the way, these are actually direct quotes that I made note of, from otherwise intelligent, clear-thinking people I know in the business world. Each of these quotes reflects a belief that is preventing the speaker from ever trying something again. And each of these quotes is a broad, absolute conclusion based on a very narrow set of unsuccessful experiences. For instance, the person who told me "we can't do direct mail" works for a business that could certainly profit from direct mail. I know that several of the company's direct competitors use mailings quite effectively. But the man's defeatist attitude based on a few early failures prevents his business from profiting in this arena. And the person who told me the Web can't sell her services is making that a self-fulfilling prophecy by failing to develop a Web site that is good enough to support e-commerce.

So you can see that allowing yourself to make broad, pessimistic generalizations from failures is a very dangerous thing. It narrows your view of the future. It shortens your strategic horizons. It turns off your marketing imagination. And it drains you of motivation and self-confidence. So how you think about and explain those failures has everything to do with whether you bounce back from them, wiser and more motivated than before, or whether you curl up in a ball and refuse to try hard again.

And it all comes down to a very simple thing: How you explain successes and failures in your own mind and in talking to the people around you. And it turns out that the majority of people have unhealthy explanatory styles that keep them from ever becoming super salespeople or superior marketers. Only the few people who naturally take to sales or who have a natural flair for entrepreneurship have truly healthy, positive explanatory styles. That's the bad news because my hunch is that you, like me, were not born with as positive an attitude toward success and failure as you need to be a sales and marketing high achiever.

Now for the good news. It's easy to change your style and adopt more positive approaches to success and failure. And when you retrain those old, unhelpful mental habits, you will find yourself coping with failures far more productively and positively. And you will find that your new, healthier attitudes naturally lead to greater success in sales and marketing, as well as life in general.

# Training Yourself for Success

So how do you train yourself to ensure that you have the most helpful attitudes toward success and failure? Well, first, you need to develop a profile of your own attitudes. Do that using the Attitudes of Success Profile I've included on the CD (CD0401). Secondly, you simply need to follow the instructions for interpreting your profile. Where your profile deviates from the profile associated with the highest levels of success in sales and marketing, you will find pointers to simple, easy exercises and tips to help you shift your attitudes.

## Learning from successes

If you know someone who is a master marketer or salesperson, I recommend you take them out for a cup of coffee and quiz them about their approach. Specifically, try to find out how they motivate themselves and how they make sure that they have a winning attitude. Much of what I've learned about marketing and sales has come from "debriefing" mentors, older people who had already achieved exceptional levels of success.

Often, it's surprising what they'll tell you. Their successes are sometimes the result of their special technical knowledge. But more often, it turns out their ability to create and maintain a winning attitude is what made the difference. That was certainly the case when I quizzed an acquaintance, someone who consistently achieves top ranking as a salesperson in his industry because of his ability to write more business than others. How does he do it? I found out almost by accident what one of his secrets was one day, as the following story (from the *Mastering Motivation Audio Workshop* my firm produces) illustrates:

John is affiliated with a big life insurance underwriter, but basically is an entrepreneur and must take full responsibility for earning his own commissions. As you may know, many people try their hand at this work, but only a very few manage to turn it into a lucrative and successful career. Well, John is very disciplined about his work and has managed to write an amazing number of insurance policies over the years, including several for my family and myself. Once when he was visiting my office, I happened to look over his shoulder at his appointment book. It was a large, spiral-bound book with plenty of room for notes on each day's square.

What caught my eye were some funny little tick marks at the bottom of each day. It was obvious John was keeping count of something on a daily basis. I asked him about it, and he laughed and said, "Oh, that's just my tallies. I use a code so people won't bug me about it, but really, all I do is keep count of the number of prospects I phone each morning, and the number of sales calls I actually go on in the course of the day. See, yesterday, for example, I made twelve prospecting calls, and I went on five sales visits."

So naturally I asked him why he kept those tallies, and he explained that he had found that the easiest way to get more business was simply to go on more sales calls, and the easiest way to do that was to make more phone calls each morning. The more people he called, the more meetings he was able to set up. So by tracking the number of prospecting calls, he reminded himself of his goal of calling a certain number each week. And by tracking the number of meetings, he could see the positive results of his efforts.

Then he laughed and explained that there was a story behind his system. It seems that back in his early days in the business, he and another salesman had been complaining and saying that they wished they could double their income by making twice as many sales. So John had pointed out that all it took was twice as many sales calls, and that the only thing keeping them from seeing twice as many customers was that it was not much fun to sit at the phone trying to set up appointments. As soon as they had a few calls lined up, they tended to quit phoning and go out and start selling.

So he challenged his friend in the following manner. They both agreed to keep an accurate tally of how many prospecting calls they made by phone each day. And they each agreed to pay the other $500 at the end of the month if they didn't make twice as many calls as they usually did.

Well, John said that he met his friend in a restaurant at the end of the month, and they both opened their books and counted up their phone calls. John had made his quota of calls, but his friend was just a tad under. So right then and there, he had to write out a check for $500.

You might think that was the end of the story, but not so. Even though he was $500 poorer, the guy told John he wanted to do it again next month. Apparently, he had made enough extra calls that his income was almost double, and the $500 loss was trivial compared to his gain. Well, it took several months of this for them both to get in the habit of making twice as many calls and clearing that hurdle they had set for themselves. But once they got in the habit, they never quit because it was such a pleasant thing to find that they were bringing in twice as much revenue as before. And although John does not need the kicker of a contest any longer to make those calls, he still keeps up with his simple information system. It serves to remind him of his goal, and with it he always makes his targets.

This story illustrates the importance of attitude to success in sales and marketing. And it shows how one record-setting salesperson went about the task of motivating himself to make more calls and close more deals. For him, attitude was so important that he made it his project to manage his own attitude by creating a contest to keep him focused on improving his own performance. And while different approaches might apply for each individual, all kinds of people can improve their sales and marketing performance if they are willing to make a project of their own attitudes!

## Learning from failures

Earlier in this chapter, I explore how you explain successes and failures to yourself. When I introduced that issue, I pointed out that it was inextricably intertwined with another issue — what you learn from failures. Now I want to take up that thread again and explore the importance of learning and adapting your methods based on past experience.

Marketing is all about learning — *all about learning*. Have I made myself clear?

Maybe. But I'm still going to say it one more time: Marketing is all about learning. Which means, among other things, that:

- ✔ The best marketing plans are learning plans, designed to try out creative ideas and see what happens.
- ✔ The best salespeople are people who have tested and refined their approach to a higher degree than others.
- ✔ The businesses that experiment and learn more rapidly than others always lead the pack in marketing, as in business in general.
- ✔ There are no hard and fast rules in marketing, only the rules you develop based on your own experiments and experiences (and expect those to change over time as well!).

So learning from failures is really the key to success in sales and marketing — and in business in general. Therefore, everyone who needs to sell or market should test continually in order to learn. Testing means making cautious experiments; then learning from the results and trying again until you gain the experience to work on a larger scale.

For example, the founder of an Internet startup came to me recently for advice on how to sell his services to advertising agencies. The business develops technology for running online sweepstakes and other sales promotions, and he figured big ad agencies would like to offer such options to their clients. But how to approach them? Who to call, how to present the company and its technologies, what sort of deal to propose, how to structure the pricing? He hadn't done anything like this before, and most likely no one had done the same thing before, so there were a lot of unknowns.

What we ended up doing was designing what I call a *learning plan* (see the file CD0402 on your CD for a simple worksheet if you want to create your own). The learning plan is different from a traditional sales or marketing plan because it does not tell you what to do. It tells you how to learn what to do. It's also different in that it is very simple and it tries to minimize the time and expense of learning what to do. The goal of a learning plan is to put you in a position to be able to make a more traditional marketing plan at the end.

✔ **What do you need to know?**

The first part of a learning plan is a simple listing of questions. Things you really would like to know with more certainty so that you can figure out how to do the sales or marketing. The president of that Internet startup needed to learn who should make those sales calls, who they should call on, how long it would take to develop each prospect, and what percentage of prospects would say yes. So these were the sorts of questions in his learning plan.

✔ **How can you most easily find out?**

The second part of a learning plan is simply a bunch of ideas for finding out the answers to your questions. Answers come from asking more experienced people, talking to prospective customers or clients, trying different approaches, and anything else you can think of that might help. Then, as soon as you have a good list of ways of seeking answers to your questions, you should simply start doing the research.

✔ **What did you learn?**

The third part of the plan is to document what you learned and see if you know enough now to proceed. For example, the president of that Internet startup talked to people in the advertising industry for ideas on who to call and how to structure the service. Then he set up a couple of meetings with prospects from ad agencies and asked them if they'd mind looking at his products and helping him figure out how they might be used by agencies.

With the input from these contacts, he was able to figure out how to approach agencies. He decided that his initial idea of hiring a professional salesperson to make the calls was misguided because only the largest agencies were likely to be interested — and they required a complex, lengthy sale involving more than one department and person in the decision-making. Also, he learned that the agencies wanted to be involved in the technical side and had in-house expertise in Web-based marketing. He realized it was better to make the initial high-level contacts himself and then to involve his technical people in the sale as the client relationship developed. As a result of his learning, he was able to design an appropriate sales strategy and plan.

### Using a learning plan

The learning plan template on your CD (filename CD0402) seems very simple at first glance, so it's easy to take it for granted and assume that it won't produce significant results. Not so! By helping you take a systematic approach to learning as you go, this simple tool can produce dramatic breakthroughs in any aspect of sales and marketing.

For example, take the case of a saleswoman who was hired by a company that makes and installs the cables and wiring needed in new commercial construction sites. Their work is complex — they design and install elaborate electronic and communications systems for large buildings and also retrofit updated systems for companies. The new saleswoman had an engineering background, so she understood the product well. But she did not feel knowledgeable about selling.

So she designed her own learning plan using a learning plan worksheet. Figure 4-1 shows one of the questions from her worksheet and the answers she obtained.

| Question(s): | Action(s): | Answer(s): |
|---|---|---|
| Which closes work best? | - Ask successful salespeople.<br>- Ask some friendly customers.<br>- Test different closes each week. | - Salespeople say trial closes and direct closes are best.<br>- Customers say low pressure and waiting for order is best.<br>- So far, direct closes haven't outsold low-pressure approaches. |

**Figure 4-1:** Sample Learning Plan Worksheet.

The worksheet row shown in this figure addresses the new saleswoman's uncertainty over how to close her sales. She found herself calling on many prospects multiple times without procuring a signed order. Sometimes her prospect would put the work out to competitive bid even though she'd made several sales calls, and then she'd have to prepare a bid and compete with other companies despite her earlier sales efforts. Was she not closing sales effectively? Should she be using other techniques?

To find out, she decided to ask more experienced, successful salespeople, to ask the few customers she had made friends with in her short time on the job, and to run a weekly experiment. The figure shows her results, which indicate a variety of answers. The experienced salespeople recommended a very direct "ask for the business early and often" approach. They said she needed to be more assertive. But the customers disagreed and said they actively disliked pushy salespeople. Instead, they recommended she make her technical information and recommendations available and simply wait until they were ready to make a purchase.

When she compared the assertive close efforts with the passive, more consultative closes, she found that they were about equally effective. It seemed like prospects in her market were not going to be rushed into a sale until they were ready. With this knowledge, she decided to avoid aggressive closing techniques and simply let them know she was available when they needed her. Her conclusion was, "Why use techniques that irritate customers, especially when they don't produce a noticeable increase in sales?"

## Being systematic about sales

You don't have to apply the learning plan method at the corporate level to benefit from it. You can easily use it for your own personal projects in sales and marketing, too. For example, suppose that you are a salesperson who wants to learn more about what kind of closing techniques work best. If you simply try whatever method seems best with each prospect, you'll win some and lose some — but learn very little.

Unless you take a systematic approach to testing different closes, you won't be sure that one close is working better than another. How to be systematic? One easy way is to decide that you'll not use a particular close at all for one whole week. Then the next week, you'll use it whenever it seems to be appropriate. At the end of two weeks, you can simply compare your close rates (number of sales divided by number of sales calls) and see which is higher. If there is a significant difference, it is probably due to the difference in your use of that closing technique.

For instance, if you find that you got the order in 42 percent of sales calls in the first week and 55 percent in the second week, you have some systematic evidence that using the closing technique pays off.

Most salespeople make hundreds of calls a year; some even make thousands of calls. Retail service personnel may speak with hundreds or thousands of shoppers. Telephone operators or telemarketers may talk to tens of thousands of people a year. And marketers may send out tens or even hundreds of thousands of letters, faxes, or e-mails. These are big numbers. Any individual doing the same thing repetitively has ample opportunity to try systematic experiments and learn from their own experience. Yet very few people ever do. If you break this pattern and become a systematic learner, your performance improvements will surprise you, and probably will surprise a lot of other people, too!

# On the CD

Check out the following items included on the CD-ROM:

- ✔ Attitudes of Success Profile (CD0401)
- ✔ Learning Plan Worksheet (CD0402)

# Chapter 5

# Using Testimonials and Customer Stories

*W*ouldn't it be nice if a dozen of the best-known and most admired people in your industry wrote you personal testimonials saying how special you are?

Wouldn't it be great if top people from the best companies in your market gave you permission to print their endorsements in your company literature and ads?

And wouldn't it be great to have excellent customer quotes, lauding your business or product and saying how superior it is to all the competition?

Each of these is an example of the power of personal references, testimonials, or quotes. If a credible, objective party says "buy," prospects are going to listen.

## Effective Use of Testimonials

Some marketers have been using customer quotes and testimonials for years, especially in direct-response print ads, brochures, and letters. But most marketers ignore this powerful technique. Modern Memoirs is an exception to the rule that marketers tend to overlook references and testimonials, and its director, Kitty Axelson-Berry, reports that quotes and examples from past clients are instrumental in attracting new customers to her writing, editing, and publishing service. Modern Memoirs specializes in what it terms commissioned personal memoirs, meaning books about you or someone important to you that are generally made for limited, personal distribution instead of for sale. Actually, the business creates all sorts of personal books, from family cookbooks to books celebrating the first years of a child's life to the classic personal memoir or family history.

Modern Memoirs' products are obviously quite personal, and they require a fair amount of personal involvement and expense as well. How does a prospective customer become comfortable with the idea of signing a contract? How do they know that the staff of Modern Memoirs will handle their project with sensitivity and skill? Knowing that other people have already done it and emerged happy with the book of their dreams is the best evidence. So Modern Memoirs uses a variety of customer quotes and stories to let past customers tell prospective customers about their business.

For example, in one of its brochures (a three-fold colored piece printed on standard 8½-x-14-inch paper), you will find photos of some previously produced books and a detailed description of one that reads:

MEMOIRS by Doris P. Lebow, a full-length memoir handbound in leather and paper, artfully combines 18 hours of as-told-to personal reflections with 29 photos, 40 letters of personal correspondence, 62 favorites recipes, three genealogy charts, two maps, and a family medical history.

That's a packed volume, and it makes a good example of the firm's work. The example gives prospective customers a very clear idea of what's possible, along with the reassurance that others have trod this path successfully before them. To include a photo and description of this work in its brochure, Modern Memoirs had to ask the client for permission. But in general, such permissions are readily granted when the client or customer is happy with the project and proud of their own work. In fact, Modern Memoirs' contracts generally include a clause giving the company permission to show the book to others as a sample of its work. (Two of the inside panels from this brochure are illustrated in Figure 5-1, and more of the brochure is on your CD. Look for file CD0501.)

### *m o d e r n    m e m o i r s*

To produce a printed work worthy of its subject, we have developed a four-step research and production process.

*First*, we conduct a series of in-person interviews with the individual, in consultation with family members and friends as appropriate. Full confidentiality is assured.

*Next*, all materials are transcribed, edited for clarity and continuity, and fleshed out with supplementary materials, including photographs.

*Then*, all text and related graphic elements are integrated and printed to laser copy for review.

*Finally*, using camera-ready flats and Syquest disk, the books are custom printed and bound in leather or fiber, according to preference.

*MEMOIRS by Doris P. Lebow, a full-length memoir handbound in leather and paper, artfully combines 18 hours of as-told-to personal reflections with 29 photos, 40 letters of personal correspondence, 62 favorite recipes, three genealogy charts, two maps and a family medical history.*

Modern Memoirs documents an individual's unique life experiences. These could include:

- Adventures
- Romances
- Customs
- Stories from childhood
- Careers
- Achievements
- Set-backs
- Turning points
- Medical history
- Genealogy charts
- Letters or manuscripts
- Ethical wills and crucial instructions

In addition to the commissioned as-told-to memoir, Modern Memoirs has developed a unique format that transforms awkward family photo and record albums into readily accessible print volumes. Using a mix of photos and text, the *Children's Book Series* specializes in preserving a child's earliest experiences, experiments and areas of expertise.

*Hendrix's Book recounts a little girl's first three-and-a-half years, in 32 pages of text, 28 photos, two drawings and a footprint.*

*Modern Memoirs also provides editing and/or publishing services for personal manuscripts of all lengths and topics.*

**Figure 5-1:** The Modern Memoirs brochure.

Before I go into the details of how to obtain and use testimonials, references, and customer stories, I want to show you one more example from the same firm. Modern Memoirs also runs a variety of workshops, often around topics related to its publishing services. And again, the key marketing issue is how to make prospects comfortable that this is the right firm to work with and that they will get something of value from the workshops. To solve this marketing problem, the firm uses a very simple, photocopied sheet of paper titled "What people have said about our workshops," which is inserted into brochures, mailings, and announcements.

# Borrowing a Page from Books

Testimonials are used frequently in the book business, where some authors plan their cover quotes before they even write their books. Publicists rush advance copies or bound galleys of books to key reviewers early in the book-production process in the hope of snagging a quote from a favorable review in a well-known newspaper or magazine. And authors network madly to line up the addresses of experts and celebrities, then shower them with letters and samples of their writing in the hope of getting cover quotes from the rich and famous. When you see several impressive quotes on the outside of a book, it's because someone — either the author or his or her publicist — has devoted dozens of hours to securing those well-chosen words.

When Harvey Mackay was writing his first book, *Swim with the Sharks Without Being Eaten Alive,* he launched a major campaign to line up celebrity endorsements. If you ask enough people, some of them are bound to say yes just because the exposure is good for their image, too. Well, Mackay asked *lots* of people for quotes, many of them well-known celebrities. And more than 40 gave their testimonials for promoting what went on to become a runaway best-seller. The reading public had the distinct impression that Mackay was already a celebrity himself, even though in truth he had networked to most of those rich and famous endorsers and didn't know them personally.

# Why Quotes Work

Why go to all the trouble to secure a few brief quotes? Because a good quote sells books, and it can sell many other sorts of products and services, too.

Basically, the idea is to let someone the prospect *believes* do the selling instead of you. You're the marketer. Nobody is going to take you seriously when you say they have to have a superior service or product.

Then you need to get some quote or story from that believable source to the prospect, at or near the point of purchase. (The point of purchase is the time and place where the prospect is making decisions affecting your sales.) When people are at the point of purchase, the timing is right. They are interested in what you have to sell, and they are ready to consider your offering seriously. At this moment, they want to believe in your product or service. If they find your claims credible, they will probably buy. But they are naturally suspicious. That's where testimonials and other evidence of product quality and believability are most powerful. And that's why testimonials are so often used on the covers of books. They can reach out to someone who has just picked the book up and is considering a purchase, but isn't quite sure whether the book will really meet his or her expectations.

When I wrote my last book, *Motivating & Rewarding Employees,* I put extra care into it so as to make sure that it offered fresh new insights and methods for managers. I'm actually very pleased with how the book came out, and felt it was the best of my more than a dozen books. But if I said so in my introduction, who'd believe me? The author is hardly an objective source. Nor is the publisher. If the publisher puts "You've got to read this book!" on the cover, prospective readers will naturally wonder why the publisher thinks it's a must read — and they are liable to conclude that the reason has more to do with the publisher's desire to sell a bunch of copies than the quality of the product.

So who could sing the praises of *Motivating & Rewarding Employees* in a credible manner? How about people whose names or titles indicate their objective expertise on the subject matter? So I sent copies of my manuscript to a dozen people who I thought might be willing to see their names on the cover, and most of them sent useful quotes back.

These quotes were very helpful in marketing the book. They help prospective readers and reviewers get a sense of what makes the product unique. They were well worth the time and effort it took to line them up. In fact, I don't have a definite way to measure it, but I'm pretty sure these quotes boosted the rate of sale of the book in bookstores by at least 25 percent.

It probably took 15 or 20 hours of work and a lot of calls, e-mails, faxes, and overnight letters to secure these quotes. I had to put together an impressive package describing the product to give contributors the feeling that they were lending their names to something that would make *them* look good, too. And in the long run, I ended up using my own personal network to secure each and every quote. Some of these people know me pretty well. Others know someone who knows both of us well. In general, it's easiest if there is some connection between you and the contributor if you want to secure a quote with relative ease.

# Using Quotes in Catalogs

I said that testimonials work well at the point of purchase when someone is considering buying a book or other product off the shelf. But there are many other possible points of purchase. Sometimes people make their purchase decisions while in front of a salesperson, sometimes it's when they are in front of their computer looking at a Web page, and sometimes it's when they are reading a direct mail piece such as a sales letter or catalog. All of these are points of purchase, too, and so testimonials or customer stories can be effective in them, as well.

Catalog shoppers often need supporting evidence when they are examining the claims about a product in a catalog. To them, a product may sound good, but is the catalog overstating the product's virtues? How can the shopper be sure? Again, a testimonial from an expert or a quote or example from a satisfied customer at this point of purchase can lift sales by helping the involved shopper believe the marketing claims.

It is particularly important when selling expensive products or services to businesses to provide enough evidence to make your claims believable.

Human Resource Development Press (HRD) publishes catalogs that sell a range of products and services to companies for use in training employees. Some of the many products in their catalog are relatively inexpensive and easy for a prospect to buy. Others are complex or expensive enough that HRD's catalog designer, Martha Cantwell, finds it helpful to include some evidence from experts or users to help make the case. For example, Figure 5-2 shows a page from an HRD Press catalog that features a fairly expensive training product and a book that ties into the product. Cantwell has given considerable space on this page to testimonials, displaying them next to each of the products that the page features. The testimonials help establish the credibility of the products.

## National Finalist at the Vision Awards!

**NEW!**  **VIDEO**

## Mastering Leadership
*By Steve Sullivan*

If you are looking for a powerful video message to add impact to your leadership and management skills workshops, preview *Mastering Leadership* today! You will find Steve Sullivan's inspiring program unparalleled in its ability to educate, entertain, and energize.

Filmed on the majestic coast of Northern California, this new 33–minute video describes the essence of leadership: energizing people by instilling a sense of purpose for the organization or team. Steve Sullivan discusses the galvanizing factors that are needed for successful leadership.

*Mastering Leadership* will add impact and inspiration to your ongoing leadership training programs. The video is perfect as a wrap-up segment, or an after lunch energizer. Or you can use the participants booklets, slide masters, and leader's guide and make *Mastering Leadership* the major component of your workshop.

*Mastering Leadership* costs less than half of comparable videos and makes a cost-effective addition to your video resource library.

*The Complete Package includes:*
*Exhilarating 33-minute video, and five participant booklets with assessments.*
*(additional booklets* **$6.95** *Order code: R92-MLPB)*
*Facilitator's Guide, Disk with slide masters.*
*(additional disks* **$65.00** *Order code: R92-MLSM)*
*One copy of* Leading at Mach 2, *written by Steve Sullivan.*
*(additional copies* **$17.95** *Order code: R92-LM2)*

*Complete Package.* **$295.00**  *Order code: R92-MLCP*

**This is what the experts are saying about *Mastering Leadership*—**

"Steve Sullivan has mastered it all."
**Dana Mead, Chairman and CEO, Tenneco**

"Extraordinary! *Mastering Leadership* was the highlight of our leadership conference."
**Tom Beckett, Director, Yale University**

"Your *Mastering Leadership* video program has made training almost as easy as breathing."
**Anna Lossius, Vice President, Fleet Bank**

"In our executive seminar series, *Mastering Leadership* was the highest rated program ever!"
**David Jones, Chairman of the Board, Southern Gas Association**

"Wow! Our people can't stop talking about your program. Welcome to the team."
**Peter FioRito, Vice President, IBM Global Services**

**—Now see for yourself!**

**LEADERSHIP**

"After reading *Selling at Mach 1*, I flew halfway across Canada to hear Steve Sullivan speak. Now that I have finished *Leading at Mach 2*, I would fly halfway around the world."
**Al Alexandruk
CEO, The Prolific Group**

## Leading at Mach 2    **NEW!**
*By Steve Sullivan*

*Leading at Mach 2* is a 23-year "work-in-progress." Not until Steve Sullivan had excelled as an Army Ranger, Senior Corporate Executive, Entrepreneur, and nationally recognized Motivator did he feel qualified to address the issue. Now, after a lifetime of getting results at accelerated speeds, this award-winning author's recipe for success is no longer a secret. If you thought leadership meant "being the boss," *Leading at Mach 2* gives you ample reason to think again.

**To Order Call 800-707-7769 or Fax 888-374-3488**    1

**Figure 5-2:** Leadership Training Products in an HRD Press catalog.

# Seeking Customer Testimonials

So if testimonials and customer stories are so effective in lifting sales at the prospect's point of purchase, why aren't they used more often? In truth, this is a relatively rare marketing strategy. Most products are marketed without testimonials. I think it's partly that most marketers are unaware of the power of the technique. It isn't taught in marketing or advertising courses at business schools. It isn't in marketing texts. And it isn't common practice among marketers and managers.

And because it is an uncommon strategy, most people are unclear about how to use it. They aren't even sure who to ask or how to ask them.

## Whom to ask

The first thing stopping many people from lining up testimonials is that they aren't sure whom they can ask for quotes. So that's the first thing to get clear. Basically, *you can ask anyone who has a legitimate, authoritative opinion* about your product, service, or business. If they obviously should have an opinion, then you can certainly ask them for their opinion. Here are some of the more common prospects to consider when seeking a testimonial, case history, or other useable contribution:

- ✔ Your customers
- ✔ Friends in management positions in businesses or in other positions of recognized authority (such as accountants, doctors, or politicians)
- ✔ Experts in your industry or technology, such as well-known authors, professors, or journalists
- ✔ Anyone who runs a consulting, real estate, or insurance firm (they are always looking for exposure and are often seen as experts)
- ✔ Anyone you can get to sample or review your offerings (such as in a test market, in-store sampling, or introductory promotional offer)
- ✔ People who are sufficiently well-known that they routinely get such requests and have an established system for handling them

You have or can make plenty of opportunities to talk to people in most of these categories. So it can be perfectly natural to ask them for their opinion on a specific question concerning your business. Take advantage of these opportunities to pop the question and see what raw testimonials you can harvest just by shaking your tree a little.

Other people whom you'd like to ask may not be within your normal circle of regular contacts. Don't despair. If they are well-known, they are no doubt used to such requests. They may have a publicist, secretary, or assistant who handles requests for testimonials or other public appearances routinely. Just call or ask around until you find out what the proper approach is and then send a professional, written request. With celebrity endorsers, it's often helpful to suggest some simple phrases or quotes that they may want to consider if they don't have the desire to write their own from scratch. Also, be sure to describe the sort of use you think you'll put their quote to, with specific reference to how neatly and professionally it will be presented and how many people of what sort you expect to see and read (or hear) it. That way, the big fish can decide more easily if this is a good exposure opportunity for him or her.

When you approach a well-known individual for a quote, your odds of success are a lot lower than when you approach your own customers or other people you already know. Also, the turnaround is going to be considerably slower. But don't worry. If you keep trying, you'll probably line up one or two at a minimum. And even if you don't, those customer quotes are often more believable and compelling than celebrity endorsements anyway.

Don't be too pushy when asking people for quotes. Some people just don't feel comfortable lending their names. Often lower-level employees in a company don't have the authority to lend their names and titles to others without clearance from their bosses, which is not that easy to secure. Other people are simply not into the idea of participating in your project and don't have any interest in seeing their names in your marketing materials. That's fine. Don't bug these noncontributors. For every one of them there's another person who loves your product or service and likes to take part in anything that gives him or her exposure. Just keep looking until you find people who are happy to contribute. They are out there for the finding. And so few people go asking for their contributions that they will probably be honored when you ask.

Oh, and please stay far away from people who raise the question of payment. Anyone who says, "Sure, I'd be willing to give you a quote. How much are you offering?" is not thinking about the opportunity in a helpful way. They don't see it as a simple favor that may come round to help them some day in the future. They are trying to milk the situation for a few quick bucks. People who think that way are likely to come up with other ways to bother you for money in the future. And besides, it isn't really an objective testimonial if you paid for it, is it? So when you bump into someone who wants to profit from your request for a quote, just thank them kindly and back out as gracefully and quickly as you can.

## *What to ask for*

The next stumbling block that stops many people from getting testimonials is that they don't know what to ask for. Basically, *you can ask people for any information or opinions that wouldn't embarrass them in public and that they can legitimately call their own.* (Do make sure that people are contributing their own words, not ones they stole from someone else.)

But (and this is a big but), your request needs to be very specific. Specificity makes your request easier to answer and less easy to object to. Specific requests include:

- Their opinion of your product or service
- A description of how they used your product or service and what happened as a result
- Their view of where the industry or product category or technology or economy (or whatever) is going
- Information about which of your products or services they use
- How often they use your product or service or how much of it they use
- Why they use it
- What they think the best things about it are
- Who they'd recommend it to
- What they'd recommend it for

And the less well you know someone, the more specific your request should be. You can always ask a close friend for a reference, and they'll generally say, "Sure, just tell me what you want me to say." But people whom you know more casually are not likely to be as easy to work with. To them, a general request for a favor like that may seem inappropriate or difficult. So be more specific as you work outward from your immediate circle of friends and associates.

Why is it so important to be specific? Think about the difference between asking someone for one of these specifics versus just asking them for a recommendation or testimonial. Let's role-play it to make the distinction clear. Imagine you know me vaguely, as one of the owners of a business from which your business buys some computer repair services. You don't normally think about me or my services unless there's a problem with your computers. But today, you've just received an e-mail from me asking for a personal quote from you recommending our service to other businesses.

What will you do with this request? Probably nothing at all. Perhaps a flat refusal, but you don't actually want to be rude. So probably nothing at all. It is also possible, faintly possible, that you'd dash off a hearty recommendation and send it back by e-mail. But that's not very likely because the request is so broad and poorly defined. What should the recommendation say? How long does it need to be? How should it be written? Asking someone for a recommendation is asking him or her to do something that feels difficult and poorly defined, and does not offer any obvious, major benefit to justify the difficulty of the task.

Now try a more specific request, using one of the suggestions from the preceding list. Imagine now that I have e-mailed not a generic request for a recommendation, but instead I've said something like,

> Dear Ms. Franklin,
>
> As one of your regular suppliers for several years, I am writing to ask if you could tell me what sort of companies you think our computer repair services are especially well suited for. Would you recommend them for large companies? Small? High-tech? General? Do you think the companies need to have a lot of technical expertise to take full advantage of our services, or not? Your opinion would be especially helpful right now as we are preparing our marketing plan and designing our marketing materials. Just a quick sentence or two is all we really need because I'm sure you are busy. Thanks so much for your input!
>
> Sincerely,
>
> Chip Smith, Owner, ABC Computer Services

This e-mail script asks for one simple, clear thing: who the customer would recommend your services to. That's a very easy question to answer for any reasonably happy customer. It is likely to get a positive response such as the following:

> Dear Chip:
>
> Got your note. Happy to help but in a hurry. Basically, I'd say ABC's services would be useful for any company within this geographic area as long as they have computers that need maintenance. By the way, can you remind Joanne that she is supposed to get us a bid on a new graphics workstation? Thanks.
>
> Anne Franklin

Congratulations! You just landed a testimonial in the raw. It may not look like much right now, but with a little work it will become a powerful marketing tool.

## Processing the testimonial

To "process" this raw testimonial, first you need to isolate and refine the language. Here's the sentence that contains the answer to your question:

"Basically, I'd say ABC's services would be useful for any company within this geographic area as long as they have computers that need maintenance."

It's a start, but it isn't quite as short or punchy as it needs to be. And it's perfectly reasonable to tighten it up a bit by cutting superfluous words (like *basically*) and by substituting briefer words or phrases for lengthy or poorly chosen ones. Just don't make it say anything that it didn't originally. You can't add "I love this company" because that thought wasn't there to start with. But you can massage it into the following form without violating the spirit of the original quote:

"ABC's services are useful to any company in the area with computers that need maintenance."

And now that I've isolated and cleaned up that off-hand sentence from the middle of your customer's busy e-mail, it is beginning to show some real promise as a marketing communication.

## Seeking permission to use the testimonial

But it is still not a finished testimonial because *you do not yet have permission* to attach its author's name to it. So you need to e-mail the source again, this time for permission to quote their earlier e-mail. You might do so using a script such as this:

> Dear Anne,
>
> Thanks so much for your e-mail. I'm attaching that bid Joanne had promised you. It took her longer than she expected, but the good news is she found some alternatives that offer the same performance at lower cost. One of our bigger suppliers is discounting several high-end models to get rid of back inventory, and we can pass the savings along to you.
>
> Your answer to my question was very helpful. Thanks for participating. It helps us refine our strategies, and I'm also considering including a few quotes from customers in our next brochure or other marketing communications. With a little editing to shorten it, the answer you gave me reads, "ABC's services are useful to any company in the area with computers that need maintenance." If you have any objection with our

referencing this quote or would like to review specific uses of it, please do let me know. Otherwise, we will include it in our upcoming brochure, along with some other quotes. Thanks again for your help.

Best,

Chip

I scripted this reply carefully to keep it low key. I don't want to put images in the customer's mind of her name and quote plastered all over late-night television or on a huge billboard beside the freeway. I want to keep it professional and cool in tone, so that she just glances at it and thinks, "Wonder why they want that? Not much of a quote really. But it is what I said after all, and what harm could there be in it?"

Note that you have two choices in how you solicit quotes. The first is to ask a specific question in order to generate a quote (as Chip did in the preceding example), and then — if you like the quote — seek permission to use it in marketing. A second approach is to ask up front for permission to use a quote, and then ask specific questions to generate one. If you are sure the person will cooperate, try the latter. If you aren't so sure what you'll get, try the former. Then you don't have to deal with the embarrassing situation of having to decline to use a quote because it isn't as positive as you'd hoped!

Assuming that you have solicited a quote first, one you like, you have more than one way to ask for permission to use it. You can "assume" permission and just write to confirm, as I illustrated in the preceding example. Or you can assume that you don't have permission and ask for it to be given. The latter approach is represented in the following example, in which I show another basic script for a follow-up by letter. This script takes a slightly different tack in other ways, too, emphasizing the positive responses from customers, which tends to make people feel good about being part of the event.

Dear X:

Thank you for your response to my questions. I appreciate your help and am frankly amazed by the many positive responses my request generated from our customers. Although we certainly intend to continue improving our services over time, it is gratifying to know that so many customers currently have positive things to say about our business.

After reviewing your response and a number of others, I am considering letting our customers speak for us in our next catalog. Specifically, I'd like to substitute brief quotes from customers, and perhaps a few longer ones as well, in place of much of the typical advertising copy. This seems like a more honest and genuine approach to telling our story than the usual one, in which copywriters who don't even use our services create the catalog for us. In addition, it should save us a little money, which will help us keep prices down in the coming quarter. And finally, it does offer an opportunity to create some additional exposure for our customers, some of whom might find that our catalog or other marketing communications offer helpful publicity for their businesses. (To that end, I am happy to include brief descriptions of our customers and their product lines in our next catalog if they want.)

In brief, I'd like to include your quote in our future marketing materials, and would appreciate it greatly if you'd confirm that this is acceptable to you in a return letter, fax, or e-mail. And in addition, if you'd like us to include some background information about your business or products, send that along as well.

Once again, thanks for your assistance. Your participation in this outreach project is greatly appreciated, as is your continued business. Do let me know if there is anything more we can do for you.

Sincerely,

All scripts used in this chapter are available on the CD for you to adapt and use in your pursuit of customer testimonials. Look for files CD0502 – CD0504.

If you don't mind being just a little bit pushy, you can end your communication to a prospective recommender by telling him to contact you if he objects to your using the quote, the way I did in my sample e-mail reply to Anne Franklin. Then if you don't hear, you can reasonably presume you have the person's permission to use it. But if you think that customers would object to that approach, then end the e-mail with a request that they respond one more time to confirm their permission to let you use their quote. Then you have to wait for their reply, and some percentage of them won't ever get back, forcing you to either give up or to go begging with a reminder e-mail or phone call. But some of them *will* return their confirmation. After all, it's in their own words, and they already sent them to you, so it's not a big step to say you have permission to quote them.

Either way, if you ask enough customers to start with (say, at least ten), in the long run you should find yourself with sufficient authority to include quotes from some of your customers in future marketing communications. If you line up even three or four quotes using this technique, you'll be in a position to harness the power of testimonials in your marketing.

What if some people get cold feet — but you liked their initial quotes? Even if some people balk at permitting you to use their names, you can still find good uses for those quotes. After all, they are legitimate quotes and you have (I hope you have!) hard copies of the source e-mails or letters or written notes on the phone conversations in your files. So you can go ahead and use the quotes, attributing them to a general description of the person and/or company. "President, financial institution" or "Bank executive" might do fine if the local bank's president ducks your requests and never confirms that you can attribute her quote to her directly. A quote is a quote, and can add value to marketing communications even if it must be attributed to an anonymous "Regular Customer."

## *Final step: Using those testimonials*

The final step is putting those quotes to good use in your marketing efforts. Put them together on a single sheet of paper where you can get a good feel for how they read and can decide what order you like to see them in.

There are really no limits to how you might use such quotes. I like to see them sprinkled in ads, brochures and catalogs. They add a lot of credibility to direct mail offers, and you might even consider sprinkling them on the outside of your envelope to increase the likelihood of its being opened.

Testimonials can also appear on Web pages to good effect. If you get enough, you can even have a button on your site labeled "Customer Testimonials" and allow viewers to click through to an entire page or more of such quotes. It's an odd thing that Web sites do not generally include any customer testimonials. Maybe it's time for you to break that mold.

# *Why Not Let Testimonials Stand on Their Own?*

Another idea is to create a flier, poster, or point-of-purchase pamphlet or sign that is made up almost entirely of testimonials. The testimonials can actually become the core of such marketing communications rather than just decorating and lending strength to communications that have other core content. I've got an example of a marketing piece that was created for my own business by Rocks Communications, in which testimonials make up an entire page. In fact, it's the second most important page — the back page of a catalog. (The most important page of a catalog is the front page, of course, followed by the back, then the inside covers and the center fold, where the thing falls open naturally. Design these to draw people into the rest of the pages — and use testimonials on these key pages because of their power to engage the reader.)

## Avoiding legal traps

Advertising is regulated in many countries, so you always have to be careful to make honest, well-supported claims in any marketing communications. This is certainly true for testimonials. A number of major ad campaigns have run into legal trouble by putting misleading or false statements into the mouths of celebrity endorsers. In a landmark case, the singer Pat Boone once endorsed an acne medicine called Acne-Statin in television ads in the U.S. He said, "With four daughters, we've tried the leading acne medication at our house, and nothing ever seemed to work until our girls met a Beverly Hills doctor and got some real help through a product called Acne-Statin." The U.S. Federal Trade Commission investigated this testimonial, and concluded that it was misleading. Not all of Boone's daughters had used the product in question, and none of them had serious acne problems. The ads were forced off the air, the company got in trouble, and Boone ran into some legal complications of his own. It's not nice to lie in advertisements, and it isn't legal, either!

You can avoid such problems if you don't do it the way Acne-Statin did. First, don't pay for your testimonials. Get only genuine quotes from happy customers or others who are expressing their honest opinion for free. Second, make sure

that they say things that are patently obvious, that reflect the truth and could be substantiated easily. Third, let them express their own opinions, rather than having them state fact. For instance, if Boone had said, "As a father of four girls, it's my strong opinion that Acne-Statin is the best product and I encourage my children to use it," then all that would have to be substantiated was that he had encouraged his children to use it. To substantiate that fact, all you'd need was a simple note in his handwriting to his daughters saying, "Why don't you try this product? I think you'll like it." And as for his opinion that the product was the best in its category, well, that's just his opinion. As long as he doesn't say the same thing about the competing products, his opinion is not likely to be challenged.

Another legal issue concerns the provider's rights to his or her quote. If I say or write something, I might have legal rights to it under copyright law. And I might make some claim to such rights if I think the quote is of value to you. So you need to make sure you get permission. In writing. And keep a record of your request as well as the customer's reply, so it is clear that you are using his or her quote as you said you would and as he or she said you could. A nicely maintained file of your correspondence is good protection against this legal trap.

# Using Customer Videos & Photos

I've already given some suggestions and examples of uses for customer quotes and testimonials. Candid customer comments or reactions on video or audio tape have many of the same virtues and uses as written testimonials. You can use them to create effective radio or television ads, and you can use them in a promotional video you distribute to prospects if you do business-to-business marketing. Some private schools and colleges now hand out videos to prospective students, and these are a great medium for some candid reactions as well as testimonials from students and alums.

I also encourage you to consider using customer footage on your Web site. The technology exists to put short (keep it short, please!) clips of video or audio recordings on sites, and make them available at the click of a button. People love to watch TV, and they will gladly sit and watch short videos on your Web site. Videos pull people into a site and increase the time they spend with you as well as increasing the credibility of your marketing claims.

Photos of customers, combined with their quotes or comments, are also powerful marketing tools. You can include them on a Web page, in a catalog, in print ads, even on the packaging of a product.

## Photographing endorsers

I like the idea of using a photo of a customer, perhaps with a short quote in his or her own words. You see this in some print advertising for consumer products, although when major advertisers do it, the presentation is so slick you're never sure whether it's a real customer or a paid model, which reduces its effectiveness. The best photos are honest, genuine ones. They show a real person, hopefully a reasonably attractive and friendly one, but not some smooth-skinned model who looks like all the other models in the fashion magazines.

If one or more customers agree to be photographed for your ad, catalog, Web page, or other marketing communication, remember that it's up to you to do all the work involved. Hire a professional photographer who routinely does portrait work outside of his or her studio. That's what you want the photographer to do with your customer, so make sure that you find a photographer with plenty of comparable work in his or her portfolio. Then arrange a time for the photographer to visit the subject at home (if it's for a retail product or service) or at work (for a business-to-business product or service). Assume it will take about an hour to get a decent shot and will cost you anywhere from $100 to $500, depending on the photographer.

And make sure that you get the subject to give you written permission to use their image in your marketing. It might be wisest to have a lawyer draw up a simple release form for them to sign.

## Making candid customer videos

They aren't very common, but television commercials using customer testimonials are among the most effective. Not flashy, but effective. They don't win design awards in the advertising industry, but they do win high believability ratings from viewers — especially if they use candid testimonials.

What's a candid testimonial? It's what a customer says and does before you tell them you are recording them. For instance, a car dealership might have a hidden video camera on the floor of its showroom, aimed at a centrally-placed new model that looks really great. Someone can monitor the camera's view from a nearby office or a hiding place on the showroom floor. When a shopper approaches the new model, you turn the camera on and hope for a good reaction. Perhaps the shopper does a double take upon opening the driver's door, says "Wow! I gotta have one of these!" and then jumps right in. And it's all captured on your video camera — I hope. Think how much more effective it would be to have a few candid reactions praising a new model than a fast-talking salesman in a cheap suit as the start of this commercial!

### Creating a candid set

You can also create more heavily managed situations designed to increase the chances of usable responses. For instance, you can set up a booth in a mall where you display samples of a retail product and invite people to interact with it. You can even have someone who knows where the camera is engage these people in conversations, asking them what they think, to make sure they deliver some lines in the right place — facing the hidden camera and/or microphone. Similarly, a business-to-business product or service can be demonstrated at a trade show, in a booth that is set up for recording. It's not really that hard to get some footage of candid customer reactions to a product or service if you do some advance planning.

### A word about video quality

Make sure that you use high-quality video cameras to record candid customer reactions. The average Super-8 home video camera does not produce as fine an image as you'd probably like to use, even for local television advertising or a company promotional video. A High-8 camera with plenty of light may be good enough and doesn't cost much more than an average Super-8 camera. And if you have access to professional-quality cameras, they are obviously better. Sometimes a local television station or college is willing to rent out cameras, and in larger cities there are many audio-video supply houses that rent equipment as well. Or if you have a big enough business that you can afford to use a professional production studio, just turn the filming over to them and tell them they better get high-quality, usable footage of customers or you won't pay them for their work.

Keep in mind the importance of good lighting. Basically, all cameras, including video cameras, take better pictures when there is *more light*. It's that simple. If you can shoot under bright indoor lights or out of doors on a nice day, you are likely to get video that looks good. If you film in a dim interior room or at night, it won't look good. Bright light not only gives a good, sharp image, but it also permits greater depth of field. What's that? It's the depth that is in focus.

In dim light, the camera has to adjust itself (or be adjusted) by opening up its aperture, the hole through which light comes in. And the wider that aperture, the more shallow the area that is in focus. So the foreground and background of a scene are blurry when there is dim light, but increase the lighting, and everything jumps into sharp focus.

There are finer points to lighting, but I don't really care about them, nor should you. Sure, the experts can fuss about shadows and try to set up reflectors and multiple lights to "fill" the scene with light. But that's not usually practical when shooting candid customer scenes. It would be nice not to have heavy shadows on the customer's face. But as long as the lit parts of the scene are lit brightly, you'll at least have decent-looking footage to use.

## *Don't forget to ask permission!*

The key is obviously to ask permission for whatever use you have in mind. Be specific and clear about what you want to do. Ask in writing, and get a written response, preferably with a signature (e-mail is a little less solid from a legal perspective). And when you are using a photo or video — in other words, the person's likeness — then you need to be extra careful about getting appropriate permission. Make it clear in the paperwork that that you will be using their likeness. And consider getting legal advice, especially if your organization makes enough money to be an attractive "deep pocket" target for legal actions.

After you record a candid customer reaction, the thing to do is to look at it immediately and see if it's any good. If it is inadequate, I'd just plan to discard it and not trouble the customer. But if it might be usable, then immediately speak to the subject. Explain that you are doing a candid camera operation and that you've caught their reactions on video. If possible, keep the video rolling as you explain so that you can record their reactions to supplement their written permission. Thank them and treat them kindly. Try to encourage their natural tendency to be amused and pleasantly surprised. If they are mad, apologize and promise you'll discard the footage. Then get rid of them and go on to the next subject. But if they don't seem to mind, secure their signed permission to use the video right away. Ask them if it's all right for you to use the tape in future marketing communications. Get their "yes" on tape and then get them to sign a permission form as well to make sure that everything is clear.

They may want to see a copy of the finished ad or whatever the product will be. That is certainly a reasonable request, and you should promise to send it to them as soon as it is finished.

If the person providing the testimonial is going to be described based on any affiliation with an organization, make sure that the person has the authority to give you permission to mention the organization's name, too. A senior executive obviously has this authority. But if you've interviewed a mail-room clerk at a big company and plan to run a quote from them in which you describe them as an employee of that company, you better check with the publicity department of the company first. They may well have a policy against endorsing products or services for all you know, and you don't want to find out about it after you've printed a thousand brochures.

# And Now for an Easy Alternative

You may want to harness the power of customer testimonials without actually securing any. That's impossible. But you can do some next-best things that work pretty well. The best alternative is to create a plausible fictional situation in which you create a customer character or characters. Then you tell a story, perhaps using their dialogue or quotes, that conveys an accurate picture of what makes your product or service great.

Basically, what you do is substitute fiction for nonfiction. Many consumer ads use fictional scenes and characters to make their point. Simply turn on a TV or radio and take in a few dozen ads, and you'll come across at least a few of this type.

It's less common to use fictional characters in business-to-business marketing, but still an accepted device. One form you can use is a brief story about a fictional customer. For example, if you are marketing ABC Computer Services, you might develop copy for print or radio use that reads as follows:

### Scene 1. Early morning in a big hotel

James Wilson woke early and put on his best suit. It was going to be a big day. Perhaps the biggest day of his working life. He was a keynote speaker at his industry's annual convention, and he knew he'd never had as big an opportunity to impress prospective customers before.

Before leaving the hotel room to head for the lecture hall, he quickly reviewed the contents of his briefcase. Yes, he had plenty of business cards and catalog sheets. And he had the disk containing his entire PowerPoint presentation. All those lovely graphics he'd slaved so hard to produce. It was all there, waiting to go. That is, assuming the convention center's computer would read his disk properly and convert it to the high-quality projections he needed to wow that audience.

### Scene 2. A hotel bar, late in the evening

Wilson is slumped over a table in a dark corner, a look of deep despair on his face. Someone he knows walks by, but he ducks his head. He's too embarrassed to talk to anyone right now. In fact, he's too embarrassed even to call the office and tell them what went wrong. Sure, he did his best. He tried to give a good presentation in spite of the total failure of the computer system. But how could he speak without those graphics and bullet points he'd planned to refer to? He wasn't used to such a large audience, and when his PowerPoint presentation wouldn't run, he panicked. Sweaty palms. Racing heart. Heck, he couldn't even remember what he'd said. The only thing he remembered for certain was the way the audience had disappeared, some of them even before he finished.

If only he had taken the time to make sure that his disk was compatible with the hotel's system. Or better yet, brought his own portable computer and projector so he wasn't dependent on those goofballs from the hotel's AV department. He wished he had someone to help him get the technology thing straight. Would have saved a lot of embarrassment. And maybe even saved his neck — which was not going to be any too safe when his boss heard about today's events!

This fictional narrative is easy to identify with if you've ever had to do public speaking for your work. It takes advantage of the fact that many people are afraid of public speaking. While it's obvious that the main character is fictional, it's also clear that his experience could happen to anyone who doesn't have the right computer systems and support behind them. ABC Computer Services could very well use copy such as the above to bring home the point that they should be consulted before anyone plans a major presentation.

You could also create dialogue between fictional characters. Radio ads in which two people talk about a product are fairly common and can work well. They often attempt to be humorous, and sometimes even are, but don't have to be. As long as they personify the feelings of the listener, they may be identified with just as strongly as the listener would identify with a real customer.

# Selling Services with Customer Stories

Services are intangible. You can't take them for a test drive or kick their wheels. You have to imagine them. When people shop for services, they often have difficulty deciding whether what they imagine is really appropriate and will have sufficient quality to meet their needs.

For example, how do you know that a bank will handle your business checking account well? You don't. You just assume that a bank with a well-known name and a well-built branch should be able to provide basic banking services. You are using two symbolic indicators of the quality of the bank's service to aid your imagination. You are relying on their brand name and their facility. You may also be influenced by other indicators of the quality of their service, such as how professional the tellers appear to be and how nice the checkbooks and checks they offer are.

Whenever people shop for a service, they rely to a significant degree on such indicators of service quality. That's why service marketers are supposed to "manage the evidence" as many a marketing professor tells his or her students. And it's good advice. But I like to add another strategy, which is to let those who actually *know* how good your service is give evidence to those who want to find out.

Customer stories and testimonials are especially powerful when marketing services. Some consulting firms use them to good effect by including brief case histories of past client work in their brochures or presentation folders. I know one firm, The Jack Morton Company, a specialist in marketing events and promotions, that uses this strategy very effectively. Some years ago now, they went to some of their best customers and got permission to write up descriptions of specific projects they did for those clients. Each project description was printed on a single, 8½-x-11-inch sheet of glossy paper and includes a color photograph to illustrate it. The clients agreed to let their names and stories be used. When future clients want to get a better idea of how this company's services work, they can simply read actual, real-life stories from past clients. Powerful evidence indeed.

In fact, Jack Morton Co.'s stories were so effective that the company gradually developed more and more of them and made them a central part of every packet it sends to prospects. They call this kind of marketing communication a Solution Sheet, and at last count they had written and produced more than a hundred of them! Naturally, no prospect wants to read a hundred such stories, but having a library of them makes it possible to pull four or five that closely match each prospect's situation and needs. Then the prospect can look at a selection of successful past projects that are very much related to what he or she wishes to do.

# On the CD

Check out the following items on your CD:

- Modern Memoirs brochure (CD0501)
- Request letters/e-mails (CD0502, CD0503, and CD0504)
- Catalog page from HRD Press (CD0505)

# Part II

# Research, Audits, and Plans

The 5th Wave                    By Rich Tennant

Bill and Irwin discover The Land of Lost Files

MY GOD! THIS IS A BUDGET AND ANALYSIS REPORT FOR THE MARKETING DEPT. OF A FORTUNE 500 COMPANY. MUST HAVE KILLED THE POOR BASTARD TO LOSE THIS.

## In this part . . .

*I*n this part, I help you do any of those nasty chores that marketers often get assigned — or assign themselves when they need to understand their customer or their program better. I show you how to do practical, on-a-budget marketing research. And I queue up a tool for you that's popular at my live trainings for sales or service people. It's called the Difficult Customer Diagnostic and shows you how to deal with hard-to-handle customers. Also included in this part are the tough but necessary chores of performing a marketing audit or writing marketing plans.

# Chapter 6

# Customer Research

- - - - - - - - - - - - - - - - - - - - - - - - - - - - - - - - - - - - - - - -

- - - - - - - - - - - - - - - - - - - - - - - - - - - - - - - - - - - - - - - -

*W*hat can you do to increase sales, reduce customer turnover, raise prices, increase profits — in short, make your sales and marketing more successful? Well, those are the sort of questions that you can answer in many ways. The most common way to tackle them in the world of marketing is to do a careful marketing audit (Chapter 7) or marketing plan (Chapter 8). Both of those are worthwhile exercises, and likely to help you see your way to some real increases in efficiency or effectiveness. But there is one other thing that I want you to try. First.

## Ask Your Customers!

Whenever you have questions, concerns, or a desire to boost performance, the first thing you need to do is *talk to your customers*. I cover a great deal of quick and easy methods for collecting customer input in the Marketing Research chapter of *Marketing For Dummies,* and I'll put two key tools from that chapter onto the CD that comes with this book for your reference, too:

- ✔ A diagram of the marketing research process which flowcharts how you should design and implement any survey or other research you do. (CD0601)

- ✔ Seven Questions to Ask When Reviewing a Survey, which will help you avoid the errors that plague most surveys and make their results vague or misleading. (CD0602)

Asking your customers is the most powerful single technique for planning or improving your marketing activities. Somewhere in customers' heads or hearts lies the answer to every question, including how to grow your company ten-fold in the next three years. You just have to get that information out of them in order to profit from it.

Oh, and they probably don't know what they know, so it's not as easy as just asking them what to do. It takes system, method, and the willingness to sift through a lot of junk information for a few pearls of wisdom or a single startling insight.

In this chapter, I add a couple of action-oriented methods to those I covered in *Marketing For Dummies* and my earlier books. (If you want to take a crash course on the basics of marketing research, try *The Portable MBA in Marketing* or *The Vest-Pocket Marketer* for background coverage.) Specifically, I'm going to queue up two research methods that, thanks to that handy CD, I can get you going on right away. And I'll also share some designs for what I call passive research tools — simple customer satisfaction cards that you can mail out or leave around to invite comments from customers. So this won't be a textbookish or lengthy coverage of customer research, but it will be a very practical one. I'll start with the tools I've queued up for your use.

# Getting to Know Your Customer

Industrial chemicals maker Cabot Corporation recently developed an informal marketing research technique that involved the use of in-depth customer interviews. The interviews were designed to identify customer concerns or suggestions and to help Cabot find out how it was viewed in the marketplace. And — here's the most original part of the project — all the interviews were conducted by Cabot's salespeople or distributors. No expensive survey research firms. No forms to send out by mail. No statistical analysis or boring bar charts. Just talking to customers.

Cabot implemented their plan as follows. People who normally made sales calls took a few days off from selling and spent the time conducting informational interviews with key customers instead. To make sure that they knew how to conduct a polite, research-oriented interview, Cabot first ran them all through a short training course.

In the course, they were given a printed guide with step-by-step instructions and questions to ask. And the training also *taught them how to ask* by having them practice in role-playing exercises. The main point that a training session like this needs to convey is that the interviews are informational only and can't be turned into disguised sales pitches. Customers will be angry if they feel they were deceived about the purpose of the meeting or telephone call. (I've also conducted some training in informal, qualitative survey techniques like this and can tell you it takes a little practice to become a good listener and a nonjudgmental interviewer.)

The reason Cabot Corporation trained their people before letting them go out and do customer interviews is that you really need to change your behavior to get good results. You cannot act like an interested party. You need to play the role of researcher if you want them to play the role of "researchee."

Just remember, no matter what they say, you don't argue with your customers. Got that? I said, *don't argue with your customers.* I don't care if their views are based on incorrect information or a false interpretation. You are doing research, not debating. For customer interviews to work, you need to avoid defensive reactions. Act like a dispassionate third party who just wants to clarify exactly what the customer thinks. Then study their reactions later and try to figure out why they think the way they do.

You can use the same technique yourself, or have your sales, marketing, or service staff use the technique, to find out what improvements to make in order to make customers happier. (I also recommend having senior managers or company owners conduct at least one in-depth customer interview per month to keep them in touch with reality.)

Try calling a few customers and asking them "if they'd be willing to participate in an informational interview to help you with your research into how to improve your product and/or service." I think you'll be pleasantly surprised at how many of them are willing and even eager to provide their input once they see that you are sincerely open to constructive criticism. Most customers feel like their opinions are not wanted. They are thrilled to find someone who cares.

To ensure that you or your people conduct successful customer interviews, try using the Customer Debriefing Form on the CD (filename CD0603), so you can adapt it to your specific needs and print multiple copies for use in interviews.

This is a form my firm has used in the past when training salespeople in what we term *active research,* which basically means any simple, hands-on ways to gather insights from your customers or others in your market. (My associate Charles Schewe calls it "walking the dog research" and advocates asking exploratory questions in casual, natural interactions with customers.) The customer debriefing is a particularly good form of action research and one I've used many times for my own business as well as for clients. Try it. I guarantee you'll learn at least one new and useful thing about your own business when you go out and ask customers to open up and give you honest feedback.

# Auditing Your Customer Service

How good is your service? One way to find out is to ask customers for an overall rating of it.

That's what surveys like the 7 X 7 survey in Figure 6-1 (and on your CD as CD0604) do. They give you an idea of whether customers think you are good, fair, or poor to do business with.

## The "7 x 7" Customer Satisfaction Survey

1 = Strongly Disagree          7 = Strongly Agree

1 2 3 4 5 6 7          I am highly satisfied with all aspects of customer service.

1 2 3 4 5 6 7          I definitely will make more purchases from this company in the future.

1 2 3 4 5 6 7          I commonly recommend this company to other customers.

1 2 3 4 5 6 7          This company is highly responsive to customer needs.

1 2 3 4 5 6 7          This company's service is faster than typical of the industry.

1 2 3 4 5 6 7          This company's employees are helpful and cooperative.

1 2 3 4 5 6 7          This company is good at resolving problems for customers.

Overall Interpretation:

Overall score = _____ out of a possible 49 points. To convert to a percentage basis, divide score by 0.49. Interpret as you might a grade in a class. For instance, a score of 42 = 85.7% which is a B and not bad, but certainly leaves room for improvement. To have service that attracts new customers and brings back old customers for more, you probably need A level performance, which means a score of 45 or above.

Item-by-item Interpretation:

If your score
is low on item:          You need to focus on improving:

1          Overall customer service; focus on the entire process and consider retraining all employees.

2          Purchase intent; focus on delivering a quality experience and product and following up to make sure users are happy with their purchase.

3          Referrals; focus on boosting positive word-of-mouth by raising overall quality and in particular by making sure you notice any problems or critical incidents and resolve each one positively.

**Figure 6-1:** A general customer satisfaction survey for your use.

4    Responsiveness; make sure you recognize and react to customer requests, complaints or problems quickly and visibly. Also train service employees to demonstrate more empathy (empathetic listening skills are needed).

5    Service speed; work on handling customer orders or needs more quickly and reliably.

6    Helpfulness; work on providing supportive service characterized by being accessible/available to customers and eager to meet their specific needs.

7    Problem resolution; make sure you have appropriate processes for identifying and resolving complaints or customer concerns, including ways of compensating customers for service interruptions.

Coyright © 1998 by Alexander Hiam & Associates

Surveys such as the template I've provided are a good idea. They allow you to "take the temperature" of customer service quickly and easily. If the answers are not near he top of the scale, you know your patient is ill.

But then what? What if customers don't like you as much as you'd like them to? How do you know what to actually *do* about it?

Well, you can always make a guess, try a change, and see if your popularity increases. And I recommend that approach. But sometimes you can't figure out what the root causes of low satisfaction or continued complaints are. Then you need to dig deeper, and that's where the Customer Service Audit comes in. It's a much more powerful tool. It will reveal things you didn't even know you didn't know.

UPS always assumed that speed of delivery was the key to success. Competitors competed on speed, and customers always said they valued speed and were upset when packages came late. So UPS understandably focused on speed. Their drivers raced in and out of offices and front porches, trying to beat the clock.

Then UPS talked to some customers who said they thought the drivers were in too much of a hurry to be friendly or helpful. Customers said they wished drivers would stop long enough to answer questions and give advice. This response revealed an entirely different dimension of customer service that the company had been ignoring in their quest for speed.

Once they realized that friendliness and helpfulness of drivers was important to customers, UPS was able to change its approach. It gave new instructions to drivers and gave them permission and training to provide more in-the-field customer relations and advice.

Probably a quarter or more of your customers aren't that happy with your company. Most of their concerns are hidden from sight unless you go looking, because less than 5 percent of unhappy customers complain. The other 95 percent of them are like the sunken part of an iceberg. They are a serious hazard to navigation, but nobody can see them. Except maybe other customers, since people are about five times more likely to tell others about bad experiences than about good experiences. So those hidden grumblers are out there spreading the bad word without your knowledge. Time to do an audit and find out what's troubling them.

## Performing a customer service audit

How are you going to get to the bottom of hidden, complex customer attitudes toward your service? An audit is the best approach. A customer service audit uses a survey to explore the specifics of what customers want, and how well you think you deliver what they want. Here's a five-step process for performing your audit.

1. **Identify specific attributes of customer service, like speed, friendliness, convenience, availability, or fast action on complaints.**

   In other words, it breaks down customer service into as many components as possible to permit you to get specific in managing it.

2. **Ask customers how important each specific attribute of service really is.**

   Some aspects of service are more important than others, and when you know what they value most, then you know where to put your efforts so as to do the most good.

3. **Ask customers how well you perform on each of those specific attributes. Do they think you are doing well or not?**

4. **Think about it.**

   Specifically, look for gaps between customer priorities and your performance. If you are performing less than wonderfully on their top-priority service attributes, then you better work on those areas right now. If you are doing wonderfully on things that they rank as low priority, then you can slack off in those areas, which may give you room to improve on their higher priorities. So think about what changes you can make to better match your service performance to customers' service priorities.

5. **Make some changes.**

   Often, surveys and analyses like this end with a nice report or to-do list. To make your audit pay off, you actually have to *make some changes* in how you deliver customer service. So make an action plan and then remind yourself to check on your execution next week, next month, and so on until you see real, lasting improvements in high-priority service specifics.

# Using the audit template

The hardest part of doing a good customer service audit is figuring out what to ask customers. This seems like an easy task, but don't be deceived. If you just ask them about the obvious things, well, maybe you miss something important that isn't obvious! So take plenty of time to *brainstorm a long list of specific aspects of customer service.* Then ask a few customers if you've covered everything and add any ideas they suggest. A good, detailed list of what customer service consists of is the start of every great customer service audit.

Here are some candidates, taken from a variety of businesses and industries, to get you started:

- Politeness of personnel
- Getting job done right the first time

- ✔ Apologizing for delays
- ✔ Prompt warranty work
- ✔ Not arguing over who's responsible
- ✔ Things ready when promised
- ✔ Things made convenient for customer
- ✔ Friendliness of personnel
- ✔ Helping to solve problems
- ✔ Providing useful information
- ✔ Being available when needed
- ✔ Performing only the requested work
- ✔ Performing only the necessary work
- ✔ Keeping things neat and clean
- ✔ Reminding customers when supplies are needed
- ✔ Reminding customers when maintenance is needed
- ✔ Responding quickly to complaints
- ✔ Responding fairly to complaints
- ✔ Matching competitors' prices
- ✔ Matching competitors' capabilities
- ✔ Answering the phone quickly
- ✔ Not pestering with irritating sales pitches
- ✔ Providing loaner equipment when yours is being repaired
- ✔ Billing accurately
- ✔ Not using rude letters to collect bills
- ✔ Not using rude phone calls to collect bills
- ✔ Not stuffing bills with junk-mail advertisements
- ✔ Providing frequent-user benefits
- ✔ Honoring frequent-user offers fairly without tricky small print
- ✔ Informing customers quickly and fully about problems
- ✔ Making up for mistakes or delays with offers of real value
- ✔ Being reliable
- ✔ Being consistent and predictable
- ✔ Being creative at problem-solving

You can copy this list or make up your own, then ask a few customers to look at it and tell you if it describes the things they care about. (The list is on your CD in a survey template with the filename CD0605.) Encourage reviewers to point out anything that might be missing. That's a good way to get the most complete list possible.

Once you have a good, long list, you can prepare a survey and systematically ask as many customers as possible to respond to it. The survey should basically look like Table 6-1, whether you plan to fill it in yourself or have them do it:

| Table 6-1 | Customer Service Survey | |
|---|---|---|
| *Customer Service Element* | *How Important Is I?* | *How Do We Do on It?* |
| Politeness of personnel | __not important<br>__slightly important<br>__important<br>__very important | __poor<br>__fair<br>__good<br>__excellent |
| Getting job done right the first time | __not important<br>__slightly important<br>__important<br>__very important | __poor<br>__fair<br>__good<br>__excellent |
| Apologizing for delays | __not important<br>__slightly important<br>__important<br>__very important | __poor<br>__fair<br>__good<br>__excellent |
| Prompt warranty work | __not important<br>__slightly important<br>__important<br>__very important | __poor<br>__fair<br>__good<br>__excellent |
| Not arguing over who's responsible | __not important<br>__slightly important<br>__important<br>__very important | __poor<br>__fair<br>__good<br>__excellent |
| Things ready when promised | __not important<br>__slightly important<br>__important<br>__very important | __poor<br>__fair<br>__good<br>__excellent |

# How do you perform the survey?

The key to performing the survey successfully is to ask a bunch of customers. The best methodology is the one that lets you do that as easily and quickly as possible. If customers are willing to fill in a written survey and return it, then let them do it. Often they don't pay much attention to such requests, in which case you'll need to ask them in person or on the phone to answer some questions for you. Face-to-face interviews in which you explain that you're auditing your customer service, then ask them to rate each statement while you fill in the form, get reasonably high participation rates. Telephone requests to do the same have somewhat lower rates, and mail requests have the lowest response rates — but are the least trouble for you, so maybe it doesn't matter if only 5 or 10 percent of mailed surveys come back.

If you aren't sure which method works best or whether a particular method of administering the survey might be biased in some way, try two or three different methods. They key is just to collect a bunch of responses. And be polite, always explaining who you (really) are, why you need the information (to improve your company's service), and asking permission to ask them some questions. Then at least you won't make any enemies, even if they decline to participate.

What's a bunch of responses? How many do you really need? Well, statistically, survey research firms often want to get several hundred or more responses. But then, they want to do fancy statistics in which they chop up the responses into little subsets by cross-tabulating one response against another, so they need big starting numbers. You probably don't. A dozen responses will tell you something useful. Two or three dozen will give you more certainty that the results represent your customers accurately. Don't be obsessive about it; just get as many as you can easily get in a few weeks of effort at most.

In *analyzing the results* of a customer service audit, look for disparities between the first and second ratings:

- ✔ If you are doing well on an important service attribute, then you can leave well enough alone.

- ✔ If you are doing poorly on an important service attribute, then you need to improve your performance on it right away.

- ✔ If you are doing well on an unimportant attribute, consider putting less effort and resources into it so you can emphasize a more important attribute.

Often you'll find that you are putting lots of energy into something that is not too important to your customers, and not putting enough energy into something else that really matters to them. That's what UPS learned in the case I described in the preceding section. And that's what the sample results in Table 6-2 indicate as well.

| Table 6-2 | Sample Results and Display Format | |
| --- | --- | --- |
| *Customer Service Element No.* | *Average Importance* | *Average Performance* |
| 1. Politeness | 3 important | 4 excellent |
| 2. Right the first time | 4 very important | 2 fair |
| 3. Apologizing for delays | 3 important | 4 excellent |
| 4. Prompt warranty work | 2 slightly important | 4 excellent |
| 5. Not arguing | 4 very important | 3 good |
| Average Scores | 3.2 | 3.4 |

This table illustrates the common problem of overperforming on some elements of customer service and underperforming on others. Note that I give each rating a number from one to four using the following conversions:

| | |
| --- | --- |
| 1 = not important | 1 = poor |
| 2 = slightly | 2 = fair |
| 3 = important | 3 = good |
| 4 = very important | 4 = excellent |

That way, it's easier to compare the results on each item. If your performance rating is equal to or above the importance rating, well, you don't have any trouble on that element. But if your performance rating number is below the importance rating, that suggests you need to make the item a higher priority.

Using numbers also permits you to calculate (average) and compare your overall performance rating with an overall importance rating for all of the elements you tested. In the example in Table 6-2, you can see that such averages can be deceptive. Performance averages higher than importance. Does this mean everything's fine? Not at all! The higher average performance rating suggests the firm is putting too much effort into some items. It's overperforming in areas where performance is not very important to customers.

If you got a high average performance rating combined with overperformance on the most important service elements, then you'd be in a position to celebrate. But as long as you see underperformance on any important elements, you know there is more opportunity to improve your service.

# A Good Example

Figure 6-2 shows an example of an excellent mail piece that asks customers what they think of the service they're getting. It is a simple, quick survey, packaged in a compellingly well designed fold-out card that catches the eye and encourages feedback. (It's a piece by Professional Marketing Associates, whose work pops up elsewhere in this book.)

| | |
|---|---|
| **1** When you call or visit is our staff friendly and courteous?<br>☐ Always ☐ Usually ☐ Never | **6** Are there any changes you'd like to see us make?<br>_____<br>_____<br>_____<br>_____ |
| **2** If and when you've had questions, have we answered them clearly and completely?<br>☐ Yes ☐ No | |
| **3** Were any details that needed to be worked out handled to your satisfaction?<br>☐ Yes ☐ No | **7** I'm pleased! Here are two people you can contact to offer a no-obligation review of their insurance coverage:<br>NAME<br>ADDRESS |
| **4** If you've had any claims, were you happy with the assistance we provided to expedite matters promptly and fairly?<br>☐ Yes ☐ No | CITY   STATE   ZIP<br>PHONE (DAY)   HOME PHONE<br>NAME<br>ADDRESS |
| **5** How would you rate our knowledge and ability to deliver the right coverage for your specific needs?<br>☐ Excellent ☐ Good ☐ Adequate ☐ Unsatisfactory | CITY   STATE   ZIP<br>PHONE (DAY)   HOME PHONE |

**Figure 6-2:** A good mailer seeking customer feedback.

# On Your CD

Check out the following items on the CD-ROM:

- ✔ The Marketing Research Process (CD0601)
- ✔ Seven Questions to Ask When Reviewing a Survey (CD0602)
- ✔ Customer Debriefing Form (template) (CD0603)
- ✔ 7 X 7 Customer Satisfaction Survey (CD0604)
- ✔ Customer Service Audit (template) (CD0605)

# Chapter 7

# Dealing with Difficult Customers

*T*he world is full of difficult customers. People who complain loudly and make unreasonable demands. People who are angry about a minor problem and won't listen to reason. People who walk away, taking their business with them, just because they didn't think they could communicate with you. And people who are difficult to sell to because they are hard to get along with or don't seem to like you.

If you could make all the problematic prospects and customers happy and eager to work with you, the benefits would be tremendous. Sales would go more smoothly and there would be more sales as well. And you or your sales and service personnel would find work a lot easier and less stressful.

There are, in fact, a number of powerful techniques for eliminating the "difficult customer" problem. They work by getting at the root causes of problems with customers or prospects. When you can accurately diagnose these problems and correct them by eliminating their causes, well, then you don't ever have to have a difficult customer. Your relations with prospects and customers will be far smoother and friendlier, and you will find it easier and more profitable to get and keep customers.

## What Makes Customers Difficult?

What are the root causes of difficulties in your (or your firm's) relationships with customers and prospects? In almost all cases, the problems arise because of communication problems with individual customers or prospects. Sometimes there is also a critical incident that upset or angered a customer or prospect, and this needs to be dealt with carefully. But in general, incidents are far easier to cope with when you get the communication style right than when you don't. So the best overall strategy for dealing with difficult customers is to focus on how to communicate with them.

Because these issues are so important and widespread, my firm does a variety of trainings and workshops addressing them. I share the best of those events with you in this chapter.

If you are having communication problems, then you need to figure out why and make adjustments in how you communicate with the customer. It is generally a matter of style. In this chapter, I show you how to figure out what style will work better than the one you currently use, and I give you a simple but powerful tool for diagnosing style-related communication problems and figuring out how to adapt your communication style so as to please the customer or prospect.

I start by taking the case of a problem in one-to-one communication. These sorts of problems arise often in the following cases:

- A salesperson's communications with a good prospect who just cannot be converted to a customer
- A salesperson's communications with an existing customer who is hard to handle and does not do as much business as possible
- A customer service person's difficulties in communicating with a customer
- A business owner's difficulties in developing good rapport with a key person at a company he or she wants to land as a customer
- A consultant's frustrations at being unable to develop closer relations with a key person at a company he or she wants to land as a customer
- A marketing manager's difficulties in communicating with and managing salespeople, distributors, or independent sales representatives

In cases like these, you usually find a difference in personal style. It might be something as simple as one person tending to be a "talker" who dominates the interactions, while the other values privacy and is uncomfortable with that style. It might be more in how the two people think about the topic they are discussing. If one is a systematic, step-by-step thinker, and the other is creative and unstructured, they will have a hard time communicating and getting along.

Such style differences are often hidden factors, hard to identify and correct, because we are rarely fully aware of our own styles or other people's styles. We tend to think that someone who has a different style from our own is pushy, unfriendly, not interested, not smart, or doesn't like us — rather than realizing that the differences are ones of style instead of substance. That's why I recommend using a diagnostic tool to find solutions to communications failures that get in the way of good sales and marketing.

# The Difficult Customer Diagnostic

The Difficult Customer Diagnostic is based on an activity I first used with a group of sales managers from a General Motors affiliate. I brought along copies of an inventory of personal style and used them to find out why these salespeople had difficulty with certain of their customers. In theory, I reasoned, interpersonal style differences could be quite important. And I knew that such assessments were great tools for diagnosing and fixing style problems in interpersonal communications because I had already used them to help work teams learn how to function together more effectively. But would the method work as well in the sales context? I asked the sales managers in my workshop to bear with me and give the idea a try.

The results were overwhelming. It was by far the most effective and popular activity I had ever run in a sales or marketing workshop. Each and every participant was truly excited about the results. It was simple and easy to run, and it produced results that pleased and informed the participants. At the end of the day, they crowded around me, wanting to talk about this particular activity rather than anything else I'd covered that day (and I'd presented a great deal of material on marketing-related topics). They also cleaned me out of extra copies of that assessment I'd brought along. Everyone wanted to take the activity back to his or her office to share with associates and to use on other customers.

In short, I knew I'd stumbled onto something big. But at that point, I was using forms designed for other applications. I had to edit them with a magic marker to make them work. And I didn't have the well-developed learning points and how-tos of a good training. So I passed the idea on to my training materials company and we went to work to develop a tool and method that was designed specifically for use in the sales and marketing context. Here it is.

## Premise of the method

Some customers are more difficult than others. When salespeople or account representatives have difficulty dealing with a particular customer or prospect, in spite of multiple efforts to "get along" or "close the sale," the problem is often one of style, not substance. There are many instances in which a salesperson has something of legitimate value to offer the customer but cannot make the sale because of a mismatch in their styles. There are also many instances in which an ongoing sales or service relationship seems to be less productive and more difficult than it should be. Again, style issues may be at fault.

In the modern workplace, employees now commonly receive training in how to flex their styles in order to cooperate more effectively with team members or other co-workers. But this simple principle is rarely applied to sales relationships. In the training activity you can go through in a moment, salespeople (or customer service representatives) have the chance to:

- ✔ Profile their most difficult customer's style and compare it to their own profile

- ✔ Key out some simple prescriptions about how to communicate more effectively with this customer

- ✔ Discover that they have significantly different style profiles from their most difficult customers

- ✔ See how to improve their ability to communicate with difficult customers in general by adapting their style to suit the customer's preferences

The immediate benefit of this exercise is to help salespeople or others in the fields of customer service and general marketing figure out what to do about a frustrating customer relationship. The long-term benefit is to help them become better at adapting their style to suit each customer's preferences. By learning to communicate in the customer's preferred style, the salesperson is able to be truly customer-oriented.

## *Flexing your style to be customer-oriented*

What does it mean to be customer-oriented? Most organizations stress adapting the offer to the customer's needs and wants. But good salespeople know they must also adapt their *style*, because different customers prefer different styles. So being customer-oriented means more than adapting the offer to the customer's needs — that's the substance of being customer-oriented. Being customer-oriented also means flexing one's interpersonal style to better meet the customer's interpersonal needs — that's the style of customer orientation.

Here is a way to illustrate this important point:

| Dimension | Customer Orientation |
| --- | --- |
| Substance | Right products, services, timing, placement |
| Style | Right communication style, relationship |

Experienced salespeople, service providers, and marketers in general already accept this point that style is as important as substance. Yet they are still likely to encounter some customers who they find difficult because of style reasons. It is often far harder to get style right than to get substance right because human personalities are subtle and difficult to diagnose. As a result:

- ✔ The majority of salespeople actually sell to people who are most like them in terms of personality profiles and communication styles. They don't close many sales to people who are different in interpersonal style. As a result, they may run into unnecessary problems with 50–60 percent of prospects.

✔ Even the most experienced and skilled salespeople encounter some customers whose interpersonal style needs they can't meet, and therefore have trouble with 10–15 percent of customers because of style needs.

✔ Top-performing salespeople in general are very good at flexing their interpersonal styles, and therefore encounter even fewer people whose style needs they cannot meet. They may have style problems with 1–5 percent of prospects and customers.

So no matter where you or your associates or employees fall in this spectrum of experience and interpersonal skills, there is still some "business left on the table" that you could be doing if you acquired additional interpersonal skills. The purpose of this chapter is to give you the advanced skills needed to understand and adapt to any and all style needs. And by focusing the activity on a specific relationship that you identify as troubling or difficult, you can make the results relevant and important in your daily working life.

## "I did it _their_ way . . ."

Flexing your style means temporarily changing to the most comfortable style for the other person, or, in other words, doing it their way.

The way to flex your style is to make small changes in behavior. The sorts of changes you need to make depend on the style differences between you and your customer. For example, if you are dealing with a very private person who might be put off by your more extroverted style, you need to:

✔ Respect their preference for peace and quiet by giving them more privacy than you need.

✔ Ask for their permission to talk with them about their purchase decision, instead of assuming they'll want to talk about it.

✔ Schedule meetings and telephone conversations at their convenience, giving them control over when they talk with you.

✔ Use more arm's-length channels of communication more fully. Write them notes, send e-mails and faxes. Prepare a written report to present your suggested solution to their problem instead of presenting it in person.

And in general, your understanding of their need for privacy will help you make sure they are comfortable around you. You'll give them more personal space, be careful not to "overstay your welcome," and make a point of listening more and leaving more gaps in the conversation to let them think about what's been said. You can solve most of your communication problems just by realizing that their greater preference for privacy is at the root of these problems.

By flexing their own style in these ways, the public, extroverted salesperson cools downs his or her style significantly. The personal, introverted customer will feel more comfortable and at ease in future interactions. The customer is less likely to form a negative opinion of the salesperson and, in fact, will probably like the salesperson. The salesperson will seem more respectful and polite, and will appear to be a better listener who is more interested in and aware of the customer's preferences and feelings. The customer will enjoy interacting with the salesperson.

People are still people, even when they communicate over the Internet. And they still need custom treatment in order to feel like their communication needs are being met. But ever try to get help from a company over the Internet? E-mailing them from their Web site is usually a disaster. Most companies send the same canned message to every query. And that message is rarely helpful. In fact, in one recent survey by editors at Sales & Marketing Management, most companies responded to customer questions over the Web by trying to send them to a toll-free telephone number. In other words, they couldn't handle the question at all.

When asked about how they handle customer questions over the Web, a spokesperson for Motorola admitted, "I know it's a little scary, but frankly, we're still working out how to handle customer questions online."

Here's a simple way to work that one out. Have competent sales or service staff read each e-mail received from a legitimate customer or prospect. Have them e-mail back immediately with a full reply or a request for more information. And also have them ask how the person would like to proceed. Switch to phone? Stick with e-mail? Get detailed information in the mail? See a salesperson? Visit a location of the business? In other words, get the communication going, and give them choices so you can find out what their style preferences are.

## What, exactly, *is* their way?

Now I want to take a look at your style and compare it to a difficult customer's style (or you may substitute a difficult distributor, associate, or anyone else you want to work better with in the future). It's important to profile your own style along with the style of your difficult customer. You'll be comparing your own style *with* theirs.

To complete a style profile, you answer some simple disagree-agree questions. These questions will give you eight separate scores, which you will then be able to plot on a simple graph in order to draw your own style profile and compare it with your customer's.

The first four sets of questions in the Difficult Customer Diagnostic you are about to complete address thinking style. The next four sets of questions address interpersonal style. Together, they determine how you work with customers and how they prefer you to work with them:

| Style Profiles: | What They Tell You: |
| --- | --- |
| Cognitive Style Profile | How you think, what you think about |
| Interpersonal Style Profile | How you relate to others, how you communicate with others |

When you look at all this information about yourself and a difficult customer, you almost always find that that you and the customer have some significant points of difference.

When you adjust your style to accommodate the customer's profile, you overcome those points of difference.

It's really a very simple method. But it only works when you've got the information needed to analyze profiles correctly. Most of the time, people are unable to "see" these key style differences until they've used a formal diagnostic tool and gained some experience with it. So I want you to do just what those GM sales managers did for me in that workshop I told you about. I want you to fill in the Difficult Customer Diagnostic form, which is shown in the next section. (Or you can print clean copies of this and the next form from your CD and use them if you want. The filenames are CD0601 and CD0602.)

## The Difficult Customer Diagnostic

Rate each of the following statements based on how well they fit your own style and the style of a specific customer you have in mind. If a statement fits very well, circle "5." If it does not fit at all, circle "1." Or circle a number between these two extremes. Here is the scale:

- 1 = not at all
- 2 = not really
- 3 = maybe, maybe not
- 4 = usually
- 5 = definitely

### 1. Ra scores

| You | How well does statement fit? | Customer |
|---|---|---|
| 1 2 3 4 5 | Throws self into project without a plan | 1 2 3 4 5 |
| 1 2 3 4 5 | Takes unstructured approach | 1 2 3 4 5 |
| 1 2 3 4 5 | Does not like to follow instructions | 1 2 3 4 5 |
| 1 2 3 4 5 | Likes to work on many things at once | 1 2 3 4 5 |
| 1 2 3 4 5 | Does things out of order | 1 2 3 4 5 |
| Total = ___ | <- yours   "Ra" scores   customer's -> | Total = ___ |

### 2. Se Scores

| You | How well does statement fit? | Customer |
|---|---|---|
| 1 2 3 4 5 | Likes detailed plans | 1 2 3 4 5 |
| 1 2 3 4 5 | Stays focused on a single goal | 1 2 3 4 5 |
| 1 2 3 4 5 | Does things in proper order | 1 2 3 4 5 |
| 1 2 3 4 5 | Follows instructions | 1 2 3 4 5 |
| 1 2 3 4 5 | Is analytical, not intuitive | 1 2 3 4 5 |
| Total = ___ | <- yours   "Se" scores   customer's -> | Total = ___ |

### 3. Di Scores

| You | How well does statement fit? | Customer |
|---|---|---|
| 1 2 3 4 5 | Seeks options and alternatives | 1 2 3 4 5 |
| 1 2 3 4 5 | Seeks new combinations | 1 2 3 4 5 |
| 1 2 3 4 5 | Has many ideas | 1 2 3 4 5 |
| 1 2 3 4 5 | Gets excited about each new thing | 1 2 3 4 5 |
| 1 2 3 4 5 | Asks unusual questions | 1 2 3 4 5 |
| Total = ___ | <- yours   "Di" scores   customer's -> | Total = ___ |

## 4. Co scores

| You | How well does statement fit? | Customer |
|---|---|---|
| 1 2 3 4 5 | Narrows down the choices | 1 2 3 4 5 |
| 1 2 3 4 5 | Organizes projects well | 1 2 3 4 5 |
| 1 2 3 4 5 | Combines projects to get them done | 1 2 3 4 5 |
| 1 2 3 4 5 | Good at finishing things | 1 2 3 4 5 |
| 1 2 3 4 5 | Finds common ground in arguments | 1 2 3 4 5 |
| Total = ___ | <- yours   "Co" scores   customer's -> | Total = ___ |

## 5. Pr scores

| You | How well does statement fit? | Customer |
|---|---|---|
| 1 2 3 4 5 | Likes to work alone | 1 2 3 4 5 |
| 1 2 3 4 5 | Not very social | 1 2 3 4 5 |
| 1 2 3 4 5 | Finds collaboration difficult | 1 2 3 4 5 |
| 1 2 3 4 5 | Distracted by too many people | 1 2 3 4 5 |
| 1 2 3 4 5 | Keeps thoughts to self | 1 2 3 4 5 |
| Total = ___ | <- yours   "Pr" scores   customer's -> | Total = ___ |

## 6. Pu scores

| You | How well does statement fit? | Customer |
|---|---|---|
| 1 2 3 4 5 | Enjoys working with others | 1 2 3 4 5 |
| 1 2 3 4 5 | Very social | 1 2 3 4 5 |
| 1 2 3 4 5 | Contributes to groups with confidence | 1 2 3 4 5 |
| 1 2 3 4 5 | Stimulated by other people | 1 2 3 4 5 |
| 1 2 3 4 5 | Likes to share ideas with others | 1 2 3 4 5 |
| Total = ___ | <- yours   "Pu" scores   customer's -> | Total = ___ |

**7. Re scores**

| You | How well does statement fit? | Customer |
|---|---|---|
| 1 2 3 4 5 | Attracts people who want to talk | 1 2 3 4 5 |
| 1 2 3 4 5 | Good at sensing how others feel | 1 2 3 4 5 |
| 1 2 3 4 5 | Open-minded | 1 2 3 4 5 |
| 1 2 3 4 5 | Asks lots of questions | 1 2 3 4 5 |
| 1 2 3 4 5 | Appreciates advice and suggestions | 1 2 3 4 5 |
| Total = ___ | <- yours    "Re" scores    customer's -> | Total = ___ |

**8. Ex scores**

| You | How well does statement fit? | Customer |
|---|---|---|
| 1 2 3 4 5 | Shares ideas with others | 1 2 3 4 5 |
| 1 2 3 4 5 | Expresses feelings well | 1 2 3 4 5 |
| 1 2 3 4 5 | Has strong opinions | 1 2 3 4 5 |
| 1 2 3 4 5 | Not afraid to disagree | 1 2 3 4 5 |
| 1 2 3 4 5 | Champions own ideas | 1 2 3 4 5 |
| Total = ___ | <- yours    "Ex" scores    customer's -> | Total = ___ |

When you finish the questions, calculate your scores by adding each set of five questions and entering the totals in the "Total = ___" sections. You get eight scores for yourself and eight scores for your customer. Each score should be somewhere between 5 and 25.

## Interpreting your scores

Transfer your scores to each bar of the scoring sheet by circling the appropriate numbers on each side of the black square on the first half of the profile sheet. Then on each bar, darken the area between your two scores to see what your style looks like. Is the bar centered or biased toward one side? (Usually, people have a clear bias.) And is the bar short, indicating a lack of flexibility, or is it long, indicating you can use both styles? (Usually, bars are fairly short.)

Next, transfer your customer's scores to the second half of the profile sheet. Darken the areas between scores to draw the customer's bars, just as you did your own.

## Your Profile

Random                                     Sequential

25 23 21 19 15 13 11 9 7 5 ■ 5 7 9 11 13 15 19 21 23 25

*How do you think?*

Divergent                                  Convergent

25 23 21 19 15 13 11 9 7 5 ■ 5 7 9 11 13 15 19 21 23 25

*What do you think about?*

Private                                    Public

25 23 21 19 15 13 11 9 7 5 ■ 5 7 9 11 13 15 19 21 23 25

*Do others use up or give you energy?*

Receptive                                  Expressive

25 23 21 19 15 13 11 9 7 5 ■ 5 7 9 11 13 15 19 21 23 25

*Do you tend to listen or talk more?*

## Your Customer's Profile

Random                                     Sequential

25 23 21 19 15 13 11 9 7 5 ■ 5 7 9 11 13 15 19 21 23 25

*How does customer think?*

Divergent                                  Convergent

25 23 21 19 15 13 11 9 7 5 ■ 5 7 9 11 13 15 19 21 23 25

*What does customer think about?*

Private                                    Public

25 23 21 19 15 13 11 9 7 5 ■ 5 7 9 11 13 15 19 21 23 25

*Do others use up or give customer energy?*

Receptive                                    Expressive

25 23 21 19 15 13 11 9 7 5 ■ 5 7 9 11 13 15 19 21 23 25

*Does customer tend to listen or talk more?*

The scoring sheet appears on the CD-ROM with the filename CD0702.

## How does your profile compare to your customer's?

Now that you've plotted your own profile and your difficult customer's profile, you simply need to compare the two and see where the biggest difference lies. On one or more of the bars, your score is probably quite different from the customer's. Your shaded area is centered toward one side while theirs is centered toward the other side. Right?

I knew it. Otherwise, they probably wouldn't be a difficult customer! Make a note of which dimensions you differ on so you can use the prescriptions I give you in a moment. For instance, are you more of a divergent thinker, while they are a strongly convergent thinker? (That's what the second line of the profiles shows.)

Go through and make a note of the one or more dimensions in which your profile is clearly different from your customer's profile. These differences are most likely the root of your difficulties.

If you'd like to see more about what each of the scores in your Difficult Customer Diagnostic mean, you can check the CD for the file named CD0703. It includes an interpretation key that gives you detailed descriptions and examples to illustrate what each of those style names mean. See if your style profile rings true when you look up the styles that dominate your profile.

## Prescribing the cure

Now you need to figure out what to do about the differences between your style and your customer's style. What you need to do is figure out how to adapt your style. For instance, if you are more of a divergent thinker, and your customer is strongly convergent, then you need to adapt the way you think and talk about business with this customer to accommodate their need for a convergent style.

For example, convergent thinkers like to focus narrowly and want to move toward closure. They don't want to keep hearing about more complexities or choices or details. They want a neat, orderly, directional process that they can see will get them to their end goal efficiently. And you can give them that. You can easily accommodate this style need once you understand it.

But that's just one example, and it may not apply to your difficult customer and you. To find out what to do to deal with *your* difficult customer, simply locate the appropriate section in the table that appears on the CD with the filename CD0704.

For you to flex your sales style in order to work well with a difficult customer, you need to prep by reviewing the appropriate cell(s) of the table before interacting with the customer. If you fear it will be difficult to keep to the guidelines in a meeting or telephone conversation, you may make some notes to glance at during the interaction. That way, you won't forget your "game plan" for taming the difficult customer.

## *Flexing your service style*

Customer service is integral to good marketing, because it builds profitable long-term relationships. The Difficult Customer Diagnostic works well in handling customer service problems and complaints where you seem to have trouble soothing the customer. Some customers just don't seem to like your style. They get increasingly irritated when you try to calm them down. Or they demand to speak to someone else. And there are often customers who become chronic complainers and never seem to be satisfied. Often the roots of these service difficulties are the differences in your cognitive or interpersonal styles that the Difficult Customer Diagnostic measures.

When you flex your service style to make sure you have excellent communications with all your customers, things go much more smoothly. For one thing, you get loyal customers who like your style and feel that they have good, open communications with you. You are also more likely to hear about any problems early on, so you can move to fix them.

Jill Barad, the president of Mattel, is well-known for her good communications skills and puts a lot of time and effort into maintaining good customer relations. According to Barad, "We go out and talk to retailers to find out what they want and what kids want." And sometimes that means finding out about a problem with one of her company's products. A Toys "R" Us executive recalls a time when some Barbie dolls weren't selling, and Barad found out about the problem right away and "came up with a 'buy one, give one to your friend' promotion that promised a second, identical doll free to anyone who bought one. That got them out of the stores." As the same executive puts it, "She realizes problems, reacts and solves them quickly."

And that's a pretty good testimonial from a major customer. Would your customers say the same about you? Well, probably some would and some wouldn't. That's why it's so important to adjust your style to each customer's preferences and make sure that you have equally stellar communications with all of them!

Form CD0705 on the CD, the Difficult Customer Diagnostic, is interpreted for use in ongoing service interactions or in coping with an escalating customer problem. The principles are the same as in the sales interactions in Form CD0704, but the application is a little different, so it's useful to have this more service-oriented table for reference, too.

# What Style Should Your Ads Use?

A really cool extension of this difficult customer activity is for profiling your marketing communications instead of yourself. In other words, look at an ad or brochure or Web site (or a bunch of them) and then fill in the "you" side of the diagnostic. Ask yourself how well each statement describes the style your marketing communications use.

Then ask yourself how well the statements describe your customers in general. Or, if you have the time and resources, turn the diagnostic into a customer survey (just block out the right-hand answer column) and collect data from fifty or more customers on their own styles. Is there a pattern? Which style profile is most common among customers? And does it clash with the style of your advertising, Web site, or whatever? If so, rework your marketing communications to match the dominant customer style needs. That way, you won't be turning customers off with your marketing materials by accident, just because of style differences.

By the way, most copywriters and designers who develop marketing materials have unusual style profiles that clash with the average customer. Designers are more random and divergent, and their work is sometimes more public or in-your-face than customers want as well. So you can use the prescriptions of the Difficult Customer Diagnostic to help shift their style to something that customers like more — and that will make it less difficult for your marketing pieces to connect with customers.

You can profit from your knowledge of your own style profile by seeking out customers who particularly like your style and share your profile. It's always easier to do business with people like you. You can use an ad, Web site, sales letter, or newsletter as an outreach device to "call for" people with profiles like your own. To do this, let the piece be an extreme example of your profile. For instance, if you are sequential, then make all the copy follow a "1, 2, 3" outline format. Most people won't enjoy reading it, but those who do are going to love your sequential style!

You can find an example of a newsletter that implements this strategy on your CD (filename CD0706). The newsletter, called "The Gut," is published by the highly creative Darby O'Brien agency, whose style profile is random, divergent, public, and expressive. And when you look at "The Gut," you see this profile expressed to an extreme. In fact, the name itself evokes the random, divergent approach to thinking. It's not analytic (convergent) or linear (sequential). A newsletter whose masthead says, "When you know what you know go with . . . 'The Gut'" is obviously reaching out to people whose style is random/divergent enough that they are willing to go with the gut!

## On Your CD

Check out the following items on the CD-ROM:

- Difficult Customer Diagnostic (CD0701)
- Interpretation Keys for the Difficult Customer Diagnostic (CD0702 and CD0703)
- How to Adapt Your Sales Style for a Difficult Customer (CD0704 and CD0705)
- The Gut (Newsletter expressing a strong style profile) (CD0706)

# Chapter 8

# Marketing Audits and Plans

*I*n this chapter, I show you how to analyze and develop your overall marketing strategies and plans by sharing two processes with you.

The first is the marketing audit, which is a systematic examination of every aspect of sales, marketing, customer service, and even of aspects of operations that affect sales and marketing. You can perform a simple audit yourself in a relatively short period of time with the audit form I've included on the CD. I also show you how to develop some high-impact agenda items to improve your marketing performance based on the results of your audit.

The second process I share with you in this chapter is marketing planning. Researching and writing a marketing plan is a serious endeavor. It takes time and effort and a lot of information-gathering and even more thinking. So not everyone has the time to do a full-blown plan. But if you do — or if circumstances require it — I think you'll find it a very enlightening activity.

And to make your planning process smoother, I include a marketing plan template on the CD, which you can use as you write.

## Performing a Marketing Audit

A marketing audit is the quickest, easiest way to take a hard, strategic look at your entire marketing process. It often reveals hidden weak spots so you can focus on strengthening them. I like to think of audits as revealing the weak links in the marketing chain.

The marketing audit on your CD (filename CD0801) is a simple Word document that you may edit to include more or different items if you want. Or — most likely — you may simply print it out and use it like a questionnaire to evaluate your organization.

It's also helpful if you can give copies of the audit form to multiple people. The senior managers. A couple of especially good and helpful customers. Some of the salespeople or service employees. You get the idea. Capture multiple perspectives and then average the results to get a more accurate picture of your marketing program.

Often, customers rank firms lower on marketing audit items than employees of the firm do. Why? Because customers may not be aware of initiatives or programs that are supposed to reach them, but don't. So when in doubt, as always, ask the customer — and trust their judgment above your own. When it comes to making the sale, it's only the customer's opinion that counts!

The audit is divided into seven areas, each with a list of a dozen or more specific questions. The questions have yes/no answers, which makes the audit quick and easy to complete. When you complete it, you simply need to count the number of yes answers in each section and enter them into an answer sheet that looks like Table 8-1. This table also appears on the CD (filename CD0802).

| Table 8-1 | Marketing Agenda Worksheets | |
|---|---|---|
| *Activity Area* | *Formula* | *Profile Score* |
| Customer acquisition | # of yeses_____ ÷ 17 = | _____ % |
| Information gathering | # of yeses_____ ÷ 16 = | _____ % |
| Marketing planning | # of yeses_____ ÷ 18 = | _____ % |
| Communications | # of yeses_____ ÷ 37 = | _____ % |
| Customer service | # of yeses_____ ÷ 14 = | _____ % |
| Organization & management | # of yeses_____ ÷ 12 = | _____ % |
| Creativity | # of yeses_____ ÷ 12 = | _____ % |
| **Overall Score Calculation** | **Total # of yeses_____ ÷ 126 =** | _____ % |

As you can see, the form guides you through the process of calculating your profile scores, which are represented as percentages for each of the seven sections of the audit. Obviously, a 100 percent score is the best. Anything less than 90 percent for a section indicates a weakness in that area that probably deserves close attention.

## Audits reveal strengths as well as weaknesses

Don't ignore your strengths while working on your weaknesses. If you score relatively high on one or two of the sections of the marketing audit, these are probably the activity areas which are working the best for you right now. Activities in these areas no doubt contribute disproportionately to any successes you now have, which means you better take good care of them! Don't divert resources from areas of strength to areas of weakness unless you are sure that you will get improvements in efficiency and effectiveness as a result. Sometimes it even makes sense to strengthen your best area first, in order to generate more surplus profits, before you try to do too much to improve a weak area.

How precisely to invest in improving your marketing is a complex strategic decision, and no audit, and certainly no book, can give you an absolute answer. Spend some time with these results and with any other inputs you can gather, thinking about your options and weighing different possibilities. And then proceed with caution, a step at a time, testing as you go to see what kind of results you get. Great marketing is the result of creative learning, not the output of any formulaic audit or plan. So when the dust settles, this audit should simply help you initiate a thoughtful, creative, intelligent learning process.

In other words, don't forget to think.

After you convert all your section scores into percents, you can easily compare them and see which areas are more lacking and therefore more deserving of immediate attention. It's a good idea to pick the one or two areas where your scores are lowest to work on. That gives you a helpful focus in your future sales and marketing efforts.

# Using Your Marketing Profile as a Planning Tool

This profile is a useful planning tool. Use it to identify areas in which you need to improve, and areas in which you have strengths you want to maintain and take advantage of.

For example, one of my associates, Charles Schewe, used a version of this audit to help a group of executives from electric utilities look at their marketing functions. The challenge they all faced was that their markets were opening up to competition for the first time due to deregulation. This challenge meant that these utilities could no longer take their customer base for granted.

Of course, you probably have never been able to take your customers for granted. Wouldn't it be nice to have regulatory protection of your market area? Ah, well, the days of regulated monopolies are ending, and even utilities have to learn to recruit and retain customers.

This situation made the marketing audit a very powerful marketing tool for these electric utilities. They found it a real eye opener, to say the least. It revealed large areas of marketing in which they simply were not active. In some of these organizations, the audit led to an agenda that will require several years or more to complete.

## Developing your marketing agenda

In your business, the results may be less radical than in the case I described in the preceding section, but I'm sure that your marketing audit can lead to an agenda of some sort. If it doesn't, then it hasn't done you any good. You have to act on insights to profit from them!

Marketing audits always seem to reveal some needs and generate some ideas for positive action. It's hard to really be fully customer-oriented, and it's very hard to create and integrate effective marketing actions in all areas of your business. So a great next step for follow-up from your audit is to review the findings again — especially in areas of particular weakness or strength — and develop some agenda items that will help you to better attract and retain customers.

I recommend that you do that thinking right now, while the experience of the audit is still fresh. If you can't come up with at least five high-priority actions for your agenda as a result of the audit, I'll eat my marketing hat. But do put a good effort into it, because I'm rather attached to my marketing hat. It's a hat I wear quite often when running my own business!

You'll find a set of templates on your CD (filename CD0803) for developing your marketing agenda based on the marketing audit you performed. (These templates are available as Word documents if you want to work within or edit them, and also as Acrobat files if you want to just print them out and work on paper copies of them.) Figure 8-1 shows you what they look like (although there are four more on the CD so you can develop a five-item agenda if you want).

## Reality check

Okay, now that you've saved me from having to eat my marketing hat by developing five good action items for your marketing agenda, I want you to do a quick reality check.

Agenda item #1 is to: _____

Mini-plan for agenda item #1:

**Who** should spearhead this action? _____

By **when** should it be completed? _____/_____/_____

What special **resources** might be needed?

    Other people?

    _____

    _____

    _____

    _____

    Money?  $_____

    Special Expertise? _____

    Special supplies/equipment? _____

What should this action **accomplish**?

    Key objective: _____

**Figure 8-1:**
A sample
planning
form.

Specifically, I want you to look at the resources those agenda items will require, namely, the people, money, special expertise, supplies, and equipment those agenda items need in your estimation to be completed. If you add up all those requirements, you have a pretty big investment — perhaps too big. You don't want to over-research as you develop your marketing capabilities. Your marketing capacities need to expand with your capabilities, or you will run into practical constraints, if not cash flow or other resource crises!

So stop and think about the combined impact of all those nice agenda items. If it's more than your organization can reasonably bear right now, then prioritize. Pick the one or few actions that you think need attention first. Or perhaps the ones you can *afford* to do first. This is real world marketing, after all, so it has to be doable or it won't get done.

And if those agenda items you do first are as good as you think they are, then they should yield increased revenues and hopefully even increased profits, which means that they will help create the resources to move on to additional improvements and additional agenda items. So the actions you take to enhance your sales and marketing as a result of the audit process should increase your resources, not reduce them. The goal is to invest in actions that bring in new business and/or retain or increase business from existing customers. Growth is the goal. And no matter how small the first steps, after you get started in the pursuit of growth through improvements in your sales and marketing, you will find that the resulting growth makes more improvements, and additional growth, possible.

# Formal Marketing Plans

A marketing audit gives you a quick sense of what areas need attention in order to boost your marketing and sales. But sometimes you need to do more than that. Sometimes you need to develop a detailed, formal marketing plan.

I get calls fairly often from readers of *Marketing For Dummies* or one of my other books on marketing asking for help with their plans. By and large, the need for planning arises from an external requirement from a bank or other funder, or from their company's annual planning and budgeting process. And the poor person who finds that he or she must suddenly generate a marketing plan usually feels at sea. For starters, it's a complex, elaborate thing to write, encompassing everything and anything that might touch customers or affect sales. In addition, it simply involves quite a lot of writing, and most people don't enjoy the idea of writing dozens of pages about anything. (Okay, so I'm a little weird that way. I *like* writing about marketing!) Anyway, I've learned that when people find they have to write a plan, they are not happy campers. They want help. Lots of help. And they want it now.

Then there is the other scenario for marketing planning. That's when someone is actually feeling ambitious enough to elect to do some careful planning and budgeting just because they hope it will improve their marketing program. Some people actually elect to do a marketing plan. Hard to believe, I know, but in fact the process is always illuminating and, if you can spare the time, well worth your while.

## How to write a marketing plan

So, how can people who have to, or just want to, go about the process of writing a good marketing plan? First, they should expect to spend at least a good hard week at it if they hope to get anything really polished and useful out the other end. It's not an easy thing to do. If you're in a hurry, stick with the simpler audit and agenda I showed you earlier in this chapter.

Second, people need to find some templates they can use to inspire them. Even a simple outline is helpful because it gives you a good idea of the sorts of things you may want to include in your plan. I'll give you several examples of marketing plan outlines in a moment to help you design your own. And in the next section of this chapter, I show you how to use a wonderful planning template contributed by an expert who trains and consults on planning and agreed to let me share his work with you.

The third thing you need to do to write a plan is to assemble your information. What do you need to know that you don't necessarily know or have right at hand? For example, do you need to:

- ✔ Ask salespeople or distributors their view of quality, trends, competition, and so on?

- ✔ Gather details of sales for the last year or more?

- ✔ Get breakdowns of sales by product, region, or other category?

- ✔ Get some general statistics on sales in your market or product category so you can see what your share is and whether you are gaining or losing share?

- ✔ Collect any information you can on where sales came from and which sales and marketing practices worked best in the last year or two?

- ✔ Get prices on printing, ad purchases, design services, or other costs you know you'll want to include in your budget?

- ✔ Quiz some customers for input about the quality of your service or products or for their ideas and suggestions on how to improve? (See Chapter 6 for how to do this.)

- ✔ Plan some sales promotions and work out projected costs and returns? (See Chapter 10 for how to do this.)

- ✔ Collect information on costs and prices for use in doing budgets and projections?

- ✔ Get information on any new products you'll be introducing during the period covered by the plan?

This shopping list of research questions may occupy you for several days or more. Simply gathering the information needed to do a good plan is a serious undertaking. And you haven't even begun to write yet! But hang on. We're going to make that part as easy as possible.

The fourth thing you need to do is roll up your sleeves and start writing. But don't just sit staring at a blank page or screen. It will be months before you have anything competent written. (I'm reminded of a quote from writer Gene Fowler: "Writing is easy. All you do is sit staring at a blank sheet of paper until the drops of blood form on your forehead.") I want you to avoid writer's block and anxiety and the lack of structure or guidance of the blank-sheet-of-paper method! And I also want to avoid the common mistake of making minor edits to last year's plan (if you have one). That doesn't force you to rethink your marketing; it just creates something that fools you and others into believing you've done real planning.

Instead, I want you to really write a plan because the writing process is also a thinking process, and it takes a lot of thinking to come up with good strategies and tactics. But to make the writing process easier, I recommend that you use a template that includes detailed instructions for each section of your plan.

## Using the marketing plan template

Your CD contains a 20-plus page planning guide and template contributed by a consultant and trainer who has helped hundreds of businesses do their plans. It is part of a new business planning workbook series by Philip T. DiPeri, managing director of the consulting firm Stonehenge International (of Amherst, Mass.; info. at stonehenge-intl.com). DiPeri's workbooks are used in entrepreneurial training programs throughout the world, and if you take a quick look at the template on the CD (filename CD0804), I think you can understand why. This template is full of his helpful advice (which appears in colored text on your screen and doesn't print when you use the template to create a plan).

You can simply review the template on your screen if you want, or print a hard copy for reference. But if you want to put it to best use, I recommend that you copy the MarketingPlan.dot file into a Microsoft Office Template Subdirectory. Then, when you go into Word, you should be able to select this template when you click on the File menu and then click on New. The template will then pop up on screen in Microsoft Word, ready for you to write your own plan using it.

There are some technical details you may need to deal with to use this template most effectively. They are described in the instructions on the first page of the template. I recommend that you read them. For example, the instructions explain how to control whether Word will print the hidden text in the template or not. And they also show you how to update the table of contents automatically using Word's "Index and Tables" command. If you are a Word whiz already, you no doubt know all this, but many people don't. Personally, I find it very helpful to have step-by-step instructions for such things.

## The template's structure

DiPeri explains that, "Three distinct components comprise every marketing plan: (1) marketing research and analysis, (2) decisions based on the research and analysis, and (3) the consequences of decisions made." In other words, you need to gather a bunch of information, think about what it means, and then decide what to do. That is the planning process this template takes you through, and because it gives you detailed instructions for each step of the way, I won't repeat them here.

When you follow the template through from beginning to end, you end up with a plan that has an outline something like this:

Executive summary

Marketing research and analysis

The product/service

The market

> Market definition
>
> Market segments
>
> Segment analysis
>
> Market size
>
> Market trends
>
> Market characteristics

Industry trends

Competitor profile

Other factors

Major planning decisions

Overall marketing strategy

Product/service offerings

Target markets

Competitive position

Price

Channels of distribution

Marketing communications

Consequences of marketing decisions

Sales forecasts

Revenue projections

Target unit costs

Marketing budgets

Expense budget

Capital budget

People and skills budgets

Contingency planning

Appendices

As you can see, this is a detailed, thorough planning template that covers just about everything that might be relevant. It is also quite traditional in the sense that it treats all the topics conventionally considered part of a marketing plan and treats them in a style and order that most experts would approve of. So if you are writing a plan for review and approval, this level of depth and approach to structure is a safe bet.

## Variations on the plan

You can lay out a marketing plan in many ways. No two plans are identical in their format and structure because no two organizations are identical in their needs or marketing positions. So don't be afraid to adapt the planning template to your own needs.

To help you visualize options, here is an example of one of the plan designs that I've collected over the years (and there are more templates in *The Vest-Pocket Marketer,* which Prentice Hall publishes for me).

**A Divisional Marketing Plan**

Situation analysis

Sales history

Market profile

Sales versus objective

Factors influencing sales

Profitability

Factors affecting profitability

Market environment

Growth rate

Trends

Changes in customer attitude

Recent or anticipated competitor actions

Government activity

Problems and opportunities

Problem areas

Opportunities

Marketing and profitability objectives

Sales

Market profile

Gross margin

Marketing strategy

Marketing programs

Product assumptions

# *Avoiding Random Activity*

Planning exercises can easily turn into almost random listings of possibilities. The poor planners run out of insights, information, and time by the time it comes to itemize details of the marketing program. The thinking often goes like this: "What sort of ads, mailings, or other marketing communications should we use? Hmm. Dunno. Maybe we should just list a bunch so we make sure that some advertising and mailings are included in the budget." That's a planning process, but not a very intelligent one!

You can do many things to promote your product or service. Lots and lots. Often people just try one thing after another, hoping to see sales increase, without any real idea of what might work, why, and how. I call this random marketing. It goes kind of like this:

"Hey, we need to do something to get more sales. Let's do some advertising."

Or maybe it goes like this:

"Our competitors are offering coupons. Should we do some coupons, too?"

Or perhaps,

"Everyone says the World Wide Web is a hot place to sell your services. We better invest in a site and buy some banner ads so we can be part of it, too."

Or, maybe, something like,

"We've never tried a frequent buyer program or a contest. Do you think we should do something like that?"

And so on. What about trying some telemarketing? Or print advertising? Or even television or radio? Direct mail might be better. Hmm. Lots of choices. But which to try? Is it entirely a matter of blind experimentation?

No. At least, it better not be unless you have a lot of time and money to waste groping around in the marketing dark. Random marketing is like the old philosophical theory that if you put enough apes at enough typewriters for long enough, eventually they would type a Shakespeare play by random chance. Same with random marketing. Eventually it might produce a winning program by chance. But you better be very patient!

The only difference between the old ape-at-the-typewriter theory and the typical approach to marketing is that nobody would be silly enough to actually try the ape experiment, whereas the majority of businesses try random marketing. And then they wonder why their plans don't produce satisfactory results.

## Goal-oriented marketing experiments

There is always an important element of creative experimentation in any marketing or planning effort, but not random experimentation. To get a good head start, you need to have *specific marketing goals* and a rough idea of the kinds of marketing activities that might achieve those goals. Then your creative experimentation can focus on learning how to achieve those marketing goals better by refining your rough ideas until you have a unique approach that produces a winning marketing program for you and your business.

The formula you develop and continue to refine through your marketing experiments will be uniquely yours. No formula works for more than one organization. Yet your formula can and should rely on certain transferable elements, certain fundamentals that hold up generally in all marketing programs. And the most easily transferable formulas have to do with marketing goals.

Specifically, you need to know that certain kinds of marketing initiatives tend to be appropriate to certain kinds of marketing goals, and not others.

What this means is that you can define the basic structure of any marketing plan or program — and narrow down those apparently random choices — simply by picking one or a few marketing objectives and then focusing on the marketing techniques that are most likely to help you achieve those objectives. A good plan should be driven by clear objectives.

What are good objectives? Whatever objectives are needed to help you achieve your mission or your growth goals. Marketing objectives might include:

- ✔ Find new customers
- ✔ Cross-sell more products to existing customers
- ✔ Introduce new products or services
- ✔ Improve the distribution of existing products or services
- ✔ Improve customer service
- ✔ Reduce customer complaints
- ✔ Boost the performance of salespeople or distributors
- ✔ Develop new channels of distribution (such as the Web)
- ✔ Fend off a competitor's challenge
- ✔ Increase the perceived value of offerings to counter a trend toward price competition
- ✔ Educate prospects about a new technology or process
- ✔ Increase the average order size
- ✔ Generate more or better leads for the sales force
- ✔ Expand into new geographic markets
- ✔ Recruit new distributors or retailers
- ✔ Change the way prospects think of your offering (reposition)

If you work through this list, checking those objectives that apply to your situation, you'll probably come up with at least one to three appropriate ones to guide your planning. If not, well, you can always make up some of your own. But please make sure that you have clear objectives before you go into any planning process. Otherwise, you might as well design your program by picking options at random.

# Planning Benchmarks for Marketing Communications

How much overall should you spend on marketing communications (MarCom) like advertising, the Web, mailings, telemarketing, or whatever you plan to use? The best approach is to build up a budget from specific objectives, and I present that method in the upcoming chapter on advertising plans. But it is also helpful to have a general sense of what the norms are in your industry. So Table 8-2 provides some statistics you can refer to.

| Table 8-2 | MarCom Spending as % of Sales |
|---|---|
| *Product or Service* | *Spending* |
| **Services:** | |
| Insurance | 0.6% |
| Advertising | 2.8% |
| Freight | 1.2% |
| Cable/pay TV | 1.0% |
| Nursing homes | 3.4% |
| Hospitals | 3.0% |
| Investment advice | 6.8% |
| Personal services | 4.0% |
| Services in general | 2.5% |
| **Products:** | |
| Ice cream | 5.4% |
| Furniture | 5.0% |
| Clothing | 5.1% |
| Auto parts/accessories | 0.8% |
| Greeting cards | 3.3% |
| Software | 4.5% |
| Periodicals (newspapers/magazines/newsletters) | 5.8% |
| Food products | 9.4% |
| Toys | 18% |
| Computer equipment | 2.5% |
| Office supplies | 4.2% |
| Building supplies | 1.2% |

| Product or Service | Spending |
| --- | --- |
| **Retail Stores:** | |
| Watches | 15.7% |
| Products in general | 4.2% |
| Department stores | 4.3% |
| Furniture stores | 9.0% |
| Clothing stores | 3.2% |
| Hotels/motels | 3.9% |
| Insurance agencies | 1.6% |
| Banks | 3.8% |
| Stockbrokers | 2.0% |
| Consumer electronics stores | 3.8% |
| Variety stores | 2.0% |
| Gift shops | 4.5% |
| Grocery stores | 1.2% |
| Restaurants/bars | 4.4% |
| **Retailers in General** | **3.4%** |

There's no harm in violating these norms. And if you want to gain share or increase significantly in size, you probably have to outspend the averages. But if your plan produces numbers that are *dramatically* different from the norms, then you really ought to go back and have a look to make sure a good reason exists for the difference!

# Where to Go from Here

In this chapter, I queue up a number of tools, techniques, and benchmarks to help you with your marketing strategy and plans. Whether you need to just diagnose the situation or develop a full-blown plan, you should find some helpful guidelines in this chapter. For more details on how to design and budget advertising plans and sales promotions, see the upcoming chapters that focus on each of these topics in depth. In addition, you'll find complimentary coverage of marketing plans in *Marketing For Dummies*, *The Portable MBA in Marketing* (John Wiley & Sons), and *The Vest-Pocket Marketer* (Prentice Hall), if you want a high level of handholding from me as you work on your plans.

I encourage you to seek additional resources, as well. For instance, William Cohen's *The Marketing Plan* (John Wiley & Sons), although written for classroom use, has a number of good examples of plans in the back of it that I recommend as benchmarks. In my experience, the more support and information you have at hand when you undertake a planning process, the better.

# On the CD

Check out the following items on the CD-ROM:

- The Marketing Audit (CD0801)
- Marketing Agenda Worksheets (CD0802)
- Marketing Agenda Templates (CD0803)
- DiPeri's Marketing Plan Template (CD0804)

# Chapter 9

# Planning and Budgeting Ad Campaigns

The marketing manager, entrepreneur, or general manager periodically faces the challenging chore of planning the advertising activities for the upcoming quarter or year. What ads should be run? How much should be spent? What will it cost — and will it pay off?

This is a challenging chore because it involves so many different considerations. What advertising media should you use? What kind of ads should you design for these media? Where and when should you run them? How many times should they be repeated, and in what sequence? When you start at the beginning with basic questions like these, you'll never come up with a good plan and budget. At least, not by sitting at your desk and thinking and writing. That's not where good plans come from. Anything you fabricate from scratch in your imagination is going to be highly speculative and unrealistic. Things won't go at all according to plan.

So back up. Take it more slowly. Build on what you know. The only good plans are ones that are based on solid experience. If you've found that direct mail works pretty well for you, and you have some letters that seem to pull, it's reasonable to plan on sending out more like them. And you can base your projections on past experience, which improves your odds of making an accurate guess about future performance.

'V, don't plan to put 25 percent of your budget
'ou don't know enough yet to make a good
'V. Budget a small amount, only as much as
_rience. And spend it learning how to make
_p with a formula that really does seem to
_sider rewriting the plan to incorporate a more

_ur advertising, make sure that you are building on expe-
_st guessing wildly. Also, make sure that you know what each
_sed to be accomplishing so that your plan has realistic returns
_ne sales and profits.

## _ng Your Goals

Why advertise? Unless you have a clear purpose, there is no point. Many businesses advertise for poorly defined reasons. I've heard lots of managers say things like, "We do some advertising just to keep ourselves visible, but I don't think it affects our sales." Or, "We try to match our competitors' advertising because customers expect it." Or, "We've always done advertising, and I don't know if it really works, but we're afraid of what might happen if we stopped."

I can reassure those nervous managers who are afraid to stop advertising. What would happen is that they would save the money they are now throwing away on advertising. I can guarantee that their advertising budget is not doing anything helpful if you don't even know what it's *supposed* to be doing. Advertising for its own sake never achieves anything worthwhile. It just fills up the media with mediocre ads that nobody really notices. Only advertising that is specifically designed and placed to achieve an important business objective is worthwhile. Other advertising (most advertising) does not accomplish anything worthwhile because it does not set out to accomplish anything worthwhile.

## What's the story on ad/sales ratios?

Okay, that's enough of my ranting and raving. It's just that so much of the advertising you see is really a waste of money that I don't want you to feel pressured into a me-too campaign that doesn't help your bottom line. In fact, I think I'll rant a little longer, because I'd like to debunk a myth that leads many otherwise sane managers into wasting their money on pointless advertising — and sometimes into underfunding really effective ads. That myth goes under the rubric of the advertising-to-sales ratio. *Advertising Age,* the weekly news bible of the North American advertising industry, publishes a periodic compilation of the ad/sales ratios of companies in a wide variety of industries. It's useful to advertising agencies to have a sense of how much they can expect companies to spend. But too often, these ratios are taken too seriously and used as guidelines in designing advertising budgets.

The idea that businesses should spend $x$ percent of their revenue on advertising is widely accepted in the field of marketing, but is totally absurd. It encourages spending for the sake of spending. "Gotta spend that 6 percent somehow. Let's blow it on some TV." It's a silly myth. There is no magic ratio of ad spending to sales. There is only advertising that pays off and advertising that doesn't. If you do poorly defined, purposeless advertising, it won't pay off, whether it is 10 percent of your sales or a fraction of a percent. If, on the other hand, you come up with advertising that really works for your business, then why would you limit it to a certain percent of sales? Far better to do as much of it as you can, building your business at an optimum rate as a result.

So, how can you make sure your advertising is the "right" kind, the kind that is profitable because it achieves important objectives? Well, an awfully good place to start is to set out one or two important objectives and then design ads to achieve those objectives. Then you simply need to track your progress toward those objectives to see if your ads work. If not, pull the darn things in a hurry, redesign, and try again. The most effective ad campaigns are the result of well-defined objectives, careful objective-driven design, and, often, redesign, until the marketers know they've got a winner. Figure 9-1 shows the process in a nutshell.

---

**The Ad Planning Process**

1. Define useful objective(s).

2. Design to objective(s).

3. Test against objective(s).

4. Redesign based on test(s).

**Figure 9-1:**
Designing
ads that
really work.

5. Maximize run of perfected ad.

6. Terminate ad as soon as it stops achieving objective(s) or as soon as the objective(s) are no longer important.

Now, I want to make clear what you should do with this six-step process. It's not a description of the typical advertising process that you can just look at and say, "Oh, okay, I guess that's how they do it. Now I'll get some people to do it for me." This is not a description of how most people create advertising. It is a prescription for avoiding the typical process in order to achieve much better results than average. So you need to use this six-step plan to truly drive your own advertising process. Whether you are working on your own, hiring experts at each step, or a combination of the two, you need to take the process in hand at each step and make sure that it does what it's supposed to do.

That means you need to remind yourself and tell others (probably over and over) that you want them first to make sure that they have a good, meaningful, profitable objective for your ad to accomplish. Then, when they have convinced you (or you've convinced yourself) that the objective is on target, you need to make sure that the design stage is driven by a pursuit of that objective. Don't let people waste your time showing you ads that look nice but are not relevant to your objective.

By the way, I'd insist on following this same process for any advertising you do for the Web or as you develop or expand a Web site. Just because stuff on the Web is virtual doesn't mean that you can get away with lower standards for it. The money you spend on the Web — and hopefully *make* on the Web — is certainly not virtual.

## Testing the design against its objective

When the design is finally appropriate and looks like it ought to achieve the objective, you still have to drive the process aggressively or you won't get a good result. Note that the next step in the process is (or should be) to test the ad against its objective. *Test* means find cheap, easy ways to see if it seems to work. Now, advertisers hate to do that. People who sell advertising hate to see you do that. Nobody wants to test; they all want to just run with it and pray it will work. But it's your money and your fate, so you must insist on testing:

- If it's a mailer, do a mock-up and test mail it to a small list. Low response rate? Redesign. Good response? Do a larger-scale mailing.

- If it's a print ad, don't let them talk you into buying 20 insertions each in five different newspapers. Just buy one or two insertions in one paper, and see what happens. If it doesn't seem to do anything and nobody notices it, redesign. If it works wonderfully, run it on a larger scale.

✔ If it's an idea for a television commercial, don't let them talk you into an expensive production and a massively expensive, multi-city, primetime run. First, try a low-cost, quick-and-dirty version of the commercial made at the studio of a local cable television station. Then test the cheap commercial cheaply, running it a few times in local markets. For a hundredth or even a thousandth the cost of a typical campaign, you can find out whether that TV ad concept is capable of achieving your objective. If not, back to the drawing board. If so, however, well, now you know enough to try risking some serious money on a larger-scale, more professional campaign.

✔ Whatever kind of ad it is, run it by some people who are representative of your target market. Ask them what they think. See if they even remember what it said. See if they feel excited about doing what the ad asked them to do. See if they understood the darn thing. And if they noticed the special offer you included. Heck, see if they even noticed what product or company the ad was for. Asking people to review your ads is a great way to get some informal, early feedback before even risking them on a quick, small-scale run in the media. Big companies use formal advertising tests with elaborate statistical analyses. Anyone can do informal ad testing, but few do.

Did you know that the largest advertisers, companies like Coca Cola, General Motors, and IBM, try out hundreds and hundreds of ads every year? Most of these ads never make it to the media or, if they do, have very short runs. They don't test well. And so they disappear before you ever see them. Some dozen ads may survive and go on to be aired or printed extensively. This result gives the impression to outside observers that these companies run each ad thousands of times. Not so! They only invest heavily in the few that survive a rigorous testing process. You need to learn from their example, not from the example set by the vast majority of businesses, which are far smaller and less sophisticated in their approach. The latter typically commit to an ad design long before they know if it really works.

When you finally find an ad that seems to work, once again you need to take charge and stick to the process. An effective ad is a rare and wonderful thing. Enjoy it. Show it off. Get the most you can out of it. Try it lots of ways and places. And don't believe what those experts tell you, because as soon as an ad begins to really work, they'll start talking you into replacing it. "Don't want the market to get saturated," they'll say. Or, "Ads rarely run for more than a few months without redesign. Have you thought about the next one yet?"

You'll know when that ad needs replacement. It will no longer achieve its objective. Sales will slip, or something else obvious will happen. You won't get as many orders or leads or calls or visitors to your Web site. But until then, give the poor thing a chance! It may take you a long time to come up with another winner. Ride this one for all it's worth.

# What Is Your Ad's Objective?

My whole approach to advertising is based on the selection of a meaningful objective for your ad to achieve. You are supposed to design and test the ad against this objective, and if it proves worthy, to use the ad hard until you achieve the objective or the ad stops working toward that objective. It's a simple, focused, businesslike approach that doesn't waste money on fluff advertising. But objective-driven advertising is only as good as the objective. So I figure I better give you some help in choosing a good objective.

Here is a selection of useful marketing objectives, each linked to an indicator you can watch to see if the ad works. To make your advertising objective-driven, simply select one (or at most two) of these objectives and keep it clearly in mind throughout the advertising process.

- ✔ **Objective:** How to know if you are achieving it?

- ✔ **Boost sales:** Sales rise when and where ad runs.

- ✔ **Generate calls:** The telephone rings off the hook.

- ✔ **Generate by-mail responses:** Responses come in by mail in large numbers the week after the ad is first seen.

- ✔ **Introduce new product:** Requests for and press coverage of new product increase significantly right after ad appears.

- ✔ **Switch customers from competing product:** Sales go up as a result of switching.

- ✔ **Encourage word of mouth:** Current and past customers begin to talk, stimulating sales to people who say they "heard about you from someone they know."

- ✔ **Increase your share of market:** Your sales grow faster than leading competitors' sales.

- ✔ **Recruit new distributors:** You hear from multiple distributors who are interested in working with you.

- ✔ **Help build sales by building image or reputation:** Sales grow gradually but definitely do grow, along with rapid improvements in image and enhanced reputation.

- ✔ **Attract more upscale buyers:** You sell higher-priced products or find you can raise your prices or no longer have to negotiate as many discounts.

- ✔ **Attract a different group of customers:** Your sales to the new group increase.

- ✔ **Cross-sell new product to current customers:** You sell more of the new product to your current customer base.

- ✔ **Get more shoppers to visit your store(s):** Store traffic and sales figures increase.

Notice that each and every objective in this selection is linked to a specific outcome that you can track to see if you've achieved the objective. If you see movement in the measure, then the ad is working toward its objective. If you don't, then the ad is not working and needs to be improved or scrapped in favor of a new design.

Notice also, however, that most of those indicators used to measure the success of an ad are going to be a little hard to measure precisely. In fact, sometimes they are very hard to measure accurately. Sure, you can track your sales with accuracy. But can you track the rise in sales resulting from one particular ad? Not unless you can hold everything else you do constant. This is great if it happens to be convenient anyway, but often, you will be playing around with many different marketing initiatives at once. So which sale came from the new ad, versus your catalog, or the latest updates to your Web page, or the trade show you were just at, or the better system you created for tracking your own leads and remembering to call them back? Sometimes you can tease out the answers, but not always.

# The Great Advertising Debate

Many marketing experts find it frustrating to try to measure the dotted lines from advertising to bottom-line objectives like boosting sales or outgrowing competitors. They find the links too vague. So they prefer to set more specific, short-term, easy-to-measure objectives for advertising. They look at things they can easily measure by surveying people who've been exposed to the ad. Things like awareness of the company and its products or services. Recall of the content of the ad. Stated intention to buy. Such measures can be made in a highly scientific, accurate manner. They are quite precise, but they may be quite meaningless. While awareness, recall or intention to buy may lead to increased sales, you don't know that they will unless you actually measure sales.

So there is a more pragmatic school of thought in advertising, a school of thought branded by many as "heretic" but one that makes a lot of sense to me. It says, better to pursue and measure vague goals that really matter than precise goals that may not be important at all. This argument even has an interesting shorthand to describe the two positions people take. The traditional big-company approach, focused on abstract, precise, but possibly meaningless measures, is termed precisely wrong, or PW, thinking. It is wrong because it doesn't focus on increasing sales or profits or other truly meaningful objectives. Its scientific approach makes it precise without making it meaningful.

And the proposed alternative is termed vaguely right, or VR, thinking. It is vague because it cannot measure one ad's impact on your sales with precision (especially in larger marketing programs). But it is right because it pursues essential bottom-line objectives. And, so the argument goes, wouldn't you rather be vaguely right than precisely wrong?

I'm persuaded by this argument, and I think most marketers should be, too. On average, you'll do far better if you stay focused on big picture objectives and avoid the subtleties of fancy advertising measures and statistics. If someone tries to sell you fancy advertising research, you can simply say to yourself, do I want to be precisely wrong or vaguely right? Then you'll have the strength of mind to save the cost of fancy advertising research. Instead, you'll run a crude test in which you try the ad briefly and look for any noticeable impact on sales.

# Budgeting Based on Objectives

So far, we've applied the sales process model to the design and selection of individual ads. But since I wrote *Marketing For Dummies,* I've gotten many calls from unhappy marketers who are stuck with the unpleasant chore of writing the advertising budget for the next quarter or year and don't know how to do it. Good news! When you design ads using this objective-driven method, you are halfway toward completing the most sophisticated and effective method for writing an advertising budget.

Larger companies with major advertising programs used to budget based on a percentage-of-sales target. In the last decade or two, most have switched to what they call an objective-and-task method. They simply decide what specific advertising is likely to achieve their objectives. Then they add it up and get their budget.

Then, perhaps, if the budget is more than the company can afford, they argue about the number and adjust it to reflect affordability. In this case, they have to accept that they will probably not achieve their full objectives.

But the basic idea is to budget based on what you estimate you'll have to do to achieve a specific objective. Let's say your objective for next year's advertising is to double your sales. You have some ideas about how to do that because you've tested some ads and found that they can bring in more sales. So now you simply need to work out a program that gets those ads in front of enough prospects to bring you all the sales you want.

To double your sales, you probably have to reach at least twice as many prospects. How much advertising in what places allow you to do that at a reasonable price using the ad designs you think will work? Work through a plan, cost it out, and see if it is profitable at the level of sales you anticipate (and perhaps at a more conservative forecast of sales, too, just to be safe). If so, then it's a go. If not, redesign.

How do you redesign an advertising plan and budget to better achieve your goals and be more affordable? Here are the main things you can fiddle with. Work on one or more of them:

- **Increase ad effectiveness.** Try different ad designs or timing or placement.

- **Decrease the cost of ads.** Try different ad designs or timing or placement.

- **Increase your profits.** Try raising prices or lowering costs so that your profit margin is greater (which probably means improving product quality in customers' eyes).

The preceding variables are the main variables that will affect the profitability of your advertising plan and budget. Play with them until it works.

It's really a simple, commonsense approach that anyone can do if they are willing to take the time to test and refine ads, and think hard about what kind of exposure those ads will need in order to accomplish specific sales goals. So next time you have to write an advertising budget, don't call me — at least not until you've tried the objective-and-task method first!

# Using an Advertising Objective Worksheet

If you need to create a budget for your advertising expenditures, I recommend you do it in two steps. First, fill in one or more Advertising Objective Worksheets, such as the one illustrated in Figure 9-2. These worksheets build up your ad plan based on an objective-and-task approach, so they are consistent with the advertising process I described earlier and they will produce a more realistic and effective plan than you're likely to get from other methods.

After filling in a worksheet, you'll have a pretty good idea of how you want to use various ads to try to achieve your goals. Then you are ready to summarize your plans in a conventional Advertising Budget, such as the one illustrated in Figure 9-3.

I've included spreadsheets on the CD for both the Advertising Objective Worksheet and the Advertising Budget (filenames CD0901 and CD0902) so that you can create these products quickly just by entering the numbers you want into these Excel spreadsheet files. The advantage of using these spreadsheets is that the formats and formulas are all worked out for you already. All you have to do is describe your specific ads by entering appropriate numbers in each boxed cell.

Advertising Objective Worksheet
Company or Product Name, time period (month, quarter or year)

| | Number of customers | Purchases per cust. | Average purchase $ | Total Sales Revenues |
|---|---|---|---|---|
| Sales goals for ad campaign: | 1000 | 2 | $8 | $ 16,000.00 |

| | Reach (# of prospects) | Percent responding | Percent of respondents who buy | Number of customers | Purchases per cust. | Average purchase $ | Revenues from Ad | Cost of Ad |
|---|---|---|---|---|---|---|---|---|
| Ad #1 | 250 | 10.0% | 80.0% | 20 | 1 | $ 39.00 | $ 780.00 | $ 250.00 |
| Ad #2 | 500 | 5.0% | 75.0% | 19 | 1.2 | $ 39.00 | $ 877.50 | $ 800.00 |
| Ad #3 | 3000 | 5.0% | 75.0% | 113 | 2 | $ 39.00 | $ 8,775.00 | $ 5,000.00 |
| Ad #4 | 250 | 10.0% | 80.0% | 20 | 1 | $ 39.00 | $ 780.00 | $ 250.00 |
| Ad #5 | 250 | 10.0% | 80.0% | 20 | 1 | $ 39.00 | $ 780.00 | $ 250.00 |
| Ad #6 | 250 | 10.0% | 80.0% | 20 | 1 | $ 39.00 | $ 780.00 | $ 250.00 |
| Ad #7 | 250 | 10.0% | 80.0% | 20 | 1 | $ 39.00 | $ 780.00 | $ 250.00 |
| Ad #8 | 250 | 10.0% | 80.0% | 20 | 1 | $ 39.00 | $ 780.00 | $ 250.00 |
| Ad #9 | 1000 | 2.0% | 75.0% | 15 | 2 | $ 39.00 | $ 1,170.00 | $ 1,000.00 |
| Ad #10 | 500 | 5.0% | 75.0% | 19 | 1.1 | $ 39.00 | $ 804.38 | $ 800.00 |
| Ad #11 | | | | 0 | | | $ - | |
| Ad #12 | | | | 0 | | | $ - | |
| Ad #13 | | | | 0 | | | $ - | |
| Ad #14 | | | | 0 | | | $ - | |
| Ad #15 | | | | 0 | | | $ - | |
| Ad #16 | | | | 0 | | | $ - | |
| Ad #17 | | | | 0 | | | $ - | |
| Ad #18 | | | | 0 | | | $ - | |
| Ad #19 | | | | 0 | | | $ - | |
| Ad #20 | | | | 0 | | | $ - | |
| **Totals** | | | | | | | $ 16,306.88 | $ 9,100.00 |

**Figure 9-2:** Advertising Objective Worksheet.

The Advertising Objective Worksheet gives you up to 20 rows to enter ads. For the sake of analysis, an ad means a specific advertisement, run in a specific medium a specific number of times. So, for instance, I might define Ad #1 in a budget for my own training materials company to be: "4-x-4-inch ad on Conflict Assessment, three months in *Training* magazine." And I might define Ad #2 to be, "Direct Mail script #22, to house list w/ new catalog." To keep track of these specifics, I write these notes about what I have in mind in the spreadsheet file itself, over to the right of the form where there is plenty of room. The print area doesn't include these notes, so you don't have to make them neat and print them out. But if you want to, you can reset the print area using the Print Area command under File at the top of your Excel window.

Advertising Budget
Company Name or Product Name, 20XX

| Month | Total | Magazines | Newspapers | TV | Radio | Web | Direct mail | Telemarketing |
|---|---|---|---|---|---|---|---|---|
| January | $0.00 | | | | | | | |
| February | $0.00 | | | | | | | |
| March | $0.00 | | | | | | | |
| April | $0.00 | | | | | | | |
| May | $0.00 | | | | | | | |
| June | $0.00 | | | | | | | |
| July | $0.00 | | | | | | | |
| August | $0.00 | | | | | | | |
| September | $0.00 | | | | | | | |
| October | $0.00 | | | | | | | |
| November | $0.00 | | | | | | | |
| December | $0.00 | | | | | | | |
| | | | | | | | | |
| Year | $0.00 | | | | | | | |
| | | | | | | | | |
| Forecast revenues | | | $0.00 | | | | | |

**Figure 9-3:** Advertising Budget Worksheet.

When you use the Advertising Objective Worksheet on your computer, you'll find that the print range also excludes some marginal ratios that are useful as you fiddle with the numbers and explore options — but not worth printing out and reporting. You can see, to the right of the Cost of Ad column, that the spreadsheet calculates the return on investment for each ad. If it is 100 percent, the ad breaks even. Its expected revenue-generating power is equal to its cost. Above 100 percent and you are making a profit on the ad. If you aren't sure which ads (combinations of a specific ad design and insertion in a medium of your choice) to use the most, then look at this column and repeat those with the highest returns on investment.

If you aren't sure what to enter under the Reach (# of prospects) column in the worksheet, ask whoever sells space or time in the advertising media of interest to you. Almost all media you might buy ad room from will have statistics on whom they reach. And they almost always give away detailed profiles of audience or readership for free to anyone who is interested in advertising with them. Note that the worksheet defines reach as number of prospects, not just number of warm bodies. Sometimes they are the same — sometimes not. For instance, if you are promoting a product that is bought mostly by women, then you'd want to enter the number of women who read a magazine into this Reach column, not the total number of people in the magazine's readership.

If you aren't sure what to enter under Cost of Ad, again, consult the people who sell advertising space. They are happy to quote you prices for various alternatives. And don't be afraid to negotiate. They might not reduce their prices, but then again, they might!

If you are including direct mail or other forms of advertising that don't involve a third party who sells access to the medium, then you need to come up with your own estimates of cost. Get quotes from the post office and from the printer or any other contractors you plan to use.

All the rest of the numbers you need to enter in the Advertising Objective Worksheet can be estimated based on your or your company's experience. If you've never done any advertising before, you'll find it nearly impossible to guess all the numbers you need. You won't have a clue what percent of those who see your ad or get your letter or view your Web site will actually respond by inquiring or sending for more information or by sending in an order. Nor will you know what percentage of those who respond to an ad actually end up closing an order. It might be 100 percent, but with some forms of advertising and some sorts of sales, it will be considerably less. Again, some experience is vital.

Similarly, you probably won't have a feel for how many repeat purchases you can count on from the average person responding to a specific ad until you've done some advertising of a similar sort to similar sorts of people. You simply have to accumulate knowledge through a series of experiments before you really understand all the variables enough to make good guesses. That's why you need to develop and test all ads using the six-step Ad Planning Process in the beginning of this chapter. It puts you on a learning path that eventually allows you to accumulate enough insight to design fairly complex and varied advertising plans. But don't expect to bypass the learning stage and produce accurate, effective plans and budgets overnight.

If you haven't done much advertising in the past, develop and test just one option at a time, learning from it and mastering it before trying to plan and budget many more. And even if you do quite a bit of advertising already, don't expect to suddenly leap into three or four new types of advertising overnight. Allow yourself time to apply the Ad Planning Process and learn as you go, adding perhaps just one new "trick" each time you redo your budget.

# Using an Advertising Budget Worksheet

When you've carefully planned and developed a number of different types of ads, perhaps in different media, you will have a good feel for how to use these ad forms in your marketing.

When you've gone on to do a careful analysis of how you might use each of these types of ads using an Advertising Objective Worksheet, then you will have a good feel for how they might add up to an advertising campaign that helps you achieve your sales goals.

Now you are finally in a position to summarize all this good thinking in the classic advertising budget, a simple listing of the totals you plan to spend in each medium by month for the coming year. Figure 9-3 shows what the form for writing your Advertising Budget looks like on your CD (filename CD0902). It's a convenient tool for summarizing your advertising plans because it already has the formulas built in it to sum each column and row and to calculate the overall annual budget for all your advertising.

But remember, you're just guessing in the dark if you fill in some numbers without having developed good ads and strategies, or having analyzed how you'll use them to achieve specific objectives. A good advertising budget is the end result of a lot of careful experimentation, learning, and analysis. When you've done this preparation, it's easy to figure out what you want to spend.

Oh, and remember what I said about advertising-to-sales ratios and how they shouldn't be used to decide what to spend? Well, now that you've done all that preparatory work, I think it's finally appropriate to take a peek at your ad/sales ratio. And so I've included an automatic calculation of it on the bottom of the Advertising Budget spreadsheet, below the portion of this spreadsheet that gets printed. If your ad/sales ratio is anywhere in the 2–12 percent range, you can probably ignore it:

- If it is smaller, you have to ask yourself whether you are being too conservative.

- If it is higher, you should stop and check your assumptions. Are you really getting a big return on that ad spending you've planned? Are the prices you've been quoted reasonable? Is the program profitable? Okay. Then never mind that high ratio. Maybe you're just making a bigger investment and getting a bigger return than the average marketer. If you've found a good way to make money, why hold back? However, when ratios get much higher than 12–15 percent, it's obvious you're spending quite a bit of your revenues on advertising. So just make sure you know why and that you are happy with that level of investment.

## On the CD

Check out the following items on the CD-ROM:

- ✔ Advertising Objective Worksheet (CD0901)
- ✔ Advertising Budget (CD0902)

# Chapter 10

# Planning Coupons and Other Sales Promotions

Many marketing experts use the term *sales promotion* to describe the use of coupons, discounts, premium items (special gifts), and other incentives to boost sales. Coupons are probably the best known and most widely used sales promotions, but plenty of other ways are available to give prospects an incentive to make the purchase. In this chapter, I look at a variety of options, explore some of the best ways (and worst ways) to use them, and end with an analytical approach that helps you figure out whether a specific incentive will prove profitable or not.

## The Importance of Profit

It's easy to make a sale if you don't care about profits. All you have to do is give the darn thing away. Cut the price enough, and almost anything will sell. Witness the junk people buy at a yard sale or flea market or in a dollar store. But in truth, you don't need sales if they lose you money instead of making you money. And sales promotions do not always make money.

In fact, some of the more common examples are hard to accept from a profit perspective. Take the periodic sale and clearance catalogs distributed by London-based Victoria's Secret, a cataloger and retailer specializing in women's lingerie and clothing. They usually print a 7 ½-x-10-inch, full-color catalog with a cover featuring some of their new items. But occasionally, they send out a version using some of the items and photos from earlier catalogs, bound up in a special sales-promotion-oriented version with a cover advertising all the special prices inside. Here's an example of the offers featured (in bold white print on a dark pink background) on one of their sale covers, a cover that actually had no photos or drawing of products, but simply contained text describing the special deals inside:

- ✔ "Sale: bras & panties 25% to 50% off!"

- ✔ "Clearance: discontinued bras $9.99 to $12.99!"

Then in smaller print, at the bottom of this cover, they added more promotional offers:

- ✔ "Save up to an additional $75 on a qualifying sale purchase — and defer payment until September when you charge your order of $75 or more to the Victoria's Secret Credit Card. See page 2."

Since the catalog shipped in spring, deferring payment until September is a fairly appealing incentive. And, obviously, the idea of a quarter to half off of normal prices is an incentive to open up the catalog and do some serious shopping. Women who make occasional purchases from regular-priced catalogs tend to respond to these sale catalogs with more and larger orders.

But is this good marketing or not?

Depends on what it costs Victoria's Secret, and what other objectives the company wishes to accomplish. And, most of all, it depends on how people react to the special offers.

- ✔ If Victoria's Secret customers get in the habit of waiting for the special sale catalog before ordering, it won't be profitable. It will simply migrate full-price customers to discount-price customers and train them to wait for a special offer. That often happens when companies experiment with price-based sales promotions. In fact, recently Victoria's Secret has done fewer sales catalogs in order to reduce this effect.

- ✔ If Victoria's Secret customers are reminded of how much they like the company's product line by this sale catalog, and not only buy from the catalog but look more closely at the next few mailings, too, then it is a huge success. This can happen, too, and does to some extent with these sales catalogs. Many customers use the sales to stock up on some basics, but still look forward to seeing new clothes in the next regular catalog. And to the extent that each season's new clothes are unique and appealing, many customers will want to purchase them in season and at full price rather than gambling that they'll end up in a sale catalog months later.

In reality, both kinds of reactions occur in any sales promotion. You do get customers who simply shop for deals and won't give you more business later on at full price. But you also may remind some customers that they like your products, and recruit other customers for the first time, building a habit of shopping with you that carries over to future non-sale purchases. And that's a great fallout from a sales promotion, one that makes even a break-even promotion worthwhile in terms of future sales and profits.

Here's another example of a sales promotion that may or may not work, depending on how people react to it. HR Direct is a catalog-based distributor of materials for personnel managers and their Human Resource Departments. (For example, they carry a line of posters you can put up in the workplace to "comply with all state posting laws.") On the cover of their Winter 1999 catalog, the company featured a special offer that read as follows:

"FREE Attaché Case with your first order! See page 2."

And inside, on page 2 (the inside cover page, where such offers are highly visible), the company included two photos with arrows and text to show off the neat features of the free attaché case under the bold headline, FREE GIFT! (I don't know why marketers always get so carried away with their exclamation points when they describe sales promotions. Consumers generally respond to the substance of the offer, not the punctuation. In fact, if you use fewer exclamation points, people may take your offer more seriously. Seriously!) Anyway, along with the inside-front-cover photo and offer of a free gift, HR Direct also included two other sales promotions:

- A "100% satisfaction guarantee with full refund privilege" in which the customer can return "any product, for any reason" for a refund or credit. This offer of an automatic refund contained no asterisks or small print qualifications, making it an attractive and credible offer that certainly helped some shoppers take the plunge.

- The page also included the words *FREE SAMPLES* in one corner, without further explanation. This teaser offer is a little confusing, but probably stimulated some people to call and ask if they could see a sample of a product. If the salesperson taking the call felt that the caller was a legitimate prospect, a free sample would be sent. And, naturally, the salesperson would take advantage of having the prospect on the phone to try to make a sale, perhaps by diagnosing other needs and suggesting other products.

HR Direct's sales promotions are all designed to do one thing: to stimulate people to respond to the catalog with an order or question, especially if they are new customers and haven't done business with the company before. This catalog was sent to purchased lists, so it reached many prospective customers whom the company wanted to encourage to make a trial purchase. The costs of an attaché case and a few free samples, along with the rare request for a refund, were a good investment for HR Direct because each new customer, on average, does a significant amount of business, including much repeat business, over a multi-year period. Using sales promotions to draw in new customers and get them to try the company's products is a good investment in this case.

Suppose that you want to try a sales promotion, such as a coupon or other discount offer, a guarantee, or a giveaway item like the attaché case HR Direct used in its program. How do you plan your giveaway? How do you project its impact on sales and profits? Will it pay off or not? One of the ways to tackle these questions is to do a profitability analysis, a technique I present along with some other planning methods and background information in the next section.

# How Promotions Affect Sales

How does a coupon, discount, or other form of sales promotion work? It basically can have one or more of four effects on the market. It may stimulate one or more of the following behaviors (according to professors Robert Blattberg of the University of Chicago and Scott Neslin of Dartmouth College, who authored an interesting text on the subject):

- **Brand switching.** The promotion encourages the consumer to purchase a new brand or do business with a new vendor.

- **Repeat purchasing.** The consumer is more likely to keep buying the product or doing business with the vendor because of the promotion.

- **Purchase acceleration.** The consumer buys sooner and/or in larger quantities as a result of the promotion. (Careful, sometimes there is a corresponding decline in purchases later on!)

- **Category expansion.** The consumer uses more products or services such as yours as a result of the promotion.

Notice that the net result of all these effects is (hopefully!) to generate more sales. That's the basic bottom line of any coupon or other sales promotion. That's why marketers call these things sales promotions. They are supposed to generate more sales! There are multiple paths to those increased sales, and sometimes the increases are long-term instead of short-term. But the whole idea is to *make more sales*. If you don't see a clear link from your coupon or discount program to increased sales, then forget it. You're wasting your time and your business's money.

# More sales, yes, but at what price?

You can generate increased sales in many ways, and not all of them are appealing. How about this for a proposal:

**Offer your products or services for free.**

In many cases, this would boost sales dramatically. But, on the other hand, it would soon drive you out of business. So the challenge is really to find ways to boost sales through your sales promotions without losing money.

That makes it a little harder, doesn't it? But I never promised marketing would be easy.

To make sure that you are doing sales promotions that make sense to your bottom line, you need to do a careful analysis of their impact on profitability. Specifically, you need to forecast the profitability of each coupon, discount, or other money-off or freebie offer.

These sales promotions cost you money. Do they generate enough new business, at a sufficient profit, to make them profitable ventures? To find out, you need to do a careful profitability analysis, as I keep saying. So in the next section, I show you how and also give you a powerful spreadsheet tool to use in your analysis. I focus on coupons, but remember that any sales promotion that cuts the price to the consumer can be analyzed just like a coupon.

# You can perform a profitability analysis on any sales promotion

The face value of a coupon is the amount you give away in exchange for purchase. Similarly, if you print coupons or in-store signs or mailers offering a buy-three-get-one-free deal, then that's the same (for computational purposes) as giving away one-third of your cost of one product for each product purchased. You can crunch the numbers using the same coupon profitability analysis spreadsheet and method.

# Planning Coupon Programs

Boy, have I got a deal for you!

These classic words or offers to the same effect are the bread and butter of many marketing initiatives. Offering a discount gives people a reason to buy. It attracts their attention. It converts vague intentions into immediate actions. It also costs you money, however, and that's not so good.

How much will it cost? Will the increased sales more than offset the cost? Don't know. Better find out. But it all depends on what happens. You need to do some careful thinking and forecasting before you offer any discounts or distribute any coupons.

If you print and distribute coupons, any number of things may happen:

- ✔ The market may ignore them.

- ✔ Some prospects may redeem them and become loyal, profitable customers.

- ✔ The coupons may be ignored by everyone except those people who constantly shop for deals — and won't become regular customers unless you *always* offer them a deal.

- ✔ Some of the coupons may be misredeemed — in which case you end up paying their face value but not winning new sales.

- ✔ Existing customers may use the coupons to buy just as much as they would have without the coupons, in which case you have just given away a useless discount.

- ✔ New sales may flood in, making you very happy — until you realize that the costs of the coupon program are high enough that you've lost money in the process of winning that new business.

In other words, you can't really be sure what will happen, and a number of bad things may result. Good things may result too, but that's not a certainty.

Enter coupon profitability analysis. If you do a careful analysis of several possible scenarios up front and crunch the numbers on each scenario, you will have a much better idea of the likely outcomes. Often, when people do a formal analysis, they are horrified at the results. They find that their initial ideas and assumptions have fatal flaws. They realize they were about to throw away some or all of their profit margins in exchange for very little new business. So I highly recommend a careful profitability analysis.

Also, if you've done some coupon programs in the past, it's a great idea to run the numbers on them and see how they worked. Were they *really* profitable or not? It's not obvious unless you do a proper analysis. And when you do, you can learn a great deal from these past efforts that will help you design more effective and profitable coupons in the future. Remember that creative experimentation — and *learning* from your experiments — is at the heart of all great marketing!

# *The basics of coupon profitability analysis*

So how do you perform a coupon profitability analysis? Basically, for those who want to do it themselves *without* my hand-holding via the tool on the CD, you need to identify all the fixed and variable costs of the coupon program. Then you need to figure out how much product you think you'll sell directly due to the redemption of coupons (that you wouldn't have sold otherwise). Third, you need to figure out how much you make by selling that product. And fourth, you need to subtract all those expenses from the profits you've earned to see whether the coupon program is profitable or not.

Now, if you are quick with numbers and accounting, go ahead and make your own analysis. But if you want to cut some serious corners, all you need to do is open the CD1001 file on your Marketing Kit CD. It runs in Microsoft Excel, which you should have on your Mac or Windows system if it has any recent version of Microsoft Office loaded on it.

I designed the spreadsheet and built in the formulas, so all you have to do is think about your coupon program and enter appropriate numbers into the blank boxes. Then read the bottom-line results. If the program is profitable, you'll get a nice black number (in U.S. dollars — please modify the dollar symbol if necessary to convert to other currencies). If the program you've defined is unprofitable, you'll get a nasty red number in brackets, in which case, you'd better try another approach and enter some different figures. Keep fiddling until you get a bottom-line profit based on reasonable assumptions.

Now, I know that's not a very detailed description of how to use the tool on the CD, so as you use it I recommend you follow the step-by-step instructions that start right here.

# *Step-by-step coupon profitability analysis*

Please use the CD1001 file from your Marketing Kit CD.

This form is built in Excel. To use it, simply fill in the boxed cells with numbers representing your plans for a coupon program. The spreadsheet calculates everything else needed to figure out what your costs and profits are. The general categories of costs are:

- **Fixed costs.** These are the costs of designing your coupon, printer's setup costs, and so on. Be sure to include all fixed costs that must be incurred in order to create the coupon and program.

✔ **Incremental costs or variable costs.** These are costs that vary with the number of coupons. Note that many such costs are conventionally measured on a cost per 1,000 coupons, instead of on a cost per individual coupon. When you get quotes from printers and the companies that handle coupon redemptions, those quotes will probably be in costs per 1,000 coupons.

The following paragraphs go through the coupon profitability analysis line by line, and I show you how to enter appropriate variables in order to see how a coupon program might work. You have to fill in 13 cells in order to complete an analysis of a future scenario or past program. I guide you through each one in turn.

**Number of coupons: _____**

How many coupons do you plan to distribute? If you are giving them out through a store or other public sites, you may not be able to guess accurately how many will be picked up. So just take your best guess, print a specific number, and then test several levels of distribution: Say, a) the entire print run, b) two-thirds of it, and c) one-P148

third of it. If the program seems like it will be profitable at all these levels, then it's probably a good idea to try it. Often, however, an offer is distributed to a mailing list of known number, or to the subscribers of a publication. In these cases, you can use basic circulation or list data to determine how many coupons you'll be distributing.

**Face value of coupons: $_____**

What are you planning to offer the users of the coupon? Typically a coupon gives a discount on the purchase of a single product. That's how this spreadsheet is set up. Enter a dollar value representing the amount the coupon is good for. For instance, if you plan to offer a $20 discount off the next purchase of a carton of your special industrial cleaning fluid, then enter $20 in this cell.

Ah, but how much should you offer to get a good response? I was afraid you'd ask that! A good but vague rule is to offer just enough to get someone's attention. If you offer too much, well, you're just giving the product away. If you offer too little, nobody will pay attention. So what should you offer? Regular coupon marketers run lots of experiments until they find some formulas that work. If you don't have any idea of what to offer, you need to run some experiments yourself. Start with a nice safe number. Safe means from a bottom-line perspective, which means something that is considerably less than your profit.

For example, let's say you make a cool new cat toy, which you sell at whole-sale to pet stores for $1.75, and which they mark up to a retail price of $2.49. When you examine your costs, you find that it costs you approximately $1.20 to make and deliver each unit, so your profit is $0.55 on each cat toy you sell. Now, it would be a costly experiment to offer a $0.55 discount, wouldn't it? But a $0.25 discount you can readily afford. On the other hand, is that enough of a discount to get anyone's attention? Maybe not. The redemption rate might be pretty low. So perhaps a $0.35 coupon is better. That still leaves a little profit to cover (hopefully) the costs of the coupon program, but offers enough off that it might get a reasonable response rate from cat owners. You may want to start there and see what happens.

**Design & consultation fees: $_____**

If you hire a graphic designer, marketing consultant, or ad agency to design your coupon, you're going to have to pay her. Enter the cost here.

**Setup costs for producing coupons: $_____**

If you are paying a printer to produce your coupons, there will be some setup costs. Enter them here. If you are buying ad space in a newspaper or other publication for your coupons, then you probably won't have to pay setup costs, so just enter a zero.

**Other fixed costs: $_____**

If you expect to incur any other up-front or other fixed costs, be sure to add them in here. Forgotten costs come back to bite!

**Production costs per 1,000 coupons: $_____**

If you are printing the coupons, your printer can give you this number. Ask him what the costs are at several different volume levels because there may be a sliding scale based on quantity. If you're inserting your coupons in a publication, just enter zero in this blank. Then the next line item is the one for you!

**Distribution costs per 1,000 coupons: $_____**

What will the newspaper, trade magazine, or coupon booklet publisher charge you for inserting your coupon in its publication? What will stores charge you for placing your coupons at the point of purchase? What will some hot Web site charge you to put your discount offer in a banner ad? If you are using someone else's service to distribute your coupon offer to prospective customers, enter her cost per 1,000 coupons here.

**Legitimate redemption rate (Percent of coupons properly redeemed): ____%**

What percentage of those coupons will actually be used toward purchase of your product? It could be 100 percent, but I doubt it. Usually a small percentage of coupons are actually redeemed. For under-a-dollar discounts on consumer non-durables, it's often just a few percent. For larger discounts and/or higher-cost items, the rates might be higher, even over 10 percent. But again, there is no substitute for experience, so if you've done similar coupon programs in the past, use them as your basis for estimating. If not, well, recognize that you are running an experiment and don't do anything on such a large scale that you'll regret the results later!

**Misredemption rate (Percent of coupons redeemed wrongly/for the wrong products): ___%**

Programs rarely work exactly as you hoped. Sometimes the store clerks or order fulfillment staff apply the coupon to the wrong product. Sometimes somebody finds some way to scam you. If there are ways for things to go wrong, they will. So build a little error into your projections and make sure it won't kill you.

The problem with misredemptions, obviously, is that you end up paying the face value of coupons but not getting a product sale in return. So they come directly off the bottom line. Fortunately, misredemption rates are generally quite low.

**Processing costs per coupon redeemed: $_____**

If you are using a totally computerized system in which the coupon is scanned or the discount is applied to a customer code number, then you don't really have any appreciable processing costs. Your system (or some store's system) just processes the things automatically. But most coupons actually end up having to be handled by someone, somewhere. And that is going to cost you money, whether you use a redemption service or hire someone to do it. When you subcontract coupon processing, the costs are generally in the 5–15 cents per coupon range. If you plan to have someone do it by hand, then estimate how many he can do per hour and work out what it will cost per coupon. Enter your estimated processing cost per coupon in this blank.

**Other variable costs per coupon: $_____**

If other incremental costs exist that I didn't think to include, put them here.

**Percentage of these sales that would have occurred anyway: ___%**

The spreadsheet calculates the number of sales from coupon redemptions. It does this based on the number of coupons and the legitimate redemption rate you entered. If, for example, you plan to distribute 100 coupons and you anticipate a 5 percent redemption rate, the spreadsheet calculates that you will sell five units as a result of the coupon program. Now, many people just chalk up all five of those units as resulting from the coupons. In other words, they give the coupon full credit for all those sales in which a coupon is redeemed. But is that fair? Maybe not. What if some regular customers would have bought anyway, but at full price instead of at the discount rate? Then your coupon isn't really bringing you their business.

So in this blank, you can account for those regular users who would have purchased anyway. Do so by estimating what percentage of all redemptions they will make up. Make it a high percentage if you think that the distribution method that you're using will reach lots of regular, loyal customers. Make it a low percentage if you think that the distribution method will reach mostly new prospects — such as users of your competitor's products. Make it zero if you are introducing a new product that doesn't have any regular users.

**Profit contribution per sale: $_____**

How much do you actually make in profits from each product that you sell? Calculate this number based only on the direct costs of making and selling one unit of the product. That's its contribution, and hopefully it is a positive contribution!

# The bottom line is . . .

That's it! When you fill in all those blanks, you get "the answer." In fact, you get a number of answers. The spreadsheet tells you what your incremental costs, variable costs, and total costs should be, assuming your estimates are correct. It also figures out how many new sales you should get as a result of redemptions of the coupon. Finally, and most importantly, the program calculates the total incremental profit. That's the amount the program will make or lose.

# Testing multiple scenarios

Because this is a spreadsheet with built-in formulas, you can and should test many different variables in order to get a feel for the range of possible outcomes. For example, I highly recommend that you test several different redemption rates. Build low-, medium-, and high-redemption-rate scenarios. Make sure that the program appears profitable at all three levels before you run it!

## Learning from experience

When the program is done and you have the actual numbers, compare each variable with your up-front forecast for it. Learn from your mistakes. Yes, you will have made mistakes. There is no way to forecast any coupon program with complete accuracy. In fact, unless you run very similar programs routinely, it is hard to forecast any program with even rough accuracy! So the name of the game is to learn from your experiences.

Here are some great questions to use in debriefing yourself and preparing to design even better coupon programs the next time around:

- Did we do enough coupons to reach our market?

- Did our method of distribution get enough coupons to our target market?

- Did we offer enough of an incentive to attract new business (indicated by sufficiently high redemption rates)?

- Did we offer more than we needed to in order to attract new business (indicated by far higher redemption rates than expected)?

- Were our fixed costs higher than we expected — and if so, how can we cut them next time?

- Were our incremental (variable) costs higher than we expected — and if so, how can we cut them next time?

- Were too many coupons misredeemed — and if so, how can we reduce errors and/or cheating in the future?

- Did it cost more than we expected to process each coupon — and if so, how can we reduce this handling cost next time?

When you look at these specific questions, you are working on the key variables that drive the profitability of coupon programs. Learning more about each of these variables and how to control them will give you more control over the bottom-line profitability of your program.

## Ah, but did it work?

There is one more question you really need to ask, one that has little to do with the profitability of the coupon program. That question is: Did the coupon achieve your broader marketing objectives? In other words: Did your coupon do one or more of the following?

✔ Help attract new customers, some of whom will become regular buyers

✔ Help ward off competition

✔ Boost sales for the period

✔ Introduce customers to a new or improved product or service

✔ Support or enhance other advertising or sales initiatives

✔ Help cushion a price increase

✔ Help cross-sell another product to existing customers

✔ Help to motivate the sales force by giving them a new sales incentive or tool

✔ Make your distributors, retailers or other intermediaries happy and more willing to push your product or service

✔ Help you gain access to greater distribution

✔ Help you migrate customers to direct or Web-based purchasing

✔ Increase repeat purchase rates

✔ Maintain or increase your market share

✔ Attract frequent switchers — those customers who are always looking for "a deal"

✔ Attract a specific, attractive segment (or group) of customers with an offer designed for and distributed to them

✔ Make a profit

As this lengthy list demonstrates, many reasons exist for distributing coupons. Sometimes marketers are willing to run a coupon program at or below break-even in order to accomplish their marketing objectives. The most important objective may *not* be to make a profit. It may be to give your salespeople an incentive or tool for boosting distribution. In this case, you may be happy to take a hit on the coupon as long as you get greater distribution because you figure that is so valuable it is worth investing in.

So in some situations, it may be just fine to lose money on a coupon program. But you need to know how much you'll lose, and you need to think through the likely longer-term returns. If another percentage point of market share is likely to make you thousands or millions of dollars over the next year, who cares if it costs you hundreds or thousands of dollars to win that share? The point is, you just need to know what your objectives are and know what the costs of your coupon program are. If the objectives justify the costs in your mind, go for it!

Or, if you want to play it safe, you can just stick to profitability as your primary goal for each coupon program. Then you will be happy to pick up small gains on any other objectives. It's up to you. After you have the information and analyses at your fingertips, you can make good decisions, try them out, learn from the results, and make even better decisions the next time.

# Some Alternative Approaches

What if you want to offer some incentive, but you don't want it to be price-based and to cost you directly on your profit margin? Here are some alternatives that usually build sales or loyalty without costing you as much of your profit margin:

## Offer free food

Face it: People love to eat, at least if the food is good, the location pleasant, and the company tolerable. So put some marketing imagination into ways of using free food as an incentive. One insurance company in California recruited its agents by offering a free seminar at the most luxurious hotels and restaurants, complete with a free meal of the agents' choice. The company promoted the offer with postcard mailings to purchased lists of agents. Then it followed up with a phone call from its call center. Its turnouts were best when the event was held at the best possible restaurants. And when the dust settled, giving away a free meal in exchange for the chance to build a long-term business relationship was really quite economical.

## Give gifts

Plenty of other alternatives exist for your sales promotions. Only your imagination limits your options, in this as in everything you do in marketing. I recommend collecting examples of clever sales promotions from other marketers — especially those who aren't in your industry and don't compete with you. When you look around at all the ideas people try in the world of marketing, you can often find something that adapts well to your business and industry.

Maybe you should try to make better use of premium items. Many businesses do. Rocks Communications, a marketing agency that appears in several earlier chapters, recommends "lumpy envelopes" with interesting, even funny, gifts inside of them. The contents can be simple and useful — or simple and zany — it's up to you. If they are three-dimensional, the envelopes will get opened. Almost 100 percent of them will end up being read, which is way above average for direct mail. And it often pays off well to spend between $0.50 and $5 to make an envelope interesting and memorable.

I know one executive of a regional moving company who had a bunch of high-quality canvas tote bags embroidered with her company's logo and phone number. She gives these out to good customers and prospects, and she reports that the bags are very popular. Also, they tie in nicely with her service, reminding people that her business can help them carry things from one place to another. She has probably gotten more repeat business and referrals from this simple gift item than she would have gotten new business from a series of print ads offering 5 percent discounts on her services. And the premium item is obviously a lot more profitable.

## Offer rewards for repeat business

I highly recommend that you look at loyalty rewards and programs. Many businesses are exploring this concept. It might be something as simple as the "coffee card" that collects stamps each time you fill up until you earn a free coffee. It might be something as complex as an airline's frequent flier club, with all its rules and benefits and tie-ins to other companies' sales promotions, too. Or maybe you can find a unique formula of your own.

# On the CD

Check out the following file on the CD-ROM:

▮ ✔ Coupon profitability analysis form (CD1001)

# Chapter 11

# Taking Advantage of Publicity

*T*his is probably the chapter that you, as a small or medium-sized business owner, feel most like skipping over because creating newsworthy stories about your business may seem out of your reach. Don't feel discouraged! Publicity is a very real part of your marketing plan and one that *is achievable* for you. I'll show you how.

A company that can implement an ongoing plan for free publicity opportunities can benefit greatly. But before I show you how publicity can increase sales, I want to talk about what publicity is. Publicity tells the story of a business or an executive or employee within the business. A good publicity campaign results in a positive public image and without doubt shows up on the profit side of the ledger.

## Publicity in Action

Imagine you own a mid-size tooling company that caters to the furniture market in North Carolina (which is often called the furniture capital of the world). Growing your business has two components:

✔ Growing your business through producing the best quality products available (satisfied customers keep coming back and refer other customers)

✔ Growing your business through name recognition to attract a whole new customer base

## Story ideas

Your publicity program is a powerful image builder. It tells the story of:

- Your new cutting-edge technology
- Your quality product or service
- The many ways your company gives back to the community
- The awards your company has won
- That your company is growing — renovating, relocating, updating
- How good your people are
- What a great leader your CEO is
- That you have started a new advertising campaign
- And any other interesting or important news about your business or the people in it

Suppose that you place a story (further in the chapter I discuss how to place a story) in the business section of the largest (by circulation) newspaper in the region. This story that you place is about the fact that you just received the most sophisticated machine in the world today to produce the kind of tools needed by the furniture industry.

The first result of this positive publicity is that new customers call you to find out more about what you can do for them. In addition, existing customers gain increased confidence because the article in the paper validates the fact that you are progressive. And another positive result is that in a tight labor market, potential employees and current employees are made aware of your cutting-edge capabilities and consider you a good company to work for. Employees want to work for the best.

So, with one carefully placed article you've increased name recognition, reinforced that you are the best, and highlighted the fact that your company is a great place to work because of the cutting-edge technology you possess. Not bad!

Another valuable use of the article is to post it on your Web site and send a copy of the article (with a cover letter and a product information sheet) to new and potential clients (note that you'll need permission from the publication for both — but permission is routinely granted). You may even do something as simple as placing a reprint of the article in the envelope that holds your employees' paychecks or customer invoices. Remember, *publicity can be merchandised internally and externally.* Don't forget to do both.

# Get Under the PR Umbrella!

In short, editorial coverage creates a publicity-marketing umbrella that other forms of marketing cannot compete with. Just think about it. Are you more likely to hear two businesspeople saying, "Hey did you see DeHart Tooling's new direct mail piece?" or "Hey, did you see that article about DeHart Tooling getting that new machine in *The Charlotte Observer?*"

So, you get the idea — publicity is special. But it doesn't have to be complicated. In this chapter, I show you how to create a workable publicity plan for your business, product, or service.

## Is it advertising?

One of the most interesting things about publicity is that people often don't understand the difference between publicity and advertising. Consider advertising that is paid for, such as posters, brochures, newsletters, billboards, direct mail, and advertisements. You write a check to have them produced and placed in front of an audience. Advertising involves *paid placement of marketing messages.* Not so publicity.

Publicity is not advertising; you do not pay for an interview on a radio or television program or for the space used to write about your company in a newspaper or magazine. If you are interviewed on a local business program, or a television comes to your company and videos a special event for the evening news, they do not send you a bill. Publicity falls onto the editorial side of any media company's business, not the advertising side. (This means not only is it free to you, but it is inherently more interesting and credible than paid-for space or time.)

Publicity is not public relations either. Public relations is an umbrella under which publicity is a tool. Public relations as a function generally includes all sorts of other stuff, such as how you relate to your community, that may or may not generate profitable publicity for you. I'm going to focus on getting you publicity — because that's what you need to promote your business.

Publicity, in short, is obtaining free editorial coverage based on factual, interesting, breakthrough, and newsworthy information about your company, product, or service.

Now, the question is, how do you do it?

## How to generate great publicity

Many companies obtain publicity by hiring a professional public relations firm. In many cases, a good public relations firm is a much better use of marketing dollars than advertising, but since publicity is not guaranteed and is based on the fact that you have a good story that is interesting to a reporter's readers, it is best to seek the advice of professionals both in public relations and advertising to get the best mix for your marketing dollars.

One way to determine whether your company is a good candidate for publicity as a focus of your marketing program is to determine whether the information you can share about your company, product, or service shows *progress*. Progress is always newsworthy.

Or your story may be interesting because it has *a local angle*. The closer the story is to a reader's home or business, the more important it is to them.

Another way to look at whether you are a good candidate for a publicity campaign is if your story is *unusual* — not the same old story recycled over and over again.

And, of course, you'll want your story to be *timely* — it makes sense considering the business conditions or the time of year. Timely means that your company is doing something before anyone else, by the way. If you are the third company to send out a press release about new ideas for holiday gifts, your story is a lot less likely to get picked up than if you are the first one to do it.

And the last option is that your company provides a needed service or is doing something significant for the local or regional area that is *important right now*.

## But isn't much of what we do newsworthy?

So the way to generate publicity is to let journalists in the media know about anything that you can point to as having news value because it represents significant progress, has a local angle, is unusual, is timely, and/or is important right now.

Sounds easy, doesn't it? I know what you are thinking:

- My company is doing lots of great things that should be newsworthy.

- But no one from the media is calling me to ask me about it. Why not?

- How the heck is the media that's important to me and my customers going to know about my business, product, or service?

Well, nobody in the media is going to cover your business unless they know what is newsworthy about it. They don't read minds, you know. So you've simply got to tell them.

# It's not newsworthy until journalists know about it

The idea of you calling a business reporter at the largest paper in your region and telling him or her about a new product or service you offer or about a sales record you have achieved or about expansion your company is making within the state is not so far-fetched. But most, really almost all, business-people never pick up the phone and call a journalist or editor to share their information. When have you ever initiated such a call? What, *never?* Those editors must be getting the idea that you don't like them. They may think that you don't *want* to be covered in the news.

Any media person needs information, and most of them need and want some help gathering that information. The days of the reporter with a steno pad and a trench coat and hat, seeking out a great story, are gone for good. Sure, reporters still have beats, but they are probably the largest companies in the area. There is no way today's business reporter can do his or her job effectively without the help of others to keep him or her informed. And under the "others" category there will be professional publicists that work at public relations firms, seasoned public relations professionals that work internally at companies, and then there can be *you.*

By becoming a liaison with the media, you can help your company accomplish one or more of the following:

- Inform people about how to choose, buy, and use your product or service
- Persuade consumers to buy your product or service
- Counteract misconceptions about your product or cause
- Get customers in your store or on your Web site
- Get information to the public on issues your organization is concerned about
- Bring people to an event or series of events
- Recruit highly qualified employees
- Attract investors

Because the reporter needs help gathering information that is not readily available, such as a breaking story about your company, it is very likely that you can get coverage about what your company is doing. Finding good stories is always a problem to a journalist. And their problem is your opportunity.

Take a look at Figure 11-1, which is a copy of a press release sent by one of the leading U.S. furniture makers to a national list of editors and reporters. (The figure shows the first page of the release, and all three pages of it are on your CD in the file CD1101.) Now, the story Broyhill Furniture Industries is pitching to the media here is not one they are likely to come up with on their own. What reporter would know that Broyhill has insights into what makes Generation Xers unique? Yet they do, and their story of what they learned about this important cohort and how they are adapting their products for it is potentially interesting to any reporter covering generational differences, new shopping patterns, or related topics. It took the imagination of the company and its publicists to figure out that there was a potentially useful news story here. But once the story was prepared and distributed to the media, many journalists picked up on it and mentioned Broyhill in the media.

## The local angle strategy

Another great way to generate publicity is to focus on what you do that has special interest to a local area or community. In many cases today, so much generic global information is available through the Internet and syndicated wire services like the Associated Press that the real gem to a reporter is a real person at a real company telling a real story with a real local angle. But you will want to do your homework before you approach the media to give you the best chance of making it in a paper (or in a magazine or on the radio or on television). Specifically, you need to prepare some thoughts and information and you need to package your contributions to the media in one or more of the forms that they are used to working with. The following sections look at what forms they like their information in and how to prepare them.

## The Media kit

The first step you should take is to develop a media kit. Some newspaper people and many publicists still call it a press kit. But, I like to call it a media kit because the press has now become more than a newspaper or other printed publication. *Media kits* are usually a folder (with two inside pockets) that includes one or several news releases about your company, photographs as they relate to the information in the releases, a background sheet that may overview interesting facts about your company including the history or milestones along the way, bios and photos of your management team, and any other information that compiles a complete overview of your company as it stands today.

**Broyhill**
*FURNITURE INDUSTRIES*

N E W S   R E L E A S E

One Broyhill Park
Lenoir, North Carolina
28633

**For Immediate Release**
**GX Slides Enclosed**

Contact: Celia Rocks (828) 322-3111
or CeliaRocks@aol.com

*"In my day, we didn't have MTV or*
*in-line skates. No. It was your basic 45*
*record that skipped and regular metal roller skates.*
*Times, they do change."*
—Anonymous

### One Size Does Not Fit All
*Broyhill offers Generation Xers yet another way to express themselves*

Lenoir, NC — When you get up this morning, you will drive to your 8:00-5:00 corporate, ladder-climbing job, in your Volvo, listening to your cassette tape, driving a document to a client . . . NOT!

Wait a minute—hold the mobile phone! Enter a new generation— one radically different than the one before—Generation X. For years, Baby Boomers have been the aim of new product developers, marketers and advertisers, with the exclusion of all others. But as the purchasing power of 65 million Generation Xers becomes increasingly evident, savvy product developers are no longer marginalizing this generation's economic clout and are quick to figure out that warmed over Baby Boomer campaigns won't do the trick.

"After doing some research, we found that the demographics, buying tastes and habits of Generation X are unmistakably different than previous generations," said Tom Lentz, VP of Marketing at Broyhill Furniture. "They have their own ideas when it comes to creativity, function and design. From these ideas, they have developed a style all their own—from the clothes they wear, to the way they look at work and the world, to the company they keep."

*-more-*

**Figure 11-1:** "One Size Does Not Fit All" press release.

The media kit can serve as the basis of your publicity program because it can always be referred to at a moment's notice for factual information about your company. The primary purpose of a media kit is to help newspeople report your story as thoroughly as possible. It saves the reporter's time and shows that you are competent and serious about providing accurate, up-to-date information. Not everything in a media kit will be used, but it sends the message that you are organized and have very positive and real information about your company.

A side note to the development of a media kit is that it is a great internal exercise to see where your company has been, where it is now, and where it is going. The process of organizing your company on paper, overviewing its history, its products, its executives, its milestones, and its sales accomplishments, is a great way to take a look at your company as a whole.

For starters, you can purchase shiny duotang (two-pocket) folders at your local office supply store or major office supply store chains. They come in many colors and usually come 25 to a box. You can insert all your information inside the folder and interchange the information as needed. Some companies even print stickers for the cover (with their company name and address on the sticker) because it is a low-cost alternative to printing directly onto a folder. (Place the sticker on the outside of the folder, centered on the front cover.)

Why be cheap? First impressions are the most important, right? I recommend that you invest a little money into this part of your publicity program and print a two-pocket folder that has your company name and logo. (Remember, you won't be buying advertising for this program, so the money you spend will be on the preparation of the materials and the time you spend doing publicity, which won't really be very much compared to buying ad space or time.)

You will find many additional uses for this printed media kit folder. When you're not using it for publicity, it makes a great folder to give customers. You can interchange price sheets and information easily. You can also use it as your employee handbook to hold information employees need. You might even find yourself bringing one to the bank when you visit your loan officer, or passing them out at the press room at a trade show. So, consider the many uses a media kit folder can provide your company and design it accordingly.

Remember to plan ahead. If you anticipate a move or a new area code coming into your city, you may want to print a smaller quantity or leave off your address and phone number from the outside and focus on your name and logo or a picture on the cover.

# *Has your Web page become your media kit?*

Sometimes a company's Web page *is* their media kit. Go to several businesses' Web pages and you are most likely to see most of the components of a media kit. You can use your site this way if you like. And some journalists will be happy to visit your site and pull off background information they need.

But I still recommend that you produce a written copy of a media kit because even in our wired world, reporters, both electronic and print, may want the convenience of a kit that they can refer to, throw in their briefcase, or put in a file.

Many companies are now developing pressrooms on their Web sites that list all of their press releases and photographs of executives or products that can be easily downloaded as a service to the media. I believe that right now we are in a transitional stage, where some media people are incredibly techno-savvy and actually would prefer everything electronically and others still prefer the option of traditional media kits and photographs that arrive on their desk via snail mail. This is not the time to make a decision about which way your company wants to go. Offer both and let the reaction to technology dictate the future of how your media kit will look over the next couple of years. Develop a media kit and also have the people that are posting the information on your Web site include the materials from your media kit.

# What's the hook?

Now for some bad news. Did you know that most media kits never get more than a passing glance from journalists? In general, media kits do not generate publicity. Not on their own. Not without a *hook,* or current, interesting story, to provide a focus for the media's coverage. So your media kit is just a foundation for generating publicity. You still have some more work to do.

The hook is the newsworthy information in your most current press release. How will you create that press release? By figuring out what is really exciting about your executives, staff, products, service, earnings, special event, or milestone. Let's see how that's done next.

# The Press Release That's Going to Get You Publicity

The best way to decide what the story should be is to ask yourself what's new at your company. So, ask yourself now, have you launched a new product? Did you add new employees? Did you have outstanding earnings for this quarter? Are you expanding in the region? Will you be merging with a new company? Is it your anniversary? Do you generate more or better marketing for less money than any of your competitors? Do some of your employees run in marathons or volunteer for a local charity? Does your business support a youth soccer team or league? Do you have an unusual employee recognition or reward program or event?

Whatever your story is, whether it is that you received a new contract with a major client or you've just received an award, you want to put it on paper in the form of a press release.

Because space and time is money, keep your press release brief, breakthrough, and newsworthy. How? Imagine you are writing a short article for the cover of your local paper.

Try to put yourself in the reporter's seat for a moment. The reporter receives hundreds of press releases a week, maybe even a day. He or she may only have an hour to read all of them. So he or she will have to make quick judgments and scan a paragraph or two. Keep in mind that he or she is also getting 30–40 e-mails a day and 20–30 voice mails. Your release has to rise to the top of this weighty pile of communications.

Make your press release as professional as possible so that you will be placed in the credible pile. Make it stand out! Here are some of the tricks. Your press release should:

- ✔ Consist of news that is really news, not just promotional material. (As I said above, newsworthy means it represents significant progress, has a local angle, is unusual, is timely, and/or is important right now.)

- ✔ Contain the name, address, telephone number, and Web site of your company in the upper left-hand corner of the first page. Also, give the name and phone number and e-mail of the person to contact (probably you) for further information.

- ✔ Be short. Yes, short! (No more than two pages.)

- ✔ Be word-processed and printed on your company letterhead on a good laser printer. If it's more than one page, use a matching second page and staple.

- ✔ Be spell-checked and read over by several different people for accuracy and typos.

Yes, I'm serious about checking it for accuracy and professional appearance. These are, in many cases, editors and writers that you are sending it to. They will *know* if it is well-written and professionally laid out and printed or not. Have several people at different levels in your company read over your release. You will be surprised by what different people may see. The third reader often finds a mistake that the first two missed or adds some insight that nobody else thought of.

If your release must go to a second page, try to end the first page with a completed paragraph, or at least a completed sentence. Type **-More-** across the bottom of the first page. Start the second page with a brief heading in the upper-left corner that includes the name of your company and page two.

Mark the end of your release with the digits **-30-**, or the number sign, **###**, repeated several times across the page. These are two versions of journalese for "that's all there is for now."

Figure 11-2 shows the first page of a press release from Egreetings.com that really tells the story for the business press. It is also on your CD in full with the filename CD1102. And for your further reference, you'll find a second press release from the same company, focusing on another newsworthy story to generate additional media coverage. The second release is titled, "Free Spanish Language Greetings from Egreetings.com Are a Big Hit on the Internet!"

## Good versus bad press releases

A good press release is professionally typed and sent out on original letterhead. It includes the name of the contact person, his phone number and e-mail, the date, and the copy: **For Immediate Release.** It also

- ✔ Has a great headline
- ✔ Is double-spaced
- ✔ Is clearly interesting

A bad press release, one that will end up in the garbage can, is

- ✔ Too long
- ✔ Missing a much-needed visual, such as a photograph, which can help tell the story
- ✔ Not newsworthy
- ✔ Too soft or self-promotional
- ✔ Poorly written with obvious mistakes
- ✔ Is incomplete and lacks valuable information that would make the story more interesting
- ✔ Shows little attention to details
- ✔ Arrives late

Egreetings Network, Inc.       Tel 415 375-4100
149 New Montgomery Street   Fax 415 375-4101
San Francisco, CA 94105        www.egreetings.com

# 𝓔greetings.com

**For Immediate Release**
Contact: Celia Rocks (828) 322-3111
or CeliaRocks@aol.com

### Business Travelers Delight Families With Free Internet Greetings
*From Egreetings.com*

San Francisco, California (February 21, 2000) — Until now, the busy business traveler has had three imperfect choices for communicating back home: a late-night phone call that often gets left on the answering machine, an e-mail message that has all the warmth of a credit report or a mailed card that usually arrives long after the traveler returns home.

But with one of the thousands of greetings from Egreetings.com, travelers can transmit their feelings at the click of a mouse—and for free. "The same characteristics that make e-mail so popular—ease of use, near instantaneous delivery and world-wide acceptance—make it ideal for the exchange of feelings and emotions that are best expressed with online greetings," said Gordon M. Tucker, Chief Executive Officer of Egreetings Network, Inc.

"For the home-sick road warrior, sending a greeting from Egreetings.com can be a welcome respite from spreadsheets and office reports," Tucker said. "And for the recipient, a digital greeting with animation, music, beautiful color and laughter is a real day-brightener, a reminder that you may be separated, but you're not forgotten."

What a great way to send your kids a personal greeting that they can easily print out and pin on their wall. The techno-savvy kids of this generation will appreciate the fact that you're in-style, up-to-date, and a super-cool parent.

*-more-*

**Figure 11-2:** Business travelers delight families with free Internet greetings from Egreetings.com.

# Is your release "news ready"?

As Figure 11-2 demonstrates, a good release will read like a news story, which is exactly the point. A good release will sound as if it's ready to be inserted in a paper. Here's how to write one that meets this important criterion.

1. A good release starts with a *headline*. A short title at the top should tell the media what your hook is. "Local business agrees to support youth soccer programs for five years." "Tooling company adds cutting-edge equipment." "Author explains the secrets of generating publicity." Whatever your hook, start right off with it so they "get it" right away.

2. Next, a good release will have a *lead paragraph* that covers the who, what, why, where, and when of the interesting subject you are sharing with the media. Then subsequent paragraphs clearly and cleanly elaborate upon that story by filling in the details or adding interesting tidbits.

   Who, what, when, where, and why. That's the journalist's mantra. Let it be yours when you write a release, because they don't have a story fit for print (or air) until they've answered those questions. In a way, you can think of that opening paragraph as providing the *bait* for your hook. And that bait is the who, what, when, where, and why that provides a journalist with all the essentials needed to turn a hook into actual editorial content.

3. Finally, a good release needs to follow through on the promise of the header and lead paragraph with a few more paragraphs of *supporting text and images*. Make sure that this supporting text is truly relevant and to the point, and not boringly repetitive. Provide some interesting or important background information. Throw in a quotable quote or two from a company representative if you like. Give some evidence to support your contention that you've actually done something important or unusual or timely. And if at all appropriate, do provide a photo or other visual to illustrate the story.

# Incubate!

Whenever you can, let your press release sit overnight before you send it. Check for accuracy, correct errors, but most of all, make sure that you have an interesting story to tell and that you tell it with all the facts you can.

# Got Kit. Got Release. Now What?

Once you have your press release (probably about two pages double-spaced) and a media kit, you need to *make a media pitch*. In other words, you've got to sell your story.

Make your first media pitch by selecting one reporter and trying the process once. Select the paper that is the main paper in your region and choose the reporter who covers the beat most affiliated with what your company does.

For example, if your company is an art gallery and is having a new exhibit, you would obviously contact the art editor at your local paper. If a reporter covers construction and development and your company just bought a huge piece of land to develop over the next two years, the connection is there.

You may also call the section of the paper that best relates to your company and *ask* who writes about your specific topic. You'll find someone is generally happy to point you to the correct contact.

Here's a list of some typical specialty areas at a large metropolitan daily.

| | |
|---|---|
| Art | Sunday Editor |
| Movies | Events Calendar |
| Books | Television |
| Music | Fashion |
| Business | Technology |
| News | Features |
| Real Estate | Theater |
| Editorial | Food |
| Science | Travel |
| Education | Foreign Affairs |
| Society | Women's Page |
| Entertainment (Criticism) | Home and Garden |
| Sports | Local |
| Entertainment (News) | |

Lots of choices, aren't there!

Before you make your approach to the most appropriate person, confirm the reporter's name, business address, and phone number via the phone. You have to be sure you know whom you want to talk to and how to contact them.

Good work! Now you know whom you want to send your press release to, why they would be interested in writing about it, and where to find them. You also have a thorough media kit on your company (in case a simple story turns into a feature article), and you have a press release that tells the breaking story that your focus is on today. You are, finally, prepared to generate some publicity. Well, almost.

## Time for a cover letter

Your next step is to put together a short, clear cover letter that tells the reporter why you think he or she should write about your company. It can go something like this:

> Dear Doug Smith:
>
> I enjoy your feature article every week as you overview construction and development in western North Carolina. I particularly enjoyed your article dated June 1, 2000, regarding the new proposed highway. I think your readers will enjoy hearing about the land my company is purchasing for development. The attached press release specifically outlines our plans.
>
> I have also enclosed a media kit, which gives you background information on our company and a visual rendering of the proposed project. These materials can be e-mailed to you or they can be obtained in the pressroom on our website. I will follow up with you shortly.
>
> Best Regards,
>
> John Builder

*Now* you are actually ready to make the contact. Put your cover letter, release, and kit into an envelope (don't fold them!) and send them via first-class mail. Then follow up with a friendly phone call in a few days to ask the contact if he or she saw your release and whether you can provide any more information. With a little luck, you'll get a positive, enthusiastic response and perhaps even be interviewed briefly right on the spot.

## Dealing with rejection

When you pitch a story, you are selling your hook to journalists. I know it's not "real" selling because you aren't asking for money. But it is akin to sales in that you need to select a target, make an approach, find a way to present your information, and ask them to do something that is beneficial to you.

And sometimes they do. But often, the media ignores you and declines to cover your story, in which case you need to deal with rejection, just as in personal selling (see Chapter 4 for helpful advice). Now, remember that rejection means nothing to the journalist, and should mean nothing to you, either. They just don't need your story right now. Or they just don't think the hook is very sharp. Or they don't think it's that relevant to their area or focus. But because you presented yourself professionally and politely, they are still happy, in fact more than happy, to see your next release or hear your next voice mail follow-up on a mailing. So rejection does not preclude later coverage.

In fact, you are more likely to be covered by a journalist who has rejected you in the past than by one who has never heard of you. Even though a journalist declines to cover a specific story, he or she generally makes a mental note of the source and puts you in a physical or at least a mental "possible sources" file. Your well-prepared, professional letter, release and kit earn you the right to be a source of news in the future. So don't let rejection worry you. You are still closer to coverage than you were before you made the contact.

And, just like a salesperson, you can always contact more journalists. Eventually, if you send out enough releases, you will strike pay dirt. So the next step for you is to compile and maintain a list of media contacts.

# Create Your Mailing List

The reason I waited so long in the chapter to talk about developing a mailing list is because it is really important to understand what you are sending prior to figuring out whom you are sending it to. In addition to the one targeted reporter at the largest paper in the area, who can probably do more for your company's exposure than all your marketing efforts combined, to really have an effective publicity program you should have a *comprehensive* list or lists.

Yes, I said lists — more than one — in fact, maybe many.

Plan your lists intelligently so that you don't waste your time or effort by approaching people who are inappropriate for your publicity goals. If you believe that one newspaper can give you enough publicity for your purposes, concentrate on the needs and requirements of that newspaper. But usually businesses need to contact a broader range of journalists and editors. There is no hard rule, so your only true guideline is *how far you want to reach out* with your message.

You'll find there are occasions when you want to make a mailing to a specific type of medium — large metropolitan dailies, smaller daily papers, weekly newspapers, trade magazines, local television, or radio. It's a good idea to begin by keeping them in separate lists so they can be easily extracted for a particular use. Also, it is easier to expand these more specific lists if your geographic areas become larger.

You may need only one or two lists of a very limited nature to begin with, but it pays to plan for future lists at this time as well. (It gives you a good understanding of what your growth potential is.) The reason for this is to establish a workable pattern for your lists: how you keep them, the type of information you collect, that sort of thing. As you prepare more and more lists, you can shuffle and combine them for temporary or immediate goals. This eliminates the need to build a new list each time you send out a mailing. The lists you may eventually be building could include:

- Company "hometown" media
- Branch offices "hometown" media
- Wire services that have a bureau where your company is based
- Daily newspapers (A list: big papers)
- Daily newspapers (B list: smaller papers)
- Weekly newspapers (C list)
- Television and radio stations (those that have business shows that might cover your company — the appropriate producers will be found within the news production department of the station)
- Trade, professional, and technical journals
- Consumer publications (usually national; look for a reporter who covers your subject and thinks you are unique)

## Where do you find the names for your list?

It's one thing to decide what sort of lists you want to compile, and quite another to actually create those lists. Where are you going to find the names of the appropriate editors and writers and other journalists?

One suggestion is to go to a local newspaper stand in your city and buy all the publications that someone who would use your products or services would read (probably you read many of them anyway). You'll find out who is writing about your subject and you can literally start a print database that way.

If you make business-to-business sales, you also want to compile a list of contacts at trade and industry publications. You can always find at least a few publications read by purchasers in any industry. Put them on your list. If you aren't sure what your customers read and what professional associations they belong to, ask them!

For radio and television programs that might offer opportunities for exposure, you can simply go through a television-programming guide published by your local paper. If you see that Channel 10 in your area offers a business-focused program every Sunday morning, you know that the producer of that program should appear on your media list.

What? You were thinking Oprah, Peter Jennings, Dan Rather, Tom Brokaw, or the front pages of *The Wall Street Journal*? Your company may be producing products or services that warrant exposure nationally. But, for learning the process of publicity, I recommend you start by focusing locally. The experience and the techniques you learn on a local basis can be used for regional and national publicity. It is far easier to go to the local media first to gain experience and confidence. And, in truth, most publicity is local and regional. Over the long run, this is where most businesses get the ongoing exposure they need.

## Or you can buy a list

A second option is simply to order a list from one of the media list–management companies in the country, such as Bacon's Information in Chicago 800-621-0561. They publish bound guides to magazines and newspapers, radio, and television. They can also pull a list for you based on your criteria and charge you only for the records they pull for you. You can obtain the records on disk, along with a printout.

So, suppose that you offer services to banks in the southeastern United States. You would ask the researcher at Bacon's to pull you a list of all the banking reporters in the Southeast at every daily and weekly newspaper and every business industry trade magazine that has a banking reporter as a starting point. You literally could, after you have that list, get to know every editor on that list by sending them your press release and media kit. These media contacts are perfect for your company because they fit the criteria of being in the right region and being specialists in the field of banking. To pay a list company to pull the list for you is probably a good starting point and probably worth what it charges.

Remember to check your list for changes each time you use it. No matter how your list originates or how you decide to update it, check your list frequently.

A note of caution: Don't oversend to your lists. Make each and every contact with the media count just as you would want every contact with you customers to count.

## Put it in the mail?

Different journalists have preferences about how they like to get their media materials. With today's explosion of information technology, you have quite a choice of distribution methods — mail, overnight service when a deadline is looming, via fax if it's extremely time sensitive, or electronically via e-mail that delivers it right to an editor's computer. Send it snail mail if it's not time-sensitive.

## Don't forget to follow up!

But no matter how you decide on the best way to contact the media, you must make a follow-up call. If you want to be successful with publicity, never send anything that you don't follow up with. Four or five days after you send your package, you will need to make a follow-up call and talk to the media person about your story line.

You may get voice mail, or you may actually get a live person on the phone. In case you actually talk with the reporter on the phone, be sure to have the media kit and press release right in front of you so that you can quickly discuss key points.

If you get voice mail, as is most common, make sure that you have practiced a solid voice mail message that goes something like this:

> "Hi Doug, this is John Builder. You may not recognize my name, but I'm the Director of Marketing at Build Right Construction Services. I read your articles all the time in the *Gotham City Observer* and sent you a press release that I think is something you can use and your readers will be interested in. As you know, my company has just purchased a tract of land, and in the package I sent to you I have overviewed our plans. You can reach me at 555-6666, right here in Gotham City, and I look forward to talking to you soon."

I can't emphasize enough the importance of calling a reporter. Don't be shy and don't think you shouldn't call because you will be bothering them. If you don't bother reporters just a little bit, they probably will not notice you or your story.

It's far easier to make that follow-up call if you have something in mind that's worth saying — and that they will find worth listening to. Find some significant detail that wasn't covered in your release (either on purpose or because it wasn't confirmed yet). Then you can feel good about calling because you have another piece of valuable information to share with the reporter.

When following up with your press release on the phone, remember that *the media needs you* to give them good stories. For all you know, that reporter is trying to figure out what to write about for her next article and you have provided her with a great service by putting together your information, sending it to her, and following up in a timely fashion to answer any questions she may have.

# Timing Is Everything

Timing is everything. One of the greatest benefits of working with a professional publicist is that they really plan ahead. Sometimes an up-and-coming publicist gets everything right except the timing. But timing is crucial. If you run a gym and you have a star body builder coming to your gym on Saturday, and you think that you are going to send a press release to the media that week, you've made a fatal error. Always give the media as much time as you can so they have time to put it on their work schedule, do the interviews, write the story, submit it to an editor for placement, and react to the timing of the event.

Whenever possible, the best policy is to make sure that your press releases are received as soon as you can possibly get the information complete on paper. Remember that you are asking for free space, and the reporter may not have any room at the last minute. Yesterday, there could have been absolutely no news and the reporter didn't know what to do. If you had just gotten your release to him a day earlier, he could have been grateful to have had it. Likewise, if you are pitching to weekly papers, or those that only come out once a month such as industry trade magazines, and if you want to pitch that a famous body builder will be at your gym on XX, you better allow time to fit in with their publication schedule — which means you need to be weeks, or even months, ahead of the event.

Don't worry if you think it will be too soon because you can always call again and/or send a reminder news flash as the event date nears. Early releases make it possible to do a more aggressive campaign on your part which includes a follow-up call, a reminder news flash, and perhaps even a last-minute e-mail reminder.

# How Do You Judge the Value of Publicity?

Advertising firms develop an advertising plan based on an overall budget. For each ad, they plug in the price of the ads appearing in each medium or outlet.

Publicity firms show their value by telling you how much it would have cost you if your free editorial would have been paid advertising. For example, Rocks Communications, a public relations firm that specializes in publicity, recently sent a memo to one of its clients that said:

> Congratulations, your product has appeared as a featured product in *Computer World Magazine*. Included was a photograph of the product, taken from our media kit, and a description of why it is so interesting. The one-page ad rate for *Computer World Magazine* is XXX. Your free editorial covered one fourth of the page, and was therefore equal in value to XXX. As you can see, the time it took to develop the media list, write the press release, send it, and pitch it was time well spent.

I think that this comparison to advertising understates the potential value of publicity. Editorial coverage in *Computer World Magazine* (as long as it isn't negative) will have a far greater impact on purchase intentions than the average ad. Basically, publicity is certainly the highest-value form of communications with your market except for direct, positive word of mouth. If you spend even half as much on publicity as you do on all your advertising, you will find that it generates business far in excess of its cost. Give it a try!

# Your Goal and Objective Plan

Putting your publicity plan on paper (and any professional publicity firm will prepare a written plan up front before they do anything for you) is a great idea.

## A simple, multi-step planning process

Here's a simple, multi-step, planning process:

1. Determine a date when somebody in your company, who has a background in writing and communication skills, will be able to gather together all the information needed to put together a media kit. Remember that your media kit will be updated and printed out throughout the year and is an ever-changing document.

2. Determine a date by which your media list will be in place.

3. Determine a date to decide what your first story is. Ask yourself (or others), "What is the good news about our company?" Develop your "hook." Think like a journalist. And do it by a specific date — or you may never get around to it!

4. Decide when you will do the first mailing. Pick a date a couple months out unless there is an urgent event or breaking news story that forces you to rush it. By that date, your first press release will be mailed to your media list.

5. *Very important:* Schedule people and time for follow-up. Over the couple weeks after your mailing, make sure that each reporter on the list is contacted personally by a phone call pitching the press release that has been sent.

This plan is a simple one, involving only those activities that I show you how to do earlier in this chapter. Five simple steps. Do them, and you are in the publicity business.

## Media contact sheet

Although your media list will most probably be in a database form so that you can merge letters and print labels, a media contact sheet placed with a printout of your list in a media binder is a valuable tool for your ongoing publicity program. Figure 11-3 shows what a media contact sheet looks like. The media contact sheet is also available on the CD-ROM (filename CD1104).

---

**Media Contact Sheet**

Name of the Reporter:
_____

Name of the Newspaper:
_____

Name of the Column:
_____

Beat:
_____

Reporter's Address and Phone Number:
_____

What Has Been Sent:
_____

Summary of Last Conversation with Reporter:
_____

---

**Figure 11-3:** Media Contact Sheet.

# Talking It to the Street

I hesitate to mention it, but there is another great way to get out there and generate some great visibility for yourself and your business without buying ads or even creating a media kit and press release. That is to simply be a public speaker at events that attract people who might become customers or might lead you to customers. When you speak at a local business club or group, a convention, or a conference, you are taking your content directly to interested people instead of relying on the media to distribute it for you.

And often, when you know you have a speaking event on the calendar, you can use it as a source of publicity by creating a press release and notifying an appropriate media list that you are making a presentation. Tell them what you'll be speaking about, why it is a new or important approach, and who the sponsor and audience are. Send it out a couple weeks ahead of the event, but not too far ahead or the media will have forgotten about it by the time the event occurs.

# More Information Needed?

I consider publicity so important to any marketing program that I cover it in my earlier book for this series, *Marketing For Dummies*, as well. One of the things I do in the earlier book that many people seem to like is to include a list of six Don'ts to keep you out of publicity trouble. You'll find a reproduction of that list on your CD here in case you want to check it out before you finalize your publicity plans (filename CD1105).

# On the CD

Check out the following files on the CD-ROM:

- Broyhill Furniture's "One Size" Press Release (CD1101)
- Egreetings.com's "Business Travelers" Press Release (CD1102)
- Egreetings.com's "Free Spanish Language Greetings" Press Release (CD1103)
- Media Contact Sheet Template (CD1104)
- Publicity Don'ts (CD1105)

# Part III

# Creating Great Marketing Communications

The 5th Wave                                    By Rich Tennant

"I opened with a big sale on 'CLOSED' signs, and no one came in. I decided to add some 'KEEP OUT' signs but still no one came in. But now I'm gonna invest in some 'BIO-HAZARD' signs — throw 'em in the window and see what happens."

# In this part . . .

In this part, I help you develop or improve your marketing communications. Whether you want coverage in the press, an effective mailing, a new look for your logo and business cards, a newsletter that generates good sales leads, or a great advertisement, you find much to assist you in this section. Along with detailed chapters on all these topics, you can find templates, inspirational examples, and lots of advice on how to do it right.

It's hard to create good marketing communications. Most efforts to communicate with and woo customers are actually unsuccessful. The majority of ads don't bring in much business. Customers ignore the vast majority of brochures or feel turned off or confused by them. Because there's plenty of room to improve marketing communications in even the best-managed companies, look closely at all your communications — and use the resources in this part before communicating with your customers again.

# Chapter 12

# Writing Great Ads and Letters

*H*ow do you go about the process of conceiving of and writing great ads, direct mail letters, brochures, or other marketing communications? In truth, there are as many ways as there are great copywriters and designers. But in this chapter, I assemble what I think are some of the most powerful and approachable tools and techniques for you to use if you want to roll up your sleeves and make your own marketing communications.

Every good marketing communication starts with ideas that make it persuasive and effective. Marketing is all about communicating your offer in a compelling manner, a manner that gets attention and shapes opinions and behaviors. And that's a tall order! We ask a lot of our marketing communications, whether they be ads, mailers, Web pages, catalogs, brochures, or other forms of communication with our customers and prospects. So it stands to reason that we need to do quite a bit of thinking in order to come up with ideas that really work. This chapter looks at some of the techniques that can really help differentiate your communications from the pack.

# Two Ways to Design for Persuasiveness

I'm going to start by showing you how to write incredibly effective copy — the words or story behind any ad or other marketing communication. Copy you can use for a print ad, a direct mail piece, a brochure or catalog, a Web page, a broadcast fax, a radio or TV commercial, or whatever. The basic strategy applies to anything, even to a personal sales presentation. And it's all based on a simple but powerful distinction between two very different ways of making a point when you communicate. Basically, you can engage and persuade people by either:

✔ Appealing to them with a compelling logical argument

✔ Appealing to them with an engaging story

Or you may use a combination of these two strategies. But the point is, these two strategies are always options when you are communicating, and thinking about which you might use is a wonderful source of inspiration whenever you need to create strong marketing communications.

## Dusting off your writing skills

Remember back in your old high school writing class when you explored the many ways of making a point through writing? For example, perhaps the assignment was to show how a character in a story feels when something bad happens to her. Well, you might just describe her feelings:

> "She was hollow. Empty inside. She felt cheated and alone. In fact, she'd never been so down in her life."

Or you might do something a little more dramatic. Create an imaginary scene that portrays her feelings:

> "She slumped against the railing of the bridge, tears streaking her cheeks, tempted by the cold waters far below."

Both approaches communicate your point that the character is having a really bad day, but they do it in very different ways.

Which way is best? It depends on what you're trying to accomplish, as well as on the context and the reader. It depends, in part, on your taste and style as well. There is not necessarily one best way to make a point, but when you recognize and experiment with alternative approaches, you are more likely to find a good way in any specific situation.

The same is true of advertising. The more ways you consider to make your point, the more likely you are to come up with an ad that really works. And, just as in literature, in advertising, you always have a choice between a dramatic or storytelling approach on the one hand, and a factual or nonfiction approach on the other. So don't forget to ask yourself which approach is appropriate.

## Are you writing an essay or a story?

It is always helpful to think about whether you want to make a factual argument in your ad or dramatize your point with some sort of story.

In fact, there is a factual and a fictional version of every marketing communication, just waiting to be discovered. Which should you use? Or should you perhaps try something that is a combination of the two forms — part fact and part fiction? Simply by posing this question, you open up many possibilities as you develop your ad or other marketing communication.

Let me illustrate the difference. Imagine that you are designing a letter you want to send to prospects of a training firm to introduce a new training program that teaches employees how to handle customer complaints effectively. Let's call this program Handling Unhappy Customers, or HUC for short. And let's assume that it really is a great program, and that companies that use it to train their employees will have happier, more loyal customers and make lots more money as a result.

But how to convince managers and training directors that HUC is a good service? What should the introductory letter say to catch their ear and get them interested in the training?

Well, first, you might rough out a letter that is factual. It makes a logical argument, such as the following:

> Dear Manager:
>
> Everyone knows it costs ten times as much to win a new customer as it does to do business with an existing customer. Yet companies routinely lose their good customers over errors or slip-ups that upset or anger those good customers and open the door to defection. What can you do to keep your customers from leaving you? What can you do to make sure that they buy more next year instead of less? What, in short, is the secret of high customer loyalty?
>
> People. It comes down to people in 99.9% of the cases, according to our extensive research. We studied the companies with the most loyal customers in a dozen different industries and in every case, these winning companies had more sensitive, better trained employees. Employees who know what to do when customers are upset or angry. Employees who know how to convert each problem into an opportunity to build loyalty instead of lose business.
>
> That's why we designed Handling Unhappy Customers (HUC), the radical new customer service training that has a measurable impact on your customer retention rates — or you get your money back!

Now, that's a pretty powerful argument. It makes the case for the HUC service quite forcefully. And most people who want to describe a new service for business-to-business sales would probably choose a factual approach based on argument, just like this copy employs.

But remember what your ninth-grade teacher told you about all the different ways of making your point! It should also be possible to present the Handling Unhappy Customers training program in a completely different manner, using the tools of the dramatist and telling a story (or stories) instead of arguing on the basis of fact. For example, you might draft some copy for that direct-mail piece that goes like this:

Dear Manager:

I want to share a little story that I think you will find interesting.

Rick, the purchasing manager for SysTech, was a man of action. He hated to waste even a minute of his or his company's precious time. Yet today, he was doing something uncharacteristic. He was doing nothing. He had been doing nothing for four and a half minutes already, and it was obviously wearing on him.

Rick was on hold. On hold with your company, to be specific. He was on hold because he had called to complain about a minor problem with the last order and been put on hold by one of your employees who didn't know how to handle the call.

In contrast, your employee was quite busy. She was busy asking anyone she could find what to do. She had no idea how to solve Rick's problem. But she had sensed the urgency in his voice, and she, too, was well aware of the ticking of the clock. Finally, after searching fruitlessly for the appropriate paperwork and getting a wide variety of unhelpful advice from her associates, your employee came back on the line. It had been five minutes and sixteen seconds since she put Rick on hold. You don't want to know what Rick said in reply when her first words to him were, "I'm sorry, Sir, but I can't find any record of that order. Are you sure you really sent it in?"

Accidents will happen, as the old saying goes. But whether you recover from them gracefully or lose a customer for life depends upon how those accidents are handled. If only that employee had received basic Handling Unhappy Customers (HUC) training, she would have known not to put poor Rick on hold, even for one minute. That violates the Adding Insult to Injury principle, which says that you must handle all unhappy customers with a high degree of consideration and support. And never, ever, put them on hold or question their word when they are upset!

But Rick doesn't care any more. He's already busy placing that order with one of your competitors. A competitor who has recently trained all its employees in the HUC program and is not likely to lose a customer over a minor problem. You may as well throw Rick's business card away. You're not likely to do business with SysTech again!

That's a dramatic approach to making your point. It creates a plausible scenario that catches the ear and draws the reader forward. It makes the reader wonder whether such dramas might not be playing themselves out right now, somewhere in his or her own business. And if so, well, that reader is certainly likely to question his or her staff's ability to handle unhappy customers. And wonder whether a little training might not, in fact, be a very wise investment. . . .

If you switch on your television, you are bound to see a number of examples of both styles of advertising within a short period of time. Some TV spots make a rational argument, presenting facts and attempting to make you believe their product claims. Others present a drama, tell a story of some kind, and attempt to affect your attitudes toward their product by making that story compelling.

## Testing the options

Which works better, an argument-based communication or a dramatic one? There is no hard and fast rule. Sometimes one works better, sometimes the other. So it is always wise to consider both options as you develop and test different versions of an ad.

To see how you might use this insight, return to the example of a company that wants to send out a letter to training managers and executives to introduce the new Handling Unhappy Customers training program. Rather than simply write the standard argument-based, factual letter, I have drafted copy for two kinds of letters — a fact-based approach and a fiction-based approach. One will work to the extent that its arguments are persuasive. The other will work to the extent that its dramatic scenario is compelling.

With both approaches in hand, you are in a position to test two very different types of letters. You could simply divide your list in half and send out two different letters, one fact-based and the other dramatic in its approach, and wait to see which gets more responses from training managers. Odds are, one or the other will pull significantly better. And if you hadn't thought to write both versions, you'd never have had a chance to learn which was best in this specific situation.

Always think "test" when you are working on a marketing communication. You can run one ad one week and another the next. You can mail or e-mail multiple letters by dividing your list into sections randomly. You can try different brochures on different customers or prospects. There is always a way to experiment and compare multiple options. And when you do, you can learn far more than most of your competitors will ever learn because most people are not thoughtful enough to design even the simplest of experiments. That's one of the reasons that most people market in the dark.

## Why not have your cake and eat it too?

Here's another way to take advantage of the insight that ads can take either a factual or dramatic approach. Why not incorporate both approaches into one ad? That way, you may be able to create a hybrid that works better than either form would on its own. At least it's worth a try. Why not go ahead and test three versions of any ad or letter instead of two:

- ✔ A straight, rational, persuasive argument based on facts
- ✔ A dramatic ad that is based almost entirely on a story or scenario
- ✔ A combination of fact-based argument and a brief story to dramatize your point

After you take the care to create a fact and a fiction version, it's no big deal to create a hybrid of the two. Then you have three options to test.

## Which approach is most effective?

I favor the combination of argument and storytelling. All else being equal, I find it often makes the most effective ad or direct mail letter. It can even be used on the World Wide Web.

For example, you can include storytelling in a Web page or an electronic newsletter. Whenever you have the opportunity to engage the prospect for long enough to communicate any details, a combination of argument and storytelling can work wonders. You can do it in a broadcast fax. You can use a picture that tells a story in a print ad, combined with written arguments. You can combine personal testimonials from happy customers with a factual description of the benefits of your offering in a brochure. There are really no limits to your ability to incorporate elements of both argument and narrative into a single marketing piece.

Even personal selling can incorporate both styles by weaving some case histories or testimonials into a sales presentation. It's amazing how seldom people actually use any form of storytelling in sales, yet it is an extremely powerful tool. In fact, I've noticed over the years that the most successful salespeople I've had the chance to observe tend to weave three or four stories into each sales presentation. They often use stories about other customers to illustrate a point. Similarly, some of the most effective sales collateral — brochures, catalog sheets, audiovisuals, and other materials referred to in the presentation — are full of stories. They may include actual case histories, customer testimonials, or generic stories written to illustrate how the product or service works. Never underestimate the power of storytelling when woven into sales presentations!

# What makes hybrid ads so effective?

I've demonstrated an obvious bias for hybrid ads, letters, sales presentations, and other communications that combine the best of fact-based argument with the best of narrative. Why is this my favorite? Because it has two things going for it.

- Creating a hybrid letter is usually the third step in a creative process. Generally, people tend to create ads or ad concepts in the order I listed them in the previous section — that is, first, the rational argument based on facts, second, the dramatic persuasion based on storytelling, and third, the hybrid that includes some of both. Why is it an advantage to use the form that you created last? Because by doing so, you spend more time and invest more effort in your ad. You really had to work hard to develop two completely different approaches and then find a good way to combine them. So the hybrid form represents more creative energy and a higher level of involvement on the marketer's part. And, in general, when you put more of yourself into an ad, you get more out of it.

- I like hybrid ads (argument plus stories) because they take advantage of the fact that we humans have both a rational and an emotional side. In fact, many scientists believe that arguments literally appeal to a different side of the brain than stories do. By combining appeals to both our rational and emotional sides, hybrid ads tend to cast the broadest net. And when both the rational and emotional appeals are working well, these ads build the highest involvement on the part of their readers, listeners, or viewers.

Think (and feel) how the owner of a mid-sized business might react upon reading a mailing from a training company that combined rational arguments about the importance of teaching good customer service with stories about customers won or lost based on employees' abilities to handle unhappy customers. The rational arguments and facts are important in convincing the reader's rational mind that the training program is legitimate and likely to be effective. But that may not be enough to stimulate action. It may not get the reader excited. A story or case history, on the other hand, may get the reader more emotionally involved. It may awaken feelings of concern or anxiety about how the reader's own employees would handle a similar situation. It may awaken feelings of desire and excitement, too, at the prospect of being able to turn upset customers into new business opportunities instead of losing them.

So the combination of rational and emotional appeals can be very powerful. And when you create hybrid ad copy using both arguments and storytelling, you can tap into both the rational and emotional sides of your prospects with relative ease. Let me show you what I mean by hybridizing the two approaches I showed you earlier for the Handling Unhappy Customers training program. I'm going to lead with the story version, for the simple reason that people often react initially on an emotional basis, then engage their rational minds. So an opening appeal to emotion is a great initial attention-getter. And a strong finish based on rational facts and arguments is a great way to cement those initial emotional responses by adding rational conviction to them. When I combine the two approaches into one, tightening them up a bit to avoid making the hybrid too lengthy, I get the following direct mail or brochure copy:

Dear Manager:

Rick, the purchasing manager for SysTech, is a man of action who hates to waste even a minute in his busy day. It is not like him to be doing nothing. But he has actually been doing nothing at all for four and a half minutes now, and it is definitely beginning to wear on him.

[Show picture of a man in shirtsleeves and a tie, phone to ear, looking at his watch in exasperation.]

Rick is on hold. On hold with your company, to be specific. He was put on hold when he had called to complain about a problem with his last order—by an employee who didn't know how to handle the call.

[Show picture of frazzled employee, phone in one hand, making a palms-up gesture as if to say I have no idea how to handle this.]

If this were a real-life situation, you can imagine that your employee would be quite busy. Perhaps busy trying to track down the paperwork and figure out how to solve Rick's problem. Finally, after searching fruitlessly for the appropriate paperwork and getting a wide variety of unhelpful advice from her associates, your employee comes back on the line. It has been five minutes and sixteen seconds since she put Rick on hold, and you don't want to know what Rick is going to say in reply when her first words to him are, "I'm sorry, Sir, but I can't find any record of your order. Are you sure you really sent it in?"

### Everything depends on the employee's response

Accidents happen, as the old saying goes. But whether you recover from them gracefully or lose a customer for life depends upon how you handle those accidents. If that employee in the preceding story had only received Handling Unhappy Customers (HUC) training, she would have known that putting Rick on hold violates the "Adding Insult to Injury Principle," which says that you must handle all unhappy customers with a high degree of consideration and support. And never, *ever*, put them on hold or question their word when they are upset!

### A major source of hidden losses

Every manager knows that it costs ten times as much to win a new customer as it does to do business with an existing customer. Yet companies routinely lose good customers like Rick over slip-ups that anger those good customers and open the door to defection.

---

**Did you know?**

A large majority of unhappy customers give very clear signs or signals that they are unhappy. Yet, according to our research, the vast majority of employees fail to pick up on those signals or respond appropriately to them.

---

What can you do to keep your customers from leaving you? What is the secret of high customer loyalty?

**People.**

It comes down to people in 99.9% of the cases, according to our research. We studied the companies with the most loyal customers in a dozen different industries and in every case, these winning companies had more sensitive, better trained employees. Employees who know what to do when customers are upset or angry. Employees who know how to convert each problem into an opportunity to build loyalty instead of lose business.

That's why we designed *Handling Unhappy Customers* (HUC), the radical new customer service training that has a measurable impact on your customer retention rates—or you get your money back!

---

"My employees are performing 100 percent better since their HUC training, and I'm getting a lot of compliments from my customers. They really notice the difference."

— Charlotte McGwire, President, Global Food Supply Inc.

---

You can take the first no-obligation step toward higher customer loyalty today by calling us or sending back the enclosed postcard to get your Course Overview booklet and video today. And if you respond before the end of the month, you will qualify for our introductory promotion, which locks in a 15 percent discount for any training events scheduled within the next six months. So please take a decisive step toward educating your employees by contacting us to preview or schedule the Handling Unhappy Customers training today.

Sincerely,

Millicent Marketer

V.P., Training Programs

Before I go into the details of the hybrid story-and-argument strategy, let me just point out a few things I've done in this example to develop it a little further than the earlier examples:

- I came up with some concepts for visuals, which I might use if the medium permits. A couple of simple black-and-white photos might work well in a two-page letter. If I adapt this copy to the brochure format, I'll probably opt for nicer full-color photos, budget permitting.

- I dropped in a few headers to break up the text, which makes it seem more readable. And the headers are intended to entice the eye, drawing the reader into each section. They also tend to reinforce the points by hitting the reader over the head with them.

- I've added two text boxes that can be read independently of the main copy. They reinforce the copy and give the reader with a short attention span something to jump to. Note that the first box offers another factual appeal. And the second is an emotional appeal based on a story. Specifically, it quotes a customer who has had a good experience with the product. Such testimonials are often very powerful and tend to be underused in marketing communications. (See Chapter 5.)

- I've added some bold and italics, to emphasize key points I was afraid might get lost given the length of this piece. Be careful with any such embellishments, however. If you get too carried away, you may make the copy look silly and reduce its credibility.

- I've finished this letter with a final paragraph containing a *call to action* — details of what to do next along with some incentive to do it now.

Developing a letter like this to a high level takes quite a bit of care, but the effort is worth it in increased responses.

### About the strategy this hybrid letter uses . . .

The combination of an opening story and hard-hitting fact-based arguments, ending with a simple call to action should generate a nice response rate. Why? Because this marketing communication pushes two powerful buttons. It appeals to emotion, and it appeals to logic. Which means it stands a good chance of creating immediate high involvement with any reader who has reason to worry about how well his or her employees handle customer problems and complaints.

You can think of attention as full involvement — which means both emotional and rational involvement combined. The preceding sample letter attempts to get attention and turn it into action by combining an emotional appeal based on a story with a rational appeal based on factual argument.

# Getting Serious about Testing

In the last section, I showed you how I combined a rational appeal with a story to make a direct mail piece I hoped would have high impact. Good strategy, but will it work? Of course you never really know until you test, but you don't have to guess in the dark. No reason to market blind, is there? To test an ad concept or evaluate ad copy, you can simply ask yourself or others how well it achieves its purpose.

And remember that the purpose of a rational, argument-based ad or letter is to persuade the rational mind. And the purpose of a narrative or story-based ad or letter is to generate a sympathetic reaction from the emotional mind. So you need to test these two different types of appeals with different sorts of criteria. And if an ad hybridizes the two appeals, then you need to test it using both sets of criteria. Here are some criteria and questions that you can use to evaluate both rational and emotional appeals.

## Rational arguments and fact-based appeals

**Criteria.** Should be convincing and persuasive. Should not lead to counter-arguments. Should be believable.

**Statements to evaluate for an ad of this type:**

- ✔ I found this ad very convincing.
- ✔ I agreed with the main points completely.
- ✔ I could think of no reasons to avoid this product/service while reading/listening to/viewing the ad.
- ✔ I did not feel like arguing with the writer/speaker.
- ✔ It made good sense to me.
- ✔ This is an important ad.

Your goal is an ad that people don't feel like arguing with. Ads that generate the fewest counter-arguments are the most persuasive.

# Emotional appeals and stories or case histories

**Criteria.** Should be engaging and interesting. Should engage feelings to a significant degree. Should be realistic and believable.

**Statements to evaluate for an ad of this type:**

- ✔ I found the ad compelling.
- ✔ It held my attention.
- ✔ I felt that it described a situation that could easily apply to me/my business.
- ✔ I liked the ad.
- ✔ The ad was definitely true to life.
- ✔ I could relate easily to the feelings of the people in this ad.

Hybrid ads involving both rational arguments and stories need to be evaluated using both sets of criteria and all twelve questions. For ads that are purely fact-oriented or purely story-oriented, you can just use the six questions that apply to their specific form. Or go ahead and evaluate each communication using all of the questions, since you can't always be sure you know what the appeal really is. Figure 12-1 shows a form you can use to evaluate marketing communications based on the need for both rational and emotional appeal. This form is also available on the CD (filename CD1201).

Notice that I alternated the items measuring effectiveness of your argument with those measuring effectiveness of your story. The story-oriented items have odd numbers, starting with item #1. The argument-oriented items have even numbers, starting with item #2. So an ad that is effective as a story will score high on the odd-numbered items, for example. And a hybrid letter, such as the one I showed you earlier for a customer training program, should score fairly high on all items and receive a high overall score.

You can use this form to check your own work and refine your drafts as you work on customer letters or any other marketing communications. Or you can take your research to a higher level by soliciting customer input. Stay tuned for details.

## Evaluation Form 1 (Argument/Story Effectiveness)

Please circle the number that best represents your feelings toward the marketing communication you have been asked to evaluate. Thank you for your help.

Scale: 1 = not at all to 5 = definitely

Item A

| #1. | 1 2 3 4 5 | I found it compelling. |
|---|---|---|
| #2. | 1 2 3 4 5 | I found it very convincing. |
| #3. | 1 2 3 4 5 | It held my attention. |
| #4. | 1 2 3 4 5 | I agreed with the main points completely. |
| #5. | 1 2 3 4 5 | I felt that it described a situation that could easily apply to me/my business. |
| #6. | 1 2 3 4 5 | I could think of no reasons to avoid this product/service. |
| #7. | 1 2 3 4 5 | I liked the ad/marketing communication. |
| #8. | 1 2 3 4 5 | I did not feel like arguing with the writer/speaker. |
| #9. | 1 2 3 4 5 | It was definitely true to life. |
| #10. | 1 2 3 4 5 | It made good sense to me. |
| #11. | 1 2 3 4 5 | I could relate easily to the feelings in it. |
| #12. | 1 2 3 4 5 | It is important. |

**Figure 12-1:**
Evaluation
Form 1
(Argument/
Story Effec-
tiveness).

## Want to do some real ad research?

It's not a bad idea to use the questions in Figure 12-1 to evaluate a marketing communication before even trying it out in the media or mailing it. If you run it by a half-dozen or more people who are similar to your target prospects, you can find out what they think and often find ways to improve the ad before spending the money and taking the risk of using it.

I recommend talking to some of your friends in the industry and to some of your most friendly customers, as well as perhaps to some people you don't know quite so well, to sign them up for ad evaluation duty. You can point out that it is quick and painless and simply involves their looking at drafts of marketing communications and then filling in a quick one-page-or-less questionnaire by circling some numbers. So it's easy duty, and it is interesting in that they get to have a peek into your marketing operations and might get some good ideas of their own. Or, you could sweeten the pot by offering participants a discount to make it more worthwhile.

It's a really wonderful thing to have a panel of even a few people to run your communications by before you finalize them. In addition to asking them to respond to some specific questions such as those I gave you earlier, you should also spend a few minutes debriefing them in person or by phone to find out what they really think about your piece. Try asking them to identify several things they like and dislike about the piece as an easy way to get them talking.

Or, if you really haven't got the time to put together an informal audience panel and test your ad, at least test it yourself and get others within the organization to test it. Any evaluation is better by far than none!

## Picking a winner

Another way to use advertising research is to develop and evaluate three or more options. I know it's more work to design three ads, letters, brochures, or whatever than to simply design one. But if you mock up three different designs and then compare them using formal scaled questions such as the ones I gave you in the previous section, you are more likely to end up picking a winner. In many ad agencies, at least three different ads are developed, and sometimes as many as a dozen. Then everyone can argue over which approach is best. If it's hard to decide, then you may have the luxury of multiple good options. But in my experience, one option often rises to the top. And it is rarely the first concept you developed. So it really does pay off to create more choices and test your options before making a decision.

In the next section, I explore another, similar model that is also used by leading ad agencies in designing and researching ads and other marketing communications. This model breaks down your options into two broad areas, as well as permitting the combination of the two areas.

# Two Ways to Design for High Involvement

Is your marketing or sales communication effective? One way to approach that question is to define effectiveness as getting high involvement from the audience. In other words, do they notice it and get interested in it — that's high involvement — or do they just blow it off without paying much mind?

Because most marketing communications are ignored by most people, involvement is an important first step toward winning the customer. You need to win their attention and interest. You need to get them involved in your effort to communicate.

You can get them involved in two ways. You can appeal to their rational side, or you can appeal to their emotional side. I discuss the difference between persuasion using rational argument and persuasion using emotionally appealing stories in the previous section. Notice the parallel. If you develop a good argument, it should generate high rational involvement as well as measuring high on the rational persuasion scale. But in this section, we aren't going to worry about the content or whether you convince people. We're just going to focus on how you build high involvement. That's sometimes a better question to ask, especially if you are designing an ad for a busy context where your biggest challenge is just to win some attention. A television spot, a magazine or newspaper ad, a banner ad for the Web, or an outdoor poster must grab attention and build involvement in a hurry or it will be passed right by. So how do you create high involvement for an ad? Here's a hypothetical example.

A picture of a crying baby will probably create emotional involvement, especially in parents of young children.

A table showing that babies fed organic baby food have fewer health problems later in life than those fed conventional baby food will get rational involvement.

Combine the two, the picture of a crying baby with the data from a study showing that organic baby food is healthier, and you've got the potential to capture full involvement by appealing to both the rational and emotional sides of those parents you want to reach.

In the two dimensions of your appeal, you can see how these two options and their combination are often represented. A number of large ad agencies actually measure rational and emotional involvement with questionnaires as a way of evaluating ads. Then they plot the results on a graph like the one shown in Figure 12-2. Ads which plot high and to the right are the ones that win the most involvement on both dimensions. And they tend to be more effective, all else being equal — especially in situations where it's hard to catch the attention of your target audience.

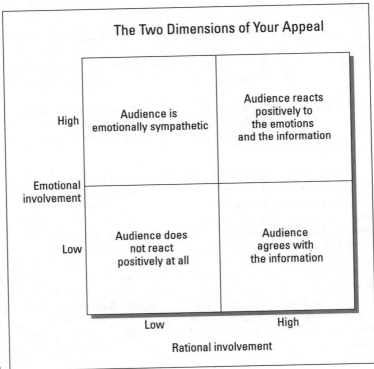

The Two Dimensions of Your Appeal

**Figure 12-2:**
The two
dimensions
of your
appeal.

So here's another way to evaluate your own marketing communications or to have a panel or group of people representing your audience evaluate them. Simply ask people to rate each ad, letter, Web page, or whatever the communication is by filling in the form shown in Figure 12-3. This form is available on your CD in case you want to print some copies. The filename is CD1202.

If you are testing multiple ads or other marketing communications, you simply ask your panel to evaluate each one using the same scale. On the CD, you'll find a form with room to evaluate up to ten options at a time, lettered from Item A to Item J.

**Evaluation Form 2 (Emotional/Rational Involvement)**

Please circle the number that best represents your feelings toward the marketing communication you have been asked to evaluate. Thank you for your help.

Scale: 1 = not at all to 5 = definitely

Item A

| #1. | 1 2 3 4 5 | I found myself caught up emotionally in it. |
|-----|-----------|---------------------------------------------|
| #2. | 1 2 3 4 5 | I was interested in the information it contained. |
| #3. | 1 2 3 4 5 | I got a definite sense of the feelings it is trying to communicate. |
| #4. | 1 2 3 4 5 | I could follow the logic of the argument easily. |
| #5. | 1 2 3 4 5 | It has a definite emotional appeal. |
| #6. | 1 2 3 4 5 | I thought it was well researched. |
| #7. | 1 2 3 4 5 | It captures my own feelings quite well. |
| #8. | 1 2 3 4 5 | It is a good source of useful ideas. |

**Figure 12-3:**
Evaluation
Form 2
(Emotional/
Rational
Involvement).

Even if you have only one or two communications to evaluate, consider including others you collect from the marketplace — especially ones you think are effective because of their track records. It is always interesting to look at the range of responses to a variety of options, and it gives you some insight into how to interpret the responses. For instance, if people rate your new brochure design at 3.9 on average, and the average for competitors' brochures is only 3.1, then you probably have a winner even though your absolute score isn't at the top of the 1–5 range.

## Scoring key

The evaluation form I provided in the preceding sections and on the CD for measuring involvement has four items that measure emotional involvement and four that measure rational involvement. To keep it simple, I made all the odd-numbered items measure emotional involvement. So all the even-numbered items measure rational involvement.

If you want to maximize involvement, you may want to score reasonably high on both the odd- and even-numbered items. But if you have a communication that is designed to be either highly emotional or highly rational in its appeal, don't expect to score high overall. Look instead for top marks on the half of the items that measure the dimension of involvement you're shooting for.

# Interpreting Your Ad Research to Select or Refine a Design

In this section, I examine the data from three different ad designs, each a draft of a possible direct response ad designed to run in the Sunday magazines of various newspapers. I'm just going to describe these ads, not show them, because I want to focus on how you interpret research about people's reactions to them.

- The first design uses an eye-catching photo and a brief story as its focus.
- The second presents several little-known facts and builds an argument for the product based on them.
- The third is a hybrid of the first two, combining a smaller photo and brief quote from a customer with a short discussion of relevant facts.

Here is how a panel of 15 prospective customers evaluated each ad on the involvement scales I gave you just a moment ago, and also on the appeal scales I presented in the earlier section on story-based versus argument-based appeals. I've simplified the results by coding them as L = low, M = medium, and H = high.

| Ads | Average Scores | | | |
|---|---|---|---|---|
| | Appeal | | Involvement | |
| | Story | Argument | Emotional | Rational |
| 1. Photo/story | H | L | H | L |
| 2. Facts/Argument | L | M | L | M |
| 3. Hybrid of 1 & 2 | M | M | M | M |

You can see that the panel's reactions to the ads are nicely summarized in a table like this. At a glance you can get a feel for the strengths and weaknesses of each of your options. The first one had high appeal as a story, and also achieved high emotional involvement. It bombed on the other scales though, reflecting its lack of hard information. The second ad got medium scores for the appeal of its argument and for its ability to involve people rationally, but bombed on the other scales because it lacked emotional impact. And the third, the hybrid, got medium scores across the board.

So which one is better? A conservative marketer would probably pick that third ad because it seems to have something for everyone. I usually favor hybrids with a combination of stories and arguments and the ability to create both rational and emotional involvement. My choice based on this data, however, is definitely the first ad. I like to see exceptionally high scores on anything, even if they require a sacrifice on other dimensions. It's just awfully hard to grab attention with an ad, so one that obviously packs an emotional punch is a good choice.

If you're still worried about ad #1's low scores on the argument and rational involvement scales, well, feel free to fiddle with it and do some more testing. Perhaps you could make it just a bit bigger and work a line or two of copy in at the bottom with some compelling facts. Even an asterisk with a footnote citing some facts or statistics might raise those low scores to the medium range without diluting its emotional impact and bringing down the other scores. So you could fiddle with it and try to formulate a better hybrid ad. But I wouldn't fiddle *too* much. An emotionally powerful ad is a rare thing, and you might mess it up if you add too much.

# Designing for Stopping Power

Another important consideration for any marketing communication is how well it screams for attention. Not all marketing communications need to shout out to their audience, but many benefit from the ability to grab attention. *Stopping power* is the ability of a marketing communication to attract immediate notice. To command attention.

My firm uses a lot of brochures. My publicists send out a brochure to anyone who is interested in background information about my firm's publications, workshops, and so on, for example. Recently, I was talked into the idea of redoing our brochure to update it and give it a little more impact. The designers for this effort were at Rocks Communications, which you will encounter in some of the other chapters of this book because they provided us with a lot of useful templates and tips for publicity. But they also do other forms of marketing communications, and, in this case, they developed a brochure that was oversized and on unusual paper and that had nothing but my firm's name on the cover.

Not only that, but they put the name in a rather unusual format. Figure 12-4 shows what it looks like.

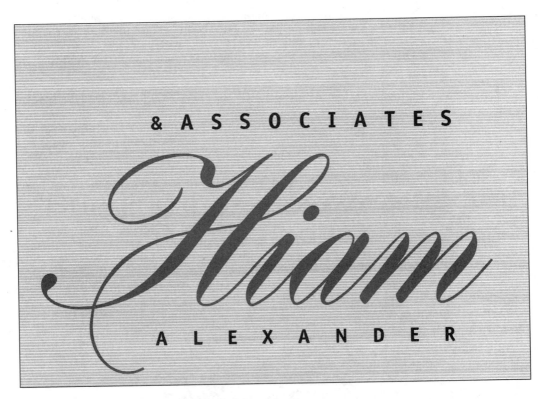

**Figure 12-4:** Alexander Hiam & Associates brochure cover.

Now, when I first looked at it, I said, "Forget it! That's not how I normally display my company name. And besides, it looks like you've put the words backwards. People will have to read it from bottom to top to figure out what it is."

## The "stop and stare" factor

But when we ran the design by a number of people, I noticed something interesting. Without variation, they all stopped and stared at it. Hard. It really arrested their attention. Maybe they were just trying to decipher it, but for whatever reason, this unusual layout really had stopping power. So I knew that if we used this design in mailings, people would not set it aside for later review and then forget it. They would hold onto it, stare at it, and, hopefully, open it up to see what the heck it was.

## Does sexy sell?

Another sure way to give any marketing communication stopping power is to put something sexy into it. A lot of naive marketers try that ploy. If you show some naked bodies in suggestive positions, sure, people will take a quick look to see what's going on. But generally sex has nothing much to do with what you are communicating, so that sort of stopping power doesn't work well. People just move on again once they realize you've tried to trick them into paying attention.

That's stopping power's great virtue. It gets you in. Even if only through a back door. And when you're in, when you have captured the attention of a prospect, then the rest of your design can go to work.

Putting a sexy photo on the outside of a direct mail envelope probably won't increase the response rate, and it might get you in a lot of trouble. Stopping power isn't really that simple.

To really generate stopping power, I reported in an earlier book, *Marketing For Dummies*, you need to give any marketing communication seven different qualities. (By the way, I got these ideas originally from Hanley Norins of Young & Rubicam.) Here are the qualities an ad needs to have in order to generate serious stopping power:

- ✔ It has to be dramatic.
- ✔ It has to demand participation.
- ✔ It has to stimulate some emotion.
- ✔ It has to make people curious.
- ✔ It should surprise people.
- ✔ It needs to communicate in an unexpected way.
- ✔ It should violate convention.

Apply these principles to the example I showed earlier, that unusual brochure cover that Rocks Communications prepared for my firm:

- ✔ The large size, unusual paper, and large, unusual lettering is definitely dramatic.
- ✔ The brochure format encourages the recipient to participate by turning the page to see what is inside — especially when the cover stimulates curiosity.

✔ This cover design is just words on paper, so what sort of emotion could it possibly stimulate? However, the use of an elegant paper and layout, combined with the almost unbusinesslike curves of those big letters, does tickle the viewer on an emotional level. There is something aesthetically pleasing about the design that hints at further pleasures within. You expect that reading this brochure will be a visually pleasant and stimulating experience.

✔ The design certainly stimulates curiosity, if only to figure out exactly what it says and what it is for.

✔ It is somewhat surprising as well, mostly because it is so different from the typical brochure used to sell business products and services at a management level.

✔ It communicates in an unexpected way. Certainly the reader does not expect to see such liberties taken with the name of a business just for the sake of design.

✔ This brochure cover certainly violates the rules. It looks nothing like typical catalogs from competing publishers and training firms. They are smaller and more conventional in size and design; they are on glossy white paper; they are very busy — full of lots of information, pitches, and pictures of products. This brochure is a foot wide, on very unusual, heavy paper, elegant and understated, and remarkably uncluttered. It stands out clearly from other brochures and catalogs competitors might send.

When I use Y&R's seven criteria for stopping power to analyze that brochure cover, I can see why it arrested the attention of all who reviewed it. It's unique and interesting enough to generate significant stopping power, which means that most of the people who take it out of an envelope will actually read it, and many of them will read it right away.

Do your marketing communications have stopping power? Maybe, but probably not. Most communications don't. In fact, if you think about it, it's impossible for most communications to have high stopping power. Stopping power requires qualities that make the communication stand out from the crowd. It is always going to be a rare trait.

When I think about stopping power, I often consider an eighth criterion that Y&R didn't include in their original formulation of the concept. I believe that *beauty also has stopping power*. A lot of stopping power. When a product design is beautiful (as is occasionally the case with a new car, for example), the thing to do is just show the product in the ads. Its beauty will make people stop and look. If you don't have an inherently beautiful product, or you have a service that cannot be easily seen and photographed, then consider finding a beautiful image to *represent* your product. (See Chapter 13 for details.)

## *Measuring stopping power*

As in the previous sections, where I use evaluation forms to give communications more appeal and involvement, you can use a simple evaluation form to measure stopping power. What you can measure, you can manage, so when you start evaluating your communications with the stopping power form, you may find yourself working more stopping power into your marketing. Any ad, letter, telemarketing script, sales presentation, Web page, fax, business card, advertisement, or other communication can be given more stopping power. And stopping power always helps get attention and give your communication the opportunity to do its job.

# *On the CD*

Check out the following files on the CD-ROM:

- ✔ Evaluation Form 1 (CD1201)
- ✔ Two Dimensions of Your Appeal (CD1202)
- ✔ Evaluation Form 2 (CD1203)

# Chapter 13

# Shortcuts to Great Advertising

reating a fabulous advertising campaign is easy. All you have to do is
hire a big agency, like Young & Rubicam, and give them an unlimited
budget to come up with incredible concepts. Then you can just sit back and
review their proposals until they come up with a real home run. (And then
you can spend several million U.S. dollars to run TV spots during the Super
Bowl and another few million to flood consumer magazines with full-page
print ads, right?) But what if you don't have the resources or budget to throw
the best designers on your project and let them loose?

Then you need to find a shortcut to great advertising. And, in truth, there are
many examples of ad campaigns that stood out by attracting exceptional interest and having exceptional impact without costing an arm and a leg. Creative
smaller ad agencies such as Darby O'Brien (in Hadley, Massachusetts) are
often asked to cobble together a high-impact campaign on a low-impact
budget. The shortcuts they find depend upon their creativity and willingness
to try unusual formulas.

Here in Figure 13-1, for example, Darby O'Brien has created a series of inexpensive black-and-white ads designed to run in local newspapers. They were
designed for a client who wanted to launch a new line of coffee, branded as
Al's Daily Grind. The positioning of this brand contrasts with the upscale,
sophisticated image of today's popular gourmet coffees. And Darby O'Brien
made the most of a limited advertising budget by photographing each ad outside using volunteers instead of paid actors (studio shots tend to be more
costly and actors have to be paid for their time and usually receive "residu-
als" or ongoing fees each time an ad runs).

**Figure 13-1:**
A powerful
but inexpen-
sive news-
paper ad
campaign.

A series of four Al's Daily Grind ads are on your CD (CD1301 through CD1303), and I urge you to study them carefully. Their bold, simple copy and gritty, real-world photography is perfect for the product's image, and also simple and clean enough to catch the eye even if reduced to fit an inexpensive small-format ad in a newspaper. Also, there is a wry, humorous undertone to these ads that unifies the series and keeps readers looking for the next one. All in all, this campaign got a lot of mileage out of relatively cheap, simple print advertising. A simple but powerful ad concept can pack a lot of punch. And simple is good if you are looking for easy or inexpensive advertising options.

# Do-It-Yourself Shortcuts

What if you *really* want to save money, and even a smaller agency is out of the question? Well, you can always work with an independent designer, someone who has a Macintosh computer and a portfolio but little in the way of overhead. You'll probably have to place the advertising yourself, but you can simply call the ad salespeople at the magazines, radio stations, television stations, or Web sites that appeal to you and ask them what you can afford. For that matter, most newspapers, magazines, television and radio stations will even do the designing for you if you don't want to spend any serious money on it. (Although you better contribute the concept and supervise their work or you'll get mediocre ads that nobody notices.)

For example, I can go to any number of local television stations in my area and get a 30-second spot ad designed and shot in their studios for less than 500 U.S. dollars. Then I can pay them to broadcast my spot to the local area for as little as a 1,000 dollars a month. That's a do-it-yourself shortcut that takes almost no knowledge and little of the marketer's time or money, yet gets out there quickly. It is often preferable to do this sort of low-budget advertising if the alternative is to do no advertising at all.

On the other hand, you are not likely to get a great ad by farming its design and production out to the cheapest provider. Sure, any newspaper or magazine is happy to lay out an ad for you if you just give them some copy. But what will it look like? Will it really catch people's eye? Will it generate much interest and action? Not too likely. When it comes to impact in advertising, you do tend to get what you pay for.

So what we really need are shortcuts to *good* advertising. Ways of creating high-impact ads simply, quickly, and cheaply. What you want to do is come up with ad concepts that are powerful but easy and cheap to execute. Those are the kind of shortcuts that could really get you ahead! Otherwise, if you simply spend less money by buying worse ads, you'll have to run a lot more of them to get the impact you need. And the end result won't be economical after all.

Creativity is the source of shortcuts. Think of something special that is easy and cheap to do, and you'll have a high impact ad for less. But that's a tall creative order, or everyone would already be doing it. So I better give you some help.

I've got two cool ideas that are not overused — in fact, not really used at all so far. They are novel approaches that rely on "found" content to give your ad more stopping power and hold attention. By using found content, they short-circuit the problem of having to develop great creative content of your own — which can be hard even for seasoned advertisers and is certainly difficult for the amateur designer.

- ✔ In the first case, I create ads that evoke a strong sense of *mood* by using words associated with that mood.

- ✔ In the second case, I create ads that communicate a mind-catching *thought* in the form of a wise quote.

I didn't have to come up with the words that give either of these ads their power, nor do you. I just went fishing in two common reference books: a thesaurus and a dictionary of quotations. You don't have to be a great writer to generate great advertising copy. You just have to go out and find it. Now, that's a real shortcut!

In the next two sections, I show you how to use these two shortcut designs. They are very flexible and adaptable. There is, in fact, no business that these templates wouldn't fit. And because the ad concepts are driven by copy, not art, they are easy to adapt to many media and relatively cheap to execute in any medium as well.

## The mood ad

The premise of the mood ad design (which can be used for any medium, from print ads to Web pages to brochures, radio, or even TV) is that you can position your offering in an appealing way by setting an emotional tone. The way the mood ad templates I've provided for you do this is through the power of language and color. (You can drop the color if you're doing black-and-white print. And you can add music or convert the words from print to voice if you're working on TV, radio, or the Web.)

I've cued up nine different print ad templates (such as the ones in Figures 13-2 and 13-3) and a brochure template (Figure 13-4) that use language to create appropriate moods. Have a look at the selection of templates on your CD to see what you've got to play with. Look for filenames CD1304 through CD1306.

These ads use an umbrella word like *reliable* along with various synonyms such as *dependable, careful,* and *trustworthy* to evoke a strong sense of feeling and associate it with your product or service offering or other marketing message. (I've created print ad templates, but you can easily turn them into scripts for radio by simply reading the list of words.)

My mood ad design is a rarely used concept in advertising, yet it is very powerful. Its rarity is one of the reasons I've included so many templates. It's always a good idea to try concepts and designs that your competitors *don't* use. And it's a very flexible strategy, capable of enhancing just about any marketing message or product offering.

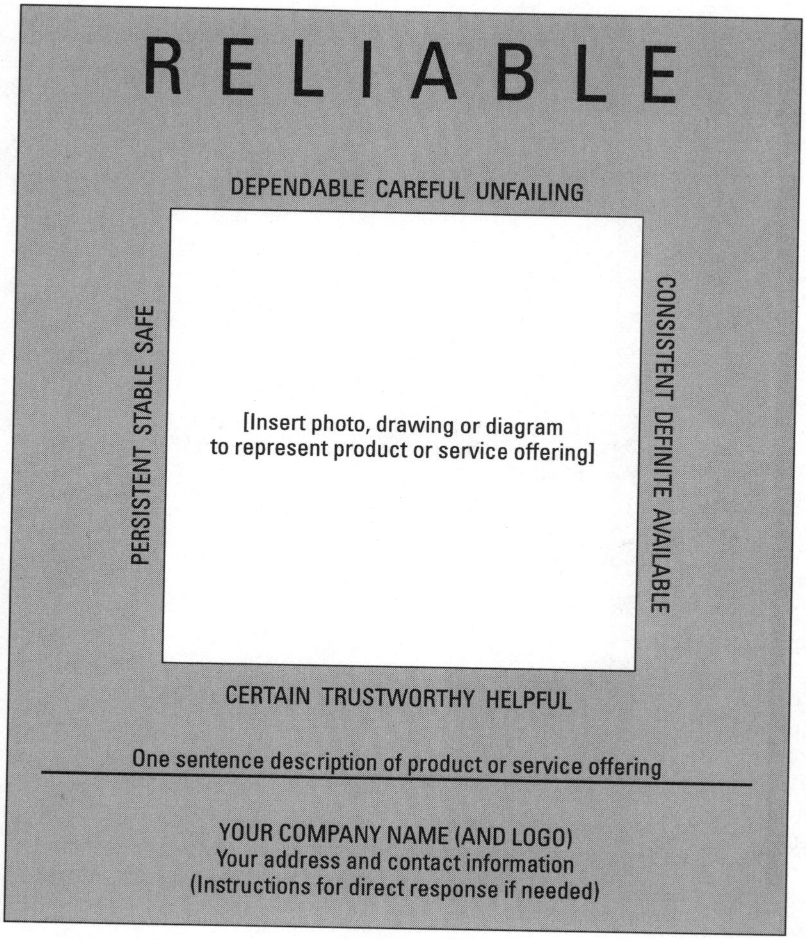

# RELIABLE

DEPENDABLE CAREFUL UNFAILING

PERSISTENT STABLE SAFE

CONSISTENT DEFINITE AVAILABLE

[Insert photo, drawing or diagram
to represent product or service offering]

CERTAIN TRUSTWORTHY HELPFUL

One sentence description of product or service offering

YOUR COMPANY NAME (AND LOGO)
Your address and contact information
(Instructions for direct response if needed)

**Figure 13-2:**
This ad
creates a
strong
sense of
trust-
worthiness,
perfect for a
business-to-
business
marketer.

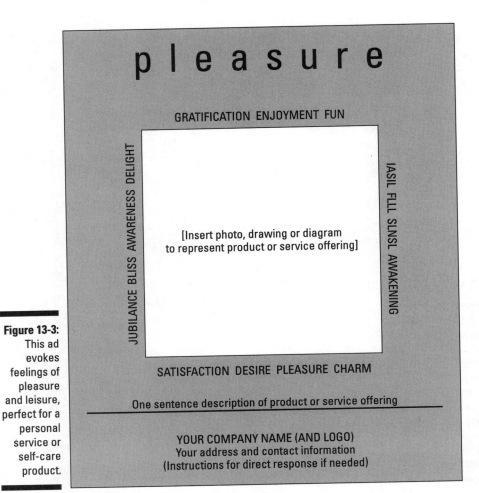

**Figure 13-3:**
This ad
evokes
feelings of
pleasure
and leisure,
perfect for a
personal
service or
self-care
product.

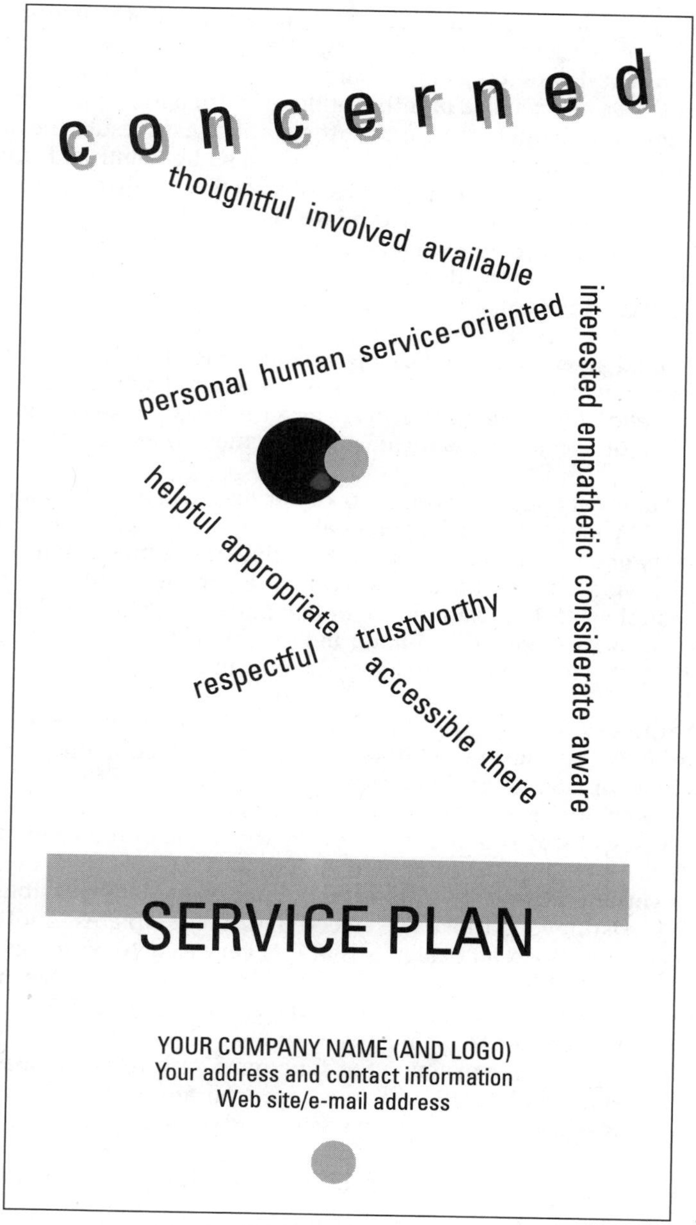

concerned

thoughtful involved available

personal human service-oriented

interested empathetic considerate aware

helpful appropriate

respectful trustworthy accessible there

**SERVICE PLAN**

YOUR COMPANY NAME (AND LOGO)
Your address and contact information
Web site/e-mail address

**Figure 13-4:**
This
brochure
template
expresses
positive
feelings
associated
with good
service.

A company specializing in the sale and installation of floor coverings in the San Francisco area used a mood ad very effectively to draw traffic to its showroom. The 4.7-inch (12 cm) square ad was printed in full color in *San Francisco Focus* magazine, a monthly affiliated with a local public radio station and given to people who support the station. As a result, the ad reached an audience of sophisticated, wealthy readers. Its headline said simply *SERENE,* and it featured a central photo of a section of attractive and unusual bamboo-wood floorboards, framed by words associated with or synonymous with the headline word. (Mood ad templates 1–9 use a similar layout.) The ad caught the eye of many readers and succeeded in attracting increased visitors to the flooring company.

But the mood ad is not limited to any specific type of product or marketer. A business-to-business marketer might employ a mood ad with an evocative word like *reliability, tenacity,* or *success* as a theme, and then show or tell how the product or service helps the customer achieve these desirable traits.

And marketers of consumer products or services can also use mood ads, although they may favor more personal words such as *vigor, pleasure, scintillating,* or *intimate.* Consumer ads can associate these mood-rich words and their synonyms with the product offering or a benefit of the product they wish to emphasize. For example, an online music and video club might pick *scintillating* as its mood-ad headline, and associate it with exciting, fascinating products that "entertain and delight" the consumer.

Note that the word *delight* ties in nicely with *scintillating* because it contains the word *light* and thus has a hidden association. When writing ad copy, always look for such links. They give strength and power to your words. If you create additional copy to expand one of the mood ad templates on your CD, try to select words that echo or evoke the mood of the headline word.

Perhaps you want to create a mood ad of your own. Many possible feelings or meanings exist beyond those I've selected for the templates. Another nice thing about this mood ad design is that it is very easy to write new ones as needed. All you really need is a book of synonyms such as a thesaurus or (my favorite for the English language) *The Synonym Finder* by J. I. Rodale, from Warner Books. Search the main entries for a word that appeals to you as a possible headline. Then examine the synonyms for it to find a dozen or more that add strength and depth to your ad. Incorporate these synonyms in the design however you wish. Here are some good design options:

✔ Wrap words around an illustration to frame it (as the templates do).

✔ List the words in a long string to form unusual and powerful body copy or script.

✔ Ask a question, then let viewers answer it by checking boxes next to words ("Is your ISP reliable? If so, then surely you'd describe it as _careful, _trustworthy, _ stable, _available, _safe, _ unfailing, _helpful, and _supportive. What? Didn't check all those boxes? Maybe you'd better give us an e-mail. That is, presuming your current service will let you.")

✔ Make a collage of words or strings of words (as in the design for a brochure cover in Figure 13-4).

These design concepts all harness the power of emotionally evocative language. Words are extraordinarily powerful. They can create a definite mood or feeling about your business or its product or service. And mood ads harness this power in simple ways that do not require sophisticated design skills or even much talent. In other words, they give you a relatively big impact considering how easy they are to create. That's the kind of marketing I like best!

## The wisdom ad

The premise of this ad design (which can be used for any print medium from display ads to direct mail letters, brochures, catalogs, and sales collateral) is that people will like ads that give them the gift of wisdom. People value wisdom because it is in short supply, and you may find it as scarce as anyone else. So where will you find servings of wisdom to include in your ads? My strategy is to go to the classics. People always like a great quote from a master writer or thinker. So the wisdom ad borrows a wise thought from literature to give the ad stopping power and increase its value to readers. Files CD 1307 through CD1309 on the CD show some wisdom ad templates.

Figure 13-5 illustrates a wisdom ad, proportioned for use as a display ad in a magazine or newspaper. (The original is 4 x 4 inches. If you plan to run an ad like this in a significantly smaller space, you'll have to use fewer, larger words, but the same basic design will still work.) This ad has no traditional headline to catch the eye. Instead it harnesses the stopping power of a thought-provoking quote. If you use short quotes and attribute them accurately to their author, you usually need not obtain reprint permission. And you can find thousands of quotes to choose from in any dictionary of quotations.

The ad shown in Figure 13-6 is another example of the use of a quote instead of a headline. Many people like such quotes and may even clip the ad just to help them remember the quote. I've written a middle section of body copy in which a short message to the reader ties the quote into some positive attribute of the marketer's offering. This takes a little creativity, but is a lot easier than writing a compelling headline or coming up with an original hook. All you have to do is find your hook in the form of an appealing quote, then tie that quote in somehow to your products or services.

"It has long been an axiom
of mine that the little things
are infinitely the most
important."

- **Sherlock Holmes**

We hope you'll take a moment to enjoy and consider
todays's word to the wise, from the famous detective
created by Sir Arthur Conan Doyle.

And perhaps you'll find this wisdom applies to our
[product/service] as well. We endeavor to perfect
the many details that our customers tell us make all
the difference between an ordinary and a
great experience.

**WORDS TO THE WISE**
from [Company Name]
[Contact Information]

**Figure 13-5:**
Print ad
relating the
timeless
quest for
truth with
the quest
for better
products.

"The real question is not
whether machines think
but whether people do."

- **B.F. Skinner**

We hope you'll take a moment to enjoy and consider
todays's word to the wise, from the famous behavioral
scientist who raised his daughter in a laboratory box.
But we don't believe Skinner's doubts are valid, at
least not when people put their minds to something
that concerns them greatly. Certainly our customers
are quite thoughtful when it comes to deciding which
[producer/service] to select. And they tell us they
appreciate our thoughtful approach to design as well.

**WORDS TO THE WISE**
from [Company Name]
[Contact Information]

**Figure 13-6:**
This ad both
amuses and
compli-
ments the
prospective
customer.

I've also designed these ads as if they are part of a series called "Words to the Wise." The idea is that you can offer readers new quotes on a regular basis, and that they will develop a habit of looking for the next word to the wise. That way, people will seek out and make a point of reading your ads.

## Yet another easy ad concept

You might also consider other devices to create sustained interest in your advertising. For instance, why not hire a starving novelist to craft an interesting short story, and then run brief installments of it in a series of ads? Engagement devices such as this are effective and are only limited by your imagination and willingness to break out of the normal advertising formulas.

## Using quotes in brochures, catalogs, and newsletters

Elsewhere in this kit, I've ranted about the value of quotes from customers. I like quotes! In general, the audience of any ad is more interested in anything that was *not* written by the ad designer or marketer. They don't care what *you* think. They know you're after their wallet. So whenever you can find a way to make a quote from someone else relevant, go for it.

And a great way to integrate relevant and compelling quotes is to go to that dictionary of quotations and find something compelling. That's the basic premise of the "wisdom ad" concept I described above, and it is also the concept behind the brochure cover design in Figure 13-7. In this design for a simple two-fold, three-panel brochure printed on regular-size 8.5-x-11-inch paper, the cover features two quotes of relevance to the service the brochure advertises.

The quotes are interesting in their own right, especially to anyone who is wrestling with how to be more successful in their career and life — and that's the target audience for this particular brochure. It is designed to promote the services of a personal coach, someone who helps people get organized and get ahead. So wise thoughts on the nature and meaning of success are very relevant to the service and will make the brochure valuable and intriguing to the target audience. It would make sense to carry the concept to the inside pages of this brochure as well by sprinkling several more good quotes around it.

"The common idea that success spoils people by making them vain, egotistic and self-complacent is erroneous; on the contrary it makes them, for the most part, humble, tolerant and kind. Failure makes people bitter and cruel."

- W. Somerset Maugham

# PERSONAL
# COACHING

HELPING CLIENTS ACHIEVE THEIR GOALS

YOUR COMPANY NAME (AND LOGO)
Your address and contact information
Web site/e-mail address

"Success is relative:
It is what we can make of
the mess we've made of things."

- T.S. Eliot

**Figure 13-7:**
A brochure
making
good use of
quotations.

Notice that by simply changing the two large-type words forming the title, you could adapt this design to many different businesses. A consultant could simply use words describing his or her business such as *computer systems* or *successful training solutions* to adapt the cover to fit the business. Then interior copy can pick up the theme of success by showing how each of the services the consultant offers helps companies achieve success. There are always creative ways to adapt a good ad concept to your particular business and market!

# Beautiful Shortcuts to Great Ads

In the preceding sections, I share concepts and templates that make use primarily of advertising copy, or the written word, for their effectiveness. Often the easiest way to create a high-impact ad cheaply and quickly is to simply write clever copy. But there are also many wonderful ways to make an impact using art. Visual appeal can transform an ordinary marketing message into an extraordinary one.

So now I want to look at some strategies for creating powerful ads, catalogs, brochures, Web pages, or other marketing communications in a hurry or on a tight budget by using beautiful visuals.

If you want to make a big impact with a gorgeous photograph but need to work fast or on a tight budget, you probably don't want to hire a professional photographer. Your best bet in a hurry is stock photography, and many vendors of it are on the Web, so don't be afraid to go shopping for a great image. Generally, you pay a fee in the low to middle hundreds of dollars for one-time usage of the image you like, selected from a large assortment on a site, CD or (more traditionally) from a book or catalog published by a stock photography house. But be careful of poor quality images. Just because they are sold by a professional firm doesn't mean they are any good! Stock photography is often expensive and sometimes of dubious quality.

To find sources of stock photography, check in the business telephone directory of New York City or any large city — which you may have to purchase from your phone company if you don't have it already. Stock photography houses are rarely listed in regular consumer "Yellow Pages" directories. Or key in "stock photography" in a search engine on the Web. Or ask for leads from a photography store manager, a professional designer or photographer, or a graphic artist. These people get marketed by stock photography houses, so they tend to have their CDs and catalogs on hand. There is a vast selection of off-the-shelf art of all kinds available for use in your marketing, but the vast majority of marketers and business managers are unaware that this treasure trove exists and don't know how to find it.

## Free stock photography? Why not!

What if you want to try your hand at using a beautiful photograph right now without having to pay anything for it? Well, it's a pretty bold demand. But I think I can help you out. My firm has for years compiled an extensive library of photographic images that we can dip into for marketing materials, trainings, and the like. Most of these are landscape and nature scenes, which means they combine beauty with flexibility. It's not hard to use, say, a photograph of a beach scene or a flower or a graceful landscape in almost any marketing campaign. As long as the picture itself is arresting or appealing, the photograph will add stopping power and improve the image of almost any communication.

Think about it this way. Every year, people buy expensive calendars featuring fine photography and then hang these calendars up where they will look at one image for a full month. And these same people are routinely exposed to many hundreds of ads each day, but do their best to ignore and forget the ads. What's the difference between the calendar they pay for and treasure and the ads they ignore? One has beautiful photographs; one doesn't. So if you want your marketing communications to be treasured instead of ignored, try giving people what they want — something beautiful.

## The marketing impact of beauty

We have a pretty big library of books on marketing and advertising here at my office, and I just went through the indexes of a bunch of them looking for the word *beauty*. It's not there. Go figure. What I figure is that most people are not designing their marketing materials (or even their products) to be beautiful. They are trying to make ads effective, or clever, or shocking, but not beautiful. So that's a strategy you can use with the confidence that you won't have a lot of competition in using this shortcut to great advertising.

And you can offer customers beauty in plenty of other ways, as well. You don't have to confine yourself to photographs! A beautiful storefront, office space, or even an especially elegant business card can create an aesthetic impact that pleases and impresses prospects and customers. Yet how many of the spaces where customers are received or served are actually made to be truly beautiful?

I want to end by sharing a photograph of a local bakery called the Henion Bakery, which makes a dramatic and appealing impact on the downtown street where it is located by growing an attractive flower garden in front of the store each spring and summer. For the cost of some seed packets and a little love and care, this business creates an unusual and beautiful presentation that tells passersby that the owners really care about their business and have the special touch that assures you of the finest products. Figure 13-8 shows a close-up of their sign covered with climbing morning glory vines. This photo is also on the CD as file CD1310. The photo was actually taken by a customer and dropped by the store with a thank-you in appreciation of the store's fine garden. So obviously somebody noticed and cared that the Henions went to the trouble of creating a beautiful garden for their customers to enjoy. (The store is run and owned by bakers David and Barbara Henion and is located in Amherst, Massachusetts.)

**Figure 13-8:**
A sign
beautified
with morning
glory
flowers.

# On the CD

Check out the following items on the CD-ROM:

- ✔ The Al's Daily Grind campaign (CD1301 through CD1303)
- ✔ Mood ad templates (CD1304 through CD1306)
- ✔ Wisdom ad templates (CD1307 through CD1309)
- ✔ The Henion Bakery's sign (CD1310)

# Chapter 14

# Business Cards, Brochures, Catalogs, and More

*W*hen you go into an important business meeting or sales call, you know that you need to look good — professional clothes; clean, attractive hair; a nice smile; good manners; and no body odor. Most people with any business experience learn to follow these rules of personal presentation fairly quickly. (More or less — I do wish that people would be a little more careful to dress conservatively and professionally whenever they have a connection or sale to make!)

But when it comes to presenting yourself at arm's length through marketing materials, people are far, far less professional. It's hard to keep in mind that your business card, letter, brochure, catalog, or other materials are *representing you* in front of potential customers. We tend to impose a lower standard on these materials than we would on ourselves if we were there in person.

But in truth, an even higher standard is necessary and appropriate. Why? Because you aren't there to make your own case. And no matter how well designed they are, marketing materials are a poor substitute for human beings. So they need to be really top-class to do the job. This chapter looks at the more important forms of marketing materials and makes sure that you're designing and using materials that help your marketing effort instead of hurting it.

(By the way, this chapter is loaded because I cover many of the principles of good design and production for printed marketing materials. You can find much here that can help you design newsletters, print ads, direct-mail letters, and anything else people read, too.)

# Business Cards

Your business card is often the first contact someone has with you or your business. Sometimes it's the only marketing communication a prospect has. So make sure that it follows the rules of good marketing communications by building both emotional and rational involvement! That means that it needs to communicate the information a prospect needs to figure out what you have and, when he needs it, how to contact you easily. That's the rational involvement goal.

## Overall impressions

But don't forget that the card also has to appeal to prospects on a basic emotional or intuitive level, too. Imagine someone looking through a pile of cards that includes many competitors of yours. Why would she pick out yours? What makes it call out to people?

Basically, you want to make sure that your card makes a powerful, positive, personal impression. (You can think of this as the PPP factor if you like!) Most cards don't. Most are quite dull. Even the ones that are clean and professional generally emphasize information and ignore the need to make an impression.

Hold on! Just because you want to make a powerful, personal impression with your card, don't do anything crazy. You don't want to make a *negative* powerful, personal impression! Strive for a sophisticated, professional image — with something different, such as a better-quality paper, a more beautiful logo, an unusual vertical layout, or a useful fact or inspirational quote printed on the back, or an attractive use of color to highlight your company name or logo. Above all, focus on a well-presented company name and logo.

You can even consider *custom cards for specific occasions.* When I go to trade shows or conferences, I sometimes have a designer or someone handy in my office make up laser-printed business cards specific to the event.

For example, I recently returned from a conference of human resource directors where I ran a workshop on identifying and developing high-potential employees. Well, I know what happens to the business cards that people collect at those events: They land in a big pile that you go through afterward, and half the time, you look at a card and say, "Now who was this person? Why do I have this card?" So I handed out cards that not only identified me and my business but also included the name of the workshop and conference. That way, people could easily recall me, no matter how big their piles of cards or how poor their memories. I'm sure I was the only presenter at that conference who actually had cards custom-made for the event, so that helps my card stand out from the others.

## Design details

In designing your cards, you want to make a good impression and include enough information on the card to make it easy for them to contact you. But at the same time, you don't want to overload them with information so that the card is confusing.

The standard size for business cards in the United States is 2 x 3½ inches. Business cards are usually printed, as opposed to being copied, largely because printing is more durable when handled a lot. How you set up the original depends entirely on how you're getting the cards made.

Business cards are printed with either flat ink or raised ink. Flat ink printing is just the standard printing; with raised ink printing, the cards are printed with an ink and then dusted with a plastic powder and heated in an oven that melts and expands the powder, giving the type a raised look and feel. Other differences to consider are that flat printing generally takes less time because it's done in-house; however, it's also usually more expensive. Because raised printing is usually sent out to a specialized facility, it's less expensive, but takes longer.

Almost all printers offer both types of printing for business cards, and the choice is largely one of taste. Personally, I don't like the look and feel of raised cards, but many people prefer them. Whichever style you choose, however, affects your design.

Business cards with flat printing are set ten-up on an 8½-x-11-inch sheet. Setting them ten-up keeps the cost down. Cards that are sent out for raised ink printing are set one-up, or you can pick from a catalog with many styles of cards and mix and match type styles, ink colors, and paper. You can even choose from a selection of generic logos.

Printers like to have space from the edge of the printing on the card to the edge of the paper. The amount of space needed varies from printer to printer — anywhere from ⅛ inch to ¼ inch. To be safe, leave ¼ inch in all directions (see Figure 14-1) because paper can sometimes shift from side to side when going through the press, and this space assures that the cutter won't clip off any text that is too close to the edge of the card.

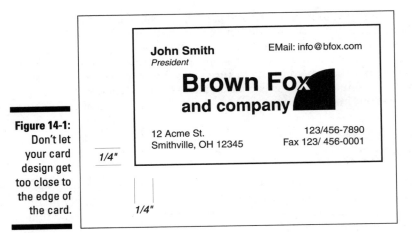

**Figure 14-1:**
Don't let
your card
design get
too close to
the edge of
the card.

Print your business cards on a heavy paper, such as #65 cover stock. It is good to use matching paper stock for your business cards, stationery, and envelopes because people associate each with the others and see all of them as part of a clearly defined, professional presentation and image (see Figure 14-2). Some papers differ in weight but match in color and finish, so you can easily match your cards with the lighter paper of your letterhead.

Some printers offer package discounts on letterhead, envelopes, and cards when ordered together, so getting them all printed at the same time is often cost-effective. You save more if using colored ink because you save on ink change charges, too.

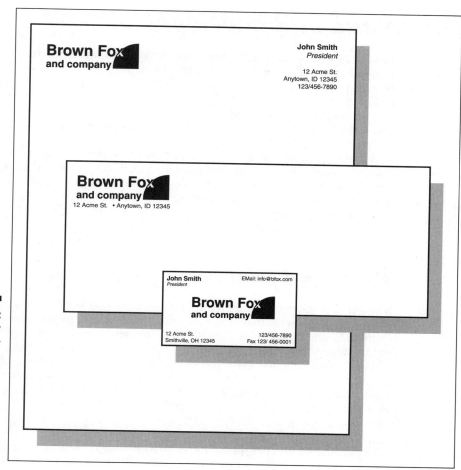

**Figure 14-2:**
Consider
how your
letterhead,
envelopes,
and busi-
ness cards
look when
seen
together.

# Letterhead and Envelopes

As with business cards, letterhead and envelopes may be the first encounter someone has with your business, and first impressions are obviously important. But even if customers have been with you for some time, the look and feel of your stationery has a subtle but powerful impact on their attitude toward you. Good letterhead can help retain a customer. So, as with business cards, letterhead is a surprisingly important marketing investment.

And don't overlook the importance of an envelop design that *calls out to be opened*. Important prospects get too much mail. Why should they pay any special attention to your envelope? Because it appears professional and impressive and looks more interesting and useful to them than the average junk mail they receive. Or does it? Better take a cold, hard look at your envelopes and see if they're up to the challenge!

## Paper and print convey an image

If you're a stockbroker or a business consultant, you may want to have an established, conservative look in your design, ink, and paper selection. Communicating a sense of stability and longevity can be important to these fields. What sort of type, ink color, and paper say this the best? Perhaps Times Roman lettering, centered in a traditional style at the head of the paper, printed in conservative black ink on an old-fashioned creamy bond containing a watermark and having some cotton fiber in it. Such a paper is more expensive than lighter, more modern papers but is consistent with a conservative, solid, sophisticated image.

What should an art therapist choose for stationery? Well, you want an image that is both playful and supportive — soft, reassuring, but a bit artistic and fun, too. How about a full-color rainbow as the logo, which brings in the artist's palette but also may evoke thoughts of calmness, good fortune, and healing (because rainbows come after storms)? As for paper, perhaps an attractive, soft, woven paper, again in a conservative off-white or creamy color, but perhaps this time with some little flecks of color in it?

You need to project a clear, strong personality in *each presentation* of a business. So you want to capture this personality in your letterhead, envelopes, and business cards. Even if you don't work with an expensive designer, take the time to explore the many options and make a thoughtful selection of paper, ink, type, and logo (if you use one). Extra care and a little extra investment here go a lot further than most people realize to help make sales and marketing successful.

# *Brochures*

"We need a brochure." That's the most common request that a marketing consultant or designer hears from clients. Seems like everybody needs a new brochure, and I think I know why. The old ones aren't working. They don't seem to have much impact. They don't look very good. They don't have the latest information or products. They don't make the phone ring off the hook. *They don't make you look good.*

People are rightly unhappy with their brochures. Most of them don't accomplish what a good brochure should:

- ✔ Get prospects excited about doing business with you.
- ✔ Communicate enough information to support a purchase decision.
- ✔ Communicate enough feeling to create a strongly positive impression or image.
- ✔ Serve as a simple catalog describing your various products or services.
- ✔ Support *all* your marketing activities, serving as a handout for salespeople, a great mail piece for prospecting, a useful update for existing customers, a good giveaway at events or trade shows, the perfect accompaniment to a formal proposal or press kit, and so on.

Whenever you're presenting yourself to the public, your brochure can break the ice for you!

To make sure that you have a brochure that does everything it can to help you sell, you first need to analyze the possible uses of that brochure. Don't design your own brochure — or ask an expert to design it — without a clear list of all its purposes. Otherwise, it won't be designed to fit those uses, and you may be disappointed with it.

Figure 14-3 displays a sample worksheet to fill in before you tackle the project of designing a new brochure.

After you identify all the likely uses for your brochure, you can think about the design requirements of each intended use — and make sure that your design incorporates those requirements.

HEADING

The quick brown fox jumped over the lazy dog, all on a summer afternoon. The quick brown fox jumped over the lazy dog, all on a summer afternoon. The quick brown fox jumped over the lazy dog, all on a summer afternoon. The quick brown fox jumped over the lazy dog, all on a summer afternoon. The quick brown fox jumped over the lazy dog, all on a summer afternoon. The quick brown fox jumped over the lazy dog, all on a summer afternoon.

The quick brown fox jumped over the lazy dog, all on a summer afternoon. The quick brown fox jumped over the lazy dog, all on a summer afternoon. The quick brown fox jumped over the lazy dog, all on a summer afternoon. The quick brown fox jumped over the lazy dog, all on a summer afternoon. The quick brown fox jumped over the lazy dog, all on a summer afternoon. The quick brown fox jumped over the lazy dog, all on a summer afternoon.

The quick brown fox jumped over the lazy dog, all on a summer afternoon. The quick brown fox jumped over the lazy dog, all on a summer afternoon. The quick brown fox jumped over the lazy dog, all on a summer afternoon. The quick brown

**Inside Panel**

HEADING

The quick brown fox jumped over the lazy dog, all on a summer afternoon. The quick brown fox jumped over the lazy dog, all on a summer afternoon. The quick brown fox jumped over the lazy dog, all on a summer afternoon. The quick brown fox jumped over the lazy dog, all on a summer afternoon. The quick brown fox jumped over the lazy dog, all on a summer afternoon. The quick brown fox

**Bulk Mailing Indetia**

**Back Panel**

Name
Address
City, State  Zip

**HEADLINE OR TITLE HERE**

Artwork or Logo

The quick brown fox jumped over the lazy dog, all on a summer afternoon. The quick brown fox jumped over the lazy dog, all on a summer afternoon. The quick brown fox jumped over the lazy dog, all on a summer afternoon. The quick brown fox jumped over the lazy dog, all on a summer afternoon. The quick brown fox jumped over the lazy dog, all on a summer afternoon. The quick brown fox jumped over the lazy dog, all on a summer afternoon. **Front Panel**

The quick brown fox jumped over the lazy dog, all on a summer afternoon. The quick brown fox jumped over the lazy dog, all on a summer afternoon. The quick brown fox jumped over the lazy dog, all on a summer afternoon. The quick brown fox jumped over the lazy dog, all on a summer afternoon. The quick brown fox jumped over the lazy dog, all on a summer afternoon.

The quick brown fox jumped over the lazy dog, all on a summer afternoon. The quick brown fox jumped over the lazy dog, all on a summer afternoon. The quick brown fox jumped over the lazy dog, all on a summer afternoon. The

**Figure 14-3:** Fill out a brochure design worksheet.

For example, say you checked "Include in letters to prospects." Now you realize that you have to figure out how it will be mailed. Will it simply fold up and have room on the outside for an address and stamp? Or will it be enclosed in an envelope — in which case you need to find out what sizes and styles you prefer and make sure that your brochure is designed to fit a standard envelope. If you plan to use it for mailings, you may want to specify an upper weight limit for it — a factor you don't need to worry about if the brochure is only meant to be handed out.

# Brochure design considerations

Freelance designer Rick Ward, who helped me with this chapter, often advises his clients to collect examples of brochures they like before coming to him to finalize their designs. That's good advice. I recommend keeping a file folder somewhere in your office labeled something like "Brochures I Like." Whenever you see an appealing brochure, toss it in that file. That way, when it comes time to think about your own brochure design, you can empty the file folder and look at lots of appealing approaches. One of them may inspire you to do something new and different that works well for you.

### Infinite materials

Brochures are unusual in the variety of options they present. You're working not just on one piece of paper but on as many as you wish to include. And you have the option of folding the paper or using separate sheets, so you can think three-dimensionally about your brochure.

In addition, you have more options for materials than you do for ads or letters. Brochures can be on regular or coated paper, but you can also get creative and use unusual cover stocks, or even get into foil paper, embossed covers, clear or opaque covers, or inside sheets, and so on. In fact, if you don't mind assembling brochures by hand, you can even include unusual materials such as cloth (how about a silk sheet between the cover and the first page?). There's nothing to stop you from using a leather or wood cover either, although I don't necessarily recommend exotic materials unless they somehow tie into your image or relate to your product line. But brochures give the marketing imagination plenty of scope!

### Sizes and shapes

That said, I suggest that you look first at simple, inexpensive, standard design options. They give plenty of room for creativity but use standard paper sizes. And you can vary these paper sizes by folding them in different ways, so you still have plenty of room for creativity. The standard precut paper sizes in many countries are as follows:

- Letter (8½ x 11 inches)
- Legal (8½ x 14 inches)
- Tabloid (11 x 17 inches)

Of these three standard sizes, the first two are the most common and easiest to work with. I recommend working within the possibilities that these two standard sizes present unless you have a good reason not to.

The first option is to use standard 8½-x-11-inch paper, which you can work with horizontally or vertically, as Figure 14-4 shows. With a little imagination, you get five excellent brochure layouts out of this standard paper size: horizontal half fold, accordion fold and tri fold, and the vertical half fold and fold over.

Similarly, you can fold a standard legal-sized sheet of paper measuring 8½ x 14 inches in many ways to create different brochure layouts. Figure 14-5 shows the same five options executed with legal-sized paper. Because of the longer length, the various folds create completely different brochures from those made with letter-size paper. For example, compare the horizontal half folds in the two figures. The smaller letter-size paper gives a vertically oriented page, whereas the longer legal-sized paper gives a chunkier, magazine-style page with the same horizontal fold.

So among these two standard (and therefore inexpensive) paper sizes and these five different folds, you have ten different brochure options. Each has a unique page size and therefore supports different approaches to page layout and design. In designing your brochure, think like a painter who first decides which size canvas to work on. The choice of canvas may be as important to the success of the painting as the design and execution of the painting itself.

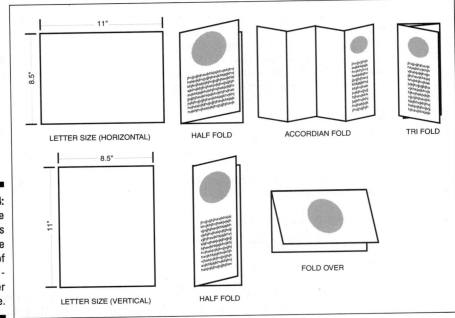

**Figure 14-4:**
Brochure
designs
using one
sheet of
8½-x-11-
inch paper
as a base.

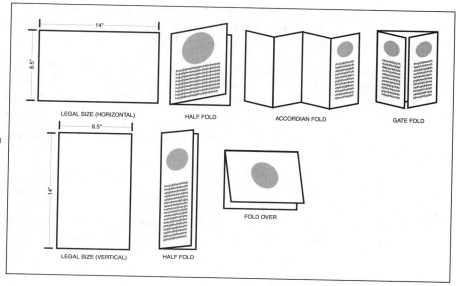

LEGAL SIZE (HORIZONTAL)    HALF FOLD    ACCORDIAN FOLD    GATE FOLD

LEGAL SIZE (VERTICAL)    HALF FOLD    FOLD OVER

**Figure 14-5:** Brochure designs using one sheet of 8½-x-14-inch paper as a base.

If you intend your finished size to be one of these standard sizes and you have bleeds (ink that runs right to the edge of the paper on one or more sides), you have to run it on oversize paper and cut it down. That's okay if you don't mind spending a bit more to get that bleed effect. But don't include it just because you didn't know better. Make sure that the bleed is really worth the added expense.

Sometimes you want your brochure to have an unusual shape or size in order to help it grab attention or make a statement, in which case the added expense of a nonstandard paper size may make sense.

If you intend to mail your brochure, it needs to fit within postal regulations and a standard envelope size, or else you have to find unusual-sized envelopes (and possibly pay extra postage). I recommend backing into your brochure specifications by starting with a search at the printer for unusual envelope sizes. That way, you won't get stuck with a great design that can't be matched with an appropriate envelope.

## Paper characteristics

Paper weight, or basis weight, is the weight in pounds of 500 sheets of 17-x-22½-inch paper. Cut-size paper usually comes in bulks of 500 sheets called a *ream.* Twenty-pound paper (written 20#) is a lighter paper than, say, 24# paper. Heavier paper is better to use if you have printing on both sides because heavier paper tends to be more opaque. You also want to choose heavier paper if your piece is going to be handled a lot, because heavier paper is more durable.

Lighter-weight paper, such as stationery paper, is called *offset paper,* and heavier card stock, such as that used for business cards, is called *cover stock.* You may use either type for a brochure. Try folding and handling different types and weights of paper before deciding. But remember that if you intend to do mass mailings of your brochure, the heavier papers will cost you more in postage. So weigh and price the postage on several options before making your decision.

You also want to consider the finish or texture of the paper you use. Paper with a texture or "grain" feels nice but may not be advisable if your brochure has a number of photos because the texture of the paper will break up the ink for the photo, making it look coarse or muddy. Stick to paper with a solid surface if you're reproducing a lot of photos to keep them sharp and clear.

## Layout tips

Printers use basically two programs for page layout: Adobe PageMaker and QuarkXPress. Your printer has at least one of these programs. In some cases, layout done in other programs can be read into one of these programs, but check with your printer beforehand to find out what its capabilities are.

When laying out the text and artwork for your brochure, keep in mind that printers need a *gripper margin* — the blank space that is needed on the end of a document so that the printing press can grab the paper and put it through the press (see Figure 14-6). Usually, the gripper margin is about ⅜ inch, but it varies with bigger presses, so check with your printer for its specific needs. This area needs to be totally blank, free from text or image.

**Figure 14-6:**
Leave a
gripper
margin
when you
lay out
brochures.

Next, think about how your text and artwork may lay out on the paper. There are no absolute rules for how many illustrations or pictures to use in any one brochure, but you can follow these general guidelines:

- ✔ Shoot for a balance between text and artwork or photos. Too much text can be boring, and a well-placed photo or illustration can break it up nicely.

- ✔ On the front panel of your brochure, place an image and/or an opening statement or paragraph to catch your reader's attention. This front panel is very important. It should draw readers to the brochure and make them want to check out the information inside. You have to catch many people's attention with this panel, so consider how people will receive it. If it's in a display rack, will the rack hide most of the cover? Maybe you want to design it to compensate for the rack.

- ✔ You may hear your printer refer to *serif* and *sans serif* typefaces. Serif typefaces have little feet-like appendages on their ends, whereas sans serif are without those feet. (This paragraph is in a serif typeface.)

- ✔ Type is measured in point size. Ten point is a small point size:

    The quick brown fox jumped over the lazy dog.

    A large point size is 24 point:

# The quick brown . . .

- ✔ Make sure that the body type is readable, no less than 10 to 12 points in size. Consider your audience. If the people reading this brochure are elderly, consider using a bigger type size, such as 14 to 18 point. If folks have a hard time seeing the type, they're not going to bother. Also avoid large areas of *reverse* type, in which the type is white or a light color on a dark background. Reverse type is much harder to read.

- ✔ Try to stick to one or two families of fonts within a brochure. Too many font styles can look sloppy and confusing. There are many styles within each family (for example, **Bold**, *Italic*, narrow, and <u>Underline</u> in the Helvetica type family) to give you plenty of variety to work with. And don't forget that you can change the size to add variety. For example, you could use all the following variations in size in a single brochure — the largest for major headers and other sizes for minor headers, the body copy, and the "fine print" details.

Helvetica 10 point

Helvetica 12 point

Helvetica 14 point

Helvetica 16 point

## Helvetica 24 point

✔ Mix up straight paragraphs with other ways of laying out text, such as checklists and tables. (Notice that I tend to work in checklists, bullets, and tables fairly often in this book.) The changes of pace you create keep the text appealing.

### Headline type

Headline type is made for just that: headlines. It's usually bigger, sometimes bolder, and sometimes ornate. It's not meant for the body of the article, which would be too hard to read. Its purpose is to grab the reader's attention and draw him or her into the article below. This type is usually used on brochure covers and paragraph headings.

### Body type

Body type is used in the body of the text. Because it needs to be simple and easy to read, it's usually (but not exclusively) restricted to serif fonts, which are easier on the eyes, especially at smaller type sizes.

### Type alignment

The way type lines up on the paper supports an image or conveys a feeling. Formal, conservative images require justified type, in which both the left and right sides are aligned. A ragged right margin gives a less formal look. Titles are often centered, and sometimes text is justified only on the right, as when it floats in open space with a photo or box to the right of it. Figure 14-7 shows you what each of these options looks like and how printers and designers refer to each option.

**Figure 14-7:**
Your options
for aligning
type on
the page.

| The quick brown fox jumped over the lazy dog. The quick brown fox jumped over the lazy dog.The quick brown fox jumped over the lazy dog. The quick brown fox jumped over the lazy dog.The quick brown fox jumped over the lazy dog. The quick brown fox jumped over the lazy dog.The quick brown fox jumped over the lazy dog. The quick brown fox jumped over the | The quick brown fox jumped over the lazy dog. The quick brown fox jumped over the lazy dog.The quick brown fox jumped over the lazy dog. The quick brown fox jumped over the lazy dog.The quick brown fox jumped over the lazy dog. The quick brown fox jumped over the lazy dog.The quick brown fox jumped over the lazy dog. The quick brown fox jumped over the | The quick brown fox jumped over the lazy dog. The quick brown fox jumped over the lazy dog.The quick brown fox jumped over the lazy dog. The quick brown fox jumped over the lazy dog. The quick brown fox jumped over the lazy dog. The quick brown fox jumped over the lazy dog.The quick brown fox jumped over the lazy dog. The quick brown fox jumped over the | The quick brown fox jumped over the lazy dog. The quick brown fox jumped over the lazy dog.The quick brown fox jumped over the lazy dog. The quick brown fox jumped over the lazy dog.The quick brown fox jumped over the lazy dog. The quick brown fox jumped over the lazy dog.The quick brown fox jumped over the lazy dog. The quick brown fox jumped over the |
|---|---|---|---|
| **JUSTIFIED LEFT (Ragged Right)** | **JUSTIFIED RIGHT (Ragged Left)** | **CENTERED** | **JUSTIFIED** |

### Text wrapping

With text wrapping, the lines of text end right where they bump into artwork. Some layout and word processing programs allow you to wrap text like this, which gives you another nice design option.

# Copy or print?

One of the first things you have to decide when producing a brochure is whether to have it copied or printed. Some of the factors that determine this include:

- ✔ If you have large runs of 1,000 pieces or more, it's better to have them printed than copied.

- ✔ Having small runs (under 1,000 pieces) printed is not cost-effective. The price per unit goes down as quantity goes up. Photocopy instead.

- ✔ Printed pieces tend to be of better quality, especially if you have a lot of photos in your piece. Photos usually don't reproduce well on a copier.

- ✔ Will the brochure be looked at once and then thrown away — or is it something a person will hold onto and possibly refer to from time to time? If it will be used one time, copying may make sense. But copied pieces do not stand up well to continuous handling. In a copier, toner dust is heated and affixed to the paper's surface. This dust, after being heated, does not fall off easily but can eventually be scratched or rubbed off. Printing, on the other hand, is far more durable as ink sinks down into the paper, locking it in and making it impossible to remove.

Figure 14-8 illustrates the differences between copying (which puts toner on the paper) and printing (which works ink into the paper).

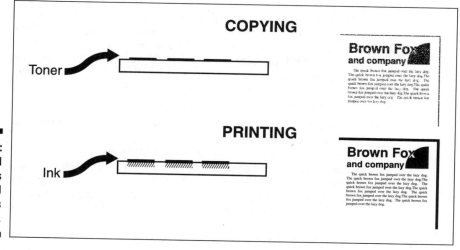

**Figure 14-8:** How copied materials and printed materials differ.

# Color

Adding color to your brochure grabs the viewer's attention and makes it more appealing to the eye, but each added color requires an additional print run and thus adds cost. There are different ways to add color.

- ✔ **PMS colors:** Printers use a universal ink color system called the Pantone Matching System. This system allows printers to match ink by referring to swatches that show the color along with the exact mixture of inks needed to obtain that color. So if you want to add color to your brochure, you need to ask a printer to let you see a set of PMS color samples so that you can select from it.

- ✔ **Four-color process:** This is the process in which full color is achieved by separating full color into four basic colors: cyan, magenta, yellow, and black. Film is shot of the image in each of these colors and is broken down into minute dots. These dots, when arranged next to each other, create the full color effect. The arrangement of these dots can be seen only with the aid of a magnifying glass, or *loupe*. The effect of the four-color process is excellent — it can reproduce fine art or photography quite accurately. But four-color printing is expensive because of the extra film work involved, as well as the need for four runs through the press.

- ✔ **Alternatives to four-color process printing:** Some alternatives allow you to have variety with color but still keep costs down. When using PMS colors, screen the color(s) at different percentages. For example, your brochure may have only two colors, such as black and blue. In a different area of the brochure where you use the color blue, use the blue screened back to 80 percent, 60 percent, and 20 percent. This gives the impression that you are using four different shades of blue, but actually it's blue at 100 percent, 80 percent, 60 percent, and 20 percent, so all the blues can be done on one run through the press. And although the shades of blue plus the black give the feeling of five colors, the brochure needs only two runs, one for black and one for blue.

- ✔ **RIP:** Another alternative for avoiding the high cost of the four-color process is to have your publication RIPped to a color copier. RIP stands for *Raster Image Processing*. Some printers have their computers hooked up to color copiers and can RIP your file to the copier and get a similar product to four-color copying. This process is especially good if you need only a few brochures. You pay an initial RIPping cost, and then you pay for each page printed at the cost of a color copy.

Avoid large fields of solid color because they add to the cost of a printed piece, and some printers have a hard time keeping the ink consistent throughout the field of color. In some cases, large solid colors can be screened to give them more consistency.

# *Artwork*

Artwork is good, right? Illustrating a brochure adds visual appeal and, if the illustrations are appropriate, makes it more persuasive. "Seeing is believing," as the saying goes! But as with type design, you need some basic technical knowledge before you're ready to select artwork for your brochure. The problem is that how you choose and prepare your graphics is determined partially by how you will produce the final output.

You have a number of overlapping categories to choose from (and of these, high resolution postscript output and vector images give you the highest quality). Here are the definitions and technical details of these three options:

✔ **High-resolution postscript output:** Any digitized artwork that has a resolution over 800 dpi (dpi is *dots per inch*; more means higher clarity or resolution). It's stored as EPS *(encapsulated postscript)* or TIFF *(Tagged Image File Format)* images. This output is done on a Postscript Imagesetter. High resolution postscript output gives you good results with offset printing, so it's recommended whenever you want a piece printed. If you use a graphic designer or artist to help you with your brochure, make sure to ask if he or she will provide the printer with high-resolution files in EPS or TIFF format.

✔ **Low-resolution postscript output:** Any digitized artwork that has a resolution in the 300–700 dpi range. This is usually used for "low end" pieces that will be copied. The original output comes from a laser printer. If you have a modern computer system in your office, you can probably generate this kind of output easily from your system. But remember it won't be suitable for printed brochures or catalogs, only for photocopies.

✔ **Bitmapped images (or "raster images"):** The way the image is digitized and stored, using small squares (pixels) arranged on a grid to represent the image. That's fine, as long as the image stays at the same size or smaller. But blow it up and those small squares grow larger, making them noticeable and giving the image a poor appearance. Figure 14-9 shows a bitmapped picture of a clock, which reproduces well, and then shows what happens when you blow up a section of that clock image. The enlargement looks terrible!

✔ **Vector images:** These get around the problems of bitmapped images by using mathematical equations to represent the lines and curves in artwork. They stay clean and clear at any level of enlargement because the computer literally redraws them to the new scale. Most logos are vector images because they're reproduced in many different sizes for different uses. Figure 14-10 shows how a vector image enlarges.

Section of bitmapped image
enlarged 400% to show pixels

**Figure 14-9:**
Don't expect
to enlarge
bitmapped
images.

**Figure 14-10:**
Vector
images
enlarge
without
losing detail.

I should also mention that the examples of bitmapped and vector art shown in Figures 14-9 and 14-10 are both examples of *line art*. Line art consists of any black-and-white image with no gray areas or screens. These images can be anything from line drawings to black-and-white logos.

You can also include forms of art other than line art — in other words, art that has grays or shades of color in it. But — wouldn't you know it? — doing so gets you into additional technical issues.

Avoid using anything that has been done in pencil, such as drawings or sketches, because these are very hard to reproduce. If you have to use a pencil drawing, the printer may suggest making a halftone print of the image to save the gray areas from burning out. Follow this advice and don't grumble about the minor added expense.

## Photography

A few guidelines exist when it comes to using photos in your brochures. Printers usually like to work from black-and-white photos that you supply (assuming that you want one- or two-color output). Color photos, especially low-contrast photos, tend to muddy up. But sometimes you have to use color photos because that's all that you have — or because you need to produce a four-color brochure. So make sure that the photos are high-contrast (lots of difference between the dark and light areas). High-contrast photos have more definition and reproduce better.

If you're planning to take (or have taken by a photographer) pictures of your products, facilities, or people, make sure to use high-contrast film. If you don't know what that is, ask at the film store. In general, slower films (with lower ASA numbers) give higher contrast and sharper images.

If you're going to photograph in color for your brochure (or catalog or ad or Web page), I recommend a slow-speed color-slide film, such as old-fashioned Kodachrome (which comes in a slow ASA 64 speed). Color slides have lots of contrast and rich tones, and they can easily be digitized into a computer. (I recently obtained a scanner from Nikon for about $1,000 that scans my color negatives and slides right into a high-quality digital file suitable for printing!)

Photographs need to be broken down into a series of dots *(halftones)* for the shaded areas to be reproduced. Without gray areas, photos would be black and white and become posterized, as Figure 14-11 demonstrates.

**Figure 14-11:**
The same photograph handled in two different ways for printing.

The halftone version of the balloon photograph in Figure 14-11 is actually a screened image in which the screen breaks up the tones into more or fewer black dots. The eye blends these back into a "whole" image, but you can see that the smooth blending of tones is an optical illusion when you blow up a portion of that image, as in Figure 14-12.

**Figure 14-12:**
When you magnify the halftone photo image of the balloon four times, you can see how the halftone handles the different shades.

## Clip art and stock photography

You can use copyright-free images, such as clip art and photos, when budget constraints eliminate the hiring of professional illustrators or photographers. These images are copyright-free, so you don't have to pay royalties or get special permission to reproduce them. They're usually available on disk or CD, and you typically pay a usage fee — but that fee is low compared to the cost of hiring an artist or photographer to create custom artwork.

Many companies sell copyright-free images — try searching the Internet or asking printers or designers for leads. Printers usually have a source for these images, but they may mark up the price. You can also purchase copyright-free images at software supply stores, as well as download them from the Internet.

## Crop and fold marks

Crop and fold marks tell printers where a piece needs to be cut or folded. They need to be marked on your original with a hairline — the smallest weight line possible — to ensure high accuracy. In the following list, I review briefly the standard terms and symbols so that you know how to communicate with your printer or binder:

- **Crop marks** are guides showing the printer where to cut a page. If your brochure needs to be printed on larger paper and then cut down (as when the ink bleeds all the way to the edge of your page or when you specify a nonstandard size), the printer uses the crop marks to cut in exactly the right place.

- **Fold marks** tell the printer where to fold the paper. (Make sure that he understands which *way* to fold the page!)

- **Score marks** indicate where the paper should be scored, or lightly cut. When you're using heavy paper, it's sometimes necessary to score before folding in order to get a clean, crisp fold. In that case, you need to mark the fold line as a score line, too.

- **Perforating** is used when a brochure includes a coupon or postcard that you want people to tear out. Perforating lines show the printer where to make the *perforations* — a series of short cuts in the paper.

Figure 14-13 shows you how the various marks described in this list are usually indicated on originals supplied to the printer.

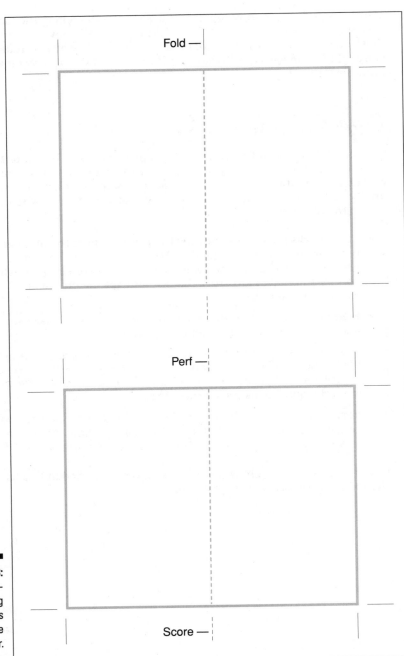

**Figure 14-13:**
Paper-
handling
instructions
to the
printer.

# Brochure benchmarks

Earlier in this chapter, I recommend that you collect examples of brochures you like. I do that myself, and I'd like to share a few designs with you that I particularly like. The first, shown in file CD1402 on the CD, is for a charter yacht, the Pleiades. Printed on an 8½-x-11-inch sheet and folded three times to make a simple mailer, this brochure features stunning photographs and plenty of color to communicate the feel of a chartered sailing voyage. It's not hard to imagine yourself vacationing on the boat, strolling a beautiful tropical beach, or enjoying the ripe tropical fruits in this brochure's well-selected photographs. (The owner of the boat hired a professional photographer to shoot the photographs.)

The writing in this brochure nicely combines the romance of a tropical vacation with practical facts that explain the details. Romantic headlines like "A ship to build a dream on" combine with factual information like "a spacious cockpit, swim platform and airy cabins" and "we're also pleased to recommend destinations and to arrange transportation and hotel or resort accommodations" to make this a hard-working marketing piece.

Please see your CD to review this and the other benchmarks I've collected for your reference. There's a simple 8½-x-14-inch brochure from the Umass Family Business Center (CD1403) that was inexpensive to produce because it's printed entirely in dark green ink. Visual interest is added by reversing some of the type on blocks of dark green. Although this brochure has a bit more in the way of solid text blocks than is ideal, the fact that the text describes upcoming events in detail makes it particularly pertinent and likely to be read. (Note also the unusual folds of this piece. It's folded horizontally in the middle and then folded up the middle again, so it seems to emerge from a very simple, clean exterior into a more involved piece than people expect.)

The next example, from Modern Memoirs, is laid out as a small, stapled booklet — demonstrating one of the product forms that this company sometimes produces for clients as well as offering a more detailed catalog of the company's offerings (CD1404). An earlier brochure than the first one, this piece has simpler, black-and-white graphics but is still quite effective.

To provide a dramatic contrast to these four benchmark examples, I also include a somewhat unusual brochure designed for my own business by Rocks Communications, the PR and marketing agency we use. They designed an intentionally unusual brochure, using oversized paper (but one that came with a matching envelope) and taking advantage of the large, wide page to give the piece an unusual look and feel. Of the many brochures my business has used over the years, this one seemed to make the biggest impression, so it's worth a look.

# Catalogs

You can think of a catalog as a simple book or an elaborate brochure. If you think of it as an elaborate brochure, you will happily discover that you already know a great deal about how to design and print catalogs because everything I just covered about brochures applies. In fact, many simpler catalog designs are indistinguishable from brochures in their basic design, use of paper, and layout. They simply focus on describing a product or service line, which makes them catalogs instead of brochures.

But more elaborate catalogs are usually made up of multiple pages stapled together. By far the most common catalog format uses sheets of tabloid (11-x-17-inch) paper, folded in half. When folded, each tabloid sheet gives you four 8½-x-11-inch pages to work with. If you use just one tabloid sheet, you have a front and a back page (they share one side of the sheet before it is folded) and two inside pages (which share the other side of the sheet).

Now imagine adding another tabloid sheet to this catalog design. It nests inside the first sheet when folded, and they are stapled together on the fold. With this two-sheet design, you have eight standard 8½-x-11-inch pages to play with — two for the front and back covers and six more on the inside of your catalog.

Add another sheet and your page count goes up by four, to 12 pages. Add another sheet, and your catalog has 16 pages you can work with. Bet it doesn't surprise you to learn that most catalogs have page counts that are multiples of four!

## Design considerations

I went into considerable detail about the design of brochures because I believe many marketers can and should roll up their sleeves and get involved in the design of their own brochures. That way, they won't be intimidated by the project and they will feel free to create and replace brochures whenever they have a need. The same is true for simpler catalogs prepared in the same style as brochures. You can design one-sheet catalogs with one or more folds and have them printed at the local print shop or photocopied quite easily. But if you want to get into more elaborate, multi-page catalogs, you need to work with specialists. Your local print shop probably can refer you to larger printers specializing in catalogs, or you can check for them on the Internet or ask businesses that already produce good catalogs whom they use.

Also consider hiring a designer who specializes in catalogs. There's more to it than the mechanics of design and layout — although that alone can become quite complex when you have many pages. The biggest challenge, however, is to sell product effectively in the pages of a catalog. How you present each purchase option (in copy and art), what you choose to feature on the covers or inside covers (where you get the most impact), whether you include an index, what sort of look and feel you go for — all of these decisions are really quite sophisticated and difficult, so I recommend that you spend the extra money for expert input. Printing a multi-page, four-color catalog costs a great deal, and mailing it is expensive, too. You may as well invest enough in the design to give yourself good odds of a profitable return on that investment!

## *Benchmark catalogs for your reference*

You can easily find good examples of multi-page, full-color catalogs by examining your mail. Catalogs from clothing retailers like J. Crew and Land's End are usually well done and can serve as benchmarks. Also look at glossy, sophisticated magazines on the newsstands for interesting approaches to graphic design that you may want to earmark for a catalog. Just as with brochures, I recommend keeping a folder of catalogs that appeal to you. You can empty it out and review the various designs the next time you need ideas.

Notice especially how good catalogs

- Use the front cover to feature special products or offers or to create an appealing mood.

- Organize their contents in intuitive ways so that readers can quickly find sections of interest.

- Vary the page layouts so that each page does not look like the last and avoids monotony.

- Give readers plenty of ways to reach the company with questions or orders, including telephone and fax numbers (and perhaps a Web site) on each page, as well as a clear, flexible order form.

- Contain clear, accurate, sufficient information about products to support purchase decisions (they answer all the customer's questions well).

- Are positive in their emotional appeal, using smiling people, enthusiastic language, bright, warm colors, or all three to create an "up" mood in readers.

I include an assortment of pages from the quarterly catalogs of Human Resource Development Press on your CD for use as a benchmark (CD1401). (I discuss these catalogs in Chapter 5, too, because some of their pages use customer quotes to good effect.) HRD Press's approach is a fine example of good business-to-business marketing of a broad product line through an informative and visually appealing catalog.

Notice how these catalog pages from HRD Press break up the space into smaller blocks by using a column or grid pattern to display multiple products on most of the pages. If you can tighten up the space used for each product without damaging the selling power of your coverage, you can generate more revenues per page. And because design, printing, and mailing costs vary with the number of pages, you discover that hard-working pages make for a more successful catalog.

Also notice how the HRD Press catalogs offer free samples of some products. That's because they're looking to build long-term, repeat-purchase relationships with businesses that buy these products. Giving away a free product is a great way to get people to consider buying more. And using free-sample offers in the catalog encourages readers to pick up the phone and respond when this catalog comes in the mail. And as long as they are calling, they often think of something else they want. . . .

According to Debra Draper of HRD Press, who manages the catalog's design and mailing, lots of people respond to these free sample offers, and many go on to become good customers. To increase the rate at which these people are converted to paying customers, she plans to design a series of follow-up letters that will be sent automatically to anyone who requests a sample. The first letter will go out with the sample, the next a couple of weeks later, and a final one a few weeks after that. The letters will include specific information about the product and how to use it. Draper plans to automate the sending of these letters to help ensure full follow-up because sometimes salespeople are busy and nobody is able to call and talk to the person who requested a sample product right away.

As you review the HRD Press samples on your CD, you may wonder how such an extensive catalog can be prepared four times each year. The answer is that it can't. Not all of it, anyway. HRD Press, like many catalog marketers, does a complete redesign only twice a year. The "guts" of its new catalog are over-printed for use in the next quarter. Then extra sheets are printed, folded, and stapled to the outside to form a new edition of the catalog. By adding a new cover sheet and one or two more sheets as a wrap around the old guts, HRD Press can feature new products, make seasonal offers, and update the look and feel of its catalog without having to reprint the entire thing.

## The list factor

To whom do you send your catalog or brochure? That's a critical question that can even override the design question. Even a poorly designed catalog, sent to the right people at the right time, may still generate a lot of business! So good lists are integral to any catalog program.

HRD Press, the featured catalog example on your CD, mails to an in-house list of over 35,000 existing customer contacts. That's a very responsive list because it's made up of past customers, and past customers are always the most likely to buy. But they supplement this list with an equal number of new names from purchased mailing lists, some of whom place an order and end up getting added to the in-house list for future mailings. The trick is always to be adding to and updating your master list.

# Spec Sheets

"Just the facts, ma'am" is what a television detective in a long-running cop show used to say. That expression has worked its way into the English vocabulary in a testament to the power of TV, but so far marketers haven't taken it to heart. Too often, we forget to communicate enough information, clearly enough, to permit someone to make an informed purchase decision.

## Content

Does your brochure present all the information needed, or is it a "fluff piece" that tries to make your offering sound good but fails to provide sufficient details? Often marketing communications are maddeningly vague to serious buyers, who want to know exactly what you do, how your equipment performs, what the specifications are, what the terms are, and so on. What, exactly, *are* the facts?

Enter the *specification,* or *spec,* sheet. It serves this purpose well, providing the hard-core, informational backup to support more imaginative or persuasive marketing materials. I believe that everyone ought to prepare spec sheets for each product or service they sell. Not all prospects will want one, but those who do will really appreciate it.

A spec sheet is a simple, clear, one-page technical description of a product (or, rarely, a service). Include one in the sales collateral for a product if technical specifications are important to buyers or prospective buyers of that product. Include a spec sheet in the collateral materials for a video monitor, fire extinguisher, food processor, outboard motor, golf club, toaster, or remote-control toy car, for example, because intermediate or ultimate buyers of these products may well want or need to know something about the product's specifications.

## Format

Spec sheets usually are 8½-x-11-inch pieces of paper with printing on only one side. Include your company name, logo, and contact information on the top or bottom of the sheet. Title it "Specifications for <product name/code>" at the top (or just beneath your company identification). Date it, because specifications often change and you may have to issue updated sheets in the future.

Use your company letterhead for a simple, quick spec sheet. Use Word's table option and a laser printer to create a simple but professional spec sheet on your letterhead.

Set the spec sheet up in two columns, the left column listing a category of specifications (size, weight, voltage, pH, and so on) and the right column giving a specific measurement for each category. Use numbered footnotes to define any ambiguous or obscure terms or units. Avoid lengthy descriptions, and don't try to "sell" the product. Spec sheets give specifications; they don't promote.

Here's a simple template for spec sheets:

Specifications for <product>

Date/date/date

| Category | Data |
|---|---|
| Category | Data |
| Category | Data |
| Category | Data |
| Category | Data |
| Category | Data |

Company Name
Address
Phone/Fax
e-mail/Web page

Spec sheets should be *clear, readable* (don't use type smaller than 11 point, please!), *accurate,* and *sufficient.* Make sure to verify all the data you include on the spec sheet, and include everything needed to describe the product.

To ensure that your specifications are sufficient, have a look at spec sheets of competing products, if possible. Also *ask customers or prospects what information they need.* If you're using units that are not universal, provide conversions (that is, give the dimensions of a product in inches and centimeters). And verify all specifications with product designers and producers. Ask them if they are *sure* of the specifications. You don't want to be wrong.

If you hire a graphic designer or advertising agency to typeset your spec sheet, leave time for a thorough check of its accuracy after the design is finalized but before it's printed. Designers often introduce errors into spec sheets. They may also attempt to "jazz up" the design of your spec sheet. Discourage this urge. Keep spec sheets clean and simple and save the creativity for other marketing materials.

# On the CD

- ✔ HRD Brochure (CD1401)
- ✔ Pleiades Brochure (CD1402)
- ✔ UMass Family Business Center Brochure (CD1403)
- ✔ Modern Memoirs Booklet (CD1404)
- ✔ Sample Business Cards (CD1405)
- ✔ Sample Newsletter (CD1406)

# Chapter 15

# Harnessing the Power of Newsletters

*N*ewsletters are a great vehicle to deliver information and bring people up to date about your company, product, or organization. Depending on the content, you can publish them monthly, quarterly, or yearly. Like brochures, letterheads, envelopes, and business cards, newsletters reflect your company's personality and should be consistent with the look and feel you have reflected in your other publications.

Keep in mind, however, that newsletters do more than simply reflect an image. They communicate more content and give you more communication options than most marketing media. In this chapter, I'm not only going to share enough technical information to help you create great newsletters, I'm also, frankly, going to do my best to talk you into treating newsletters as a very powerful and important marketing medium.

You'll often hear people talk about *relationship marketing* — a buzzword that generally means building a more genuine, meaningful, lasting business relationship with your customer. To my mind, the newsletter fits in wonderfully with this strategy. It gives you many opportunities to explain yourself, and to give readers useful information, entertainment, and other "gifts" on the printed page (or via e-mail — more on that later).

But to produce a good newsletter, you need to master a few technical details. The design of newsletters is not hard, but without a working technical vocabulary, you may find it difficult to do a good job. I start by looking at the technical side of newsletters, and then I go on to examine some options and examples.

# The Elements of a Newsletter

The following sections describe the most important parts of a newsletter.

## Masthead

The masthead is the area that appears at the top of the newsletter. The design of the masthead should remain consistent throughout all your newsletters, changing only the date and volume/issue numbers. Consistency in the masthead brings identification to that publication. If you change it every publishing, people will wonder who or what organization is distributing it every time they receive it.

Mastheads usually, but not always, contain:

- The name of the newsletter — usually done in a headline typeface — that reflects the nature of its contents
- The name of the person or organization who publishes the newsletter
- Date of issue as well as issue and volume numbers

In addition, the masthead should grab attention and set a positive tone for the newsletter. Put time and care into the choice of name and the way you display it. Later in the chapter (and on the CD), I show you some exemplary newsletters. Take note of their different approaches to masthead design. Although each does it differently, it's obvious each approach reflects care and thought.

## Articles

When you decide which articles to include in your newsletter, make sure that you cover a *variety* of topics. You want to have something of interest to everyone.

Make sure that your stories contain solid nuggets of useable information, such as when and where events are, what happened (news is always of interest), what *will* happen (forecasts are always of interest), and how to do things successfully (how-to tips and lists are great). Also make sure you *tell stories*. Who did what, when and why, how they did it, and what happened. People read the news for stories, and the same is true with newsletters. Include case histories, interviews with people who are telling their stories, or simple news stories describing an event or happening. Good newsletter articles tell interesting, relevant stories.

Lay out articles in such a way that they capture the reader's attention and invite them to read further. Break them up with new paragraphs at least once every two or three column inches. Interrupt long flows of text with headers, tables, bullet points, or an illustration.

Try to use interesting sentences, especially at the beginning of each paragraph or section. If the first sentence grabs the reader, you will probably have his or her attention for the rest of the paragraph. How can you ensure that each paragraph and each major section of a newsletter article has a catchy, engaging, attention-grabbing introductory sentence?

Only one way to be sure: That is to go back and write (or rewrite) those catchy opening sentences *after* you've written the article. Take a half hour or more just to craft good lead sentences that queue up the content of their paragraph or section. Sentences that stimulate the imagination by asking an interesting question or challenging a common assumption are also good. Let me show you what I mean. Imagine you are editing an article for a company newsletter that has the following paragraph in it:

> The Divisional Quality Improvement Team leaders got together last week for a leadership training event that included classroom study, a self-assessment of their leadership styles, and two hours of "experiential training" on a high ropes course. The training was sponsored by Corporate Headquarters and lasted for six hours. It took place at Sleepy Hollow Retreat Center in Headlesston, Indiana.

Now that's an example of the kind of writing that consigns most corporate newsletters to the recycle bin. If you have time, you could get some quotes from people about how scary that high ropes course was and how it really taught them what true teamwork is all about. Maybe someone overcame a fear of falling, so you can bring a personal story in. Content can always be improved when you put on your storyteller's hat. But even if you don't have time to perfect this article, you can do a great deal simply by adding good introductory sentences here and there.

Although you cannot quickly do much about this writer's deadly recitation of straight facts, you can at least craft an opening sentence that gives the paragraph a little more relevance and interest. For instance, you might amend it as follows:

> *What lengths — and especially heights — will our volunteer team leaders go to in order to improve their own performance?* The Divisional Quality Improvement Team leaders got together last week for a leadership training event that included classroom study, a self-assessment of their leadership styles, and two hours of "experiental training" on a high ropes course. The training . . . and so on.

By adding a catchy opener to the paragraph, you greatly increase the rate of readership for that paragraph.

## *Headers (Like this one)*

Headers (or headings) should be set in a larger and bolder type than the body of the article. A header should not be too wordy, but it must contain enough description to invite the viewer to read on. This book has many examples, so I don't need to go on at length about my views as to how a header should be written. Just read a bunch of mine, and you'll at least see how I like to do it.

You can use headline type for your headers or take bold type from the same family of type that is used in the body. Figure 15-1 illustrates some of the choices that printers (and some desktop publishing systems) offer for headline typestyles.

# Kabel BT

# Bauhaus BT

# Aurora Condensed

# METROPOLITAINESD

**Figure 15-1:** Headline typestyles.

It is good not to use too many typestyles in a single publication. In general, I recommend sticking to one type style for most of your copy. But the exception is headers. If you like, you can try a contrasting style for the headers. Sometimes it adds an appealing contrast to the design.

Figure 15-2 shows an example of a header added to the paragraph I worked on earlier. The header is set in 14 point Helvetica, and the body copy is set in 11 point Times, to illustrate the impact of contrasting styles as well as sizes.

**Figure 15-2:** Header and body copy.

## Team leaders on the ropes

What lengths–and especially heights–will our volunteer team leaders go to in order to improve their own performance? The Divisional Quality Improvement Team leaders got together last week for a leadership training event which included classroom study, a self-assessment of their leadership styles, and two hours of "experimental training" on a high ropes course. . . .

Use plenty of headers. When in doubt, break up a story with more headers. People have short attention spans, especially if the writing isn't the greatest in the world. So give them more, smaller chunks to read, each wrapped up nicely in a good header.

## Type

The body of the article should use a readable type set large enough to read easily — which means no less than 10 point and preferably 12 point. Also, a serif font style will prove more readable than a sans serif style.

*Serifs* are the little decorations at the ends of the lines in this font (the one you are reading right now). Times and Palatino are popular and attractive serif fonts. Helvetica is the most popular sans serif font. Save it for headers, not body copy in general, since serif fonts are easier on the eye. Figure 15-3 illustrates the difference between serif and sans serif letters.

If the type is too hard to read, and people have to work at it, you will lose their attention.

**Figure 15-3:** Serif and sans serif letters.

## Columns

Use columns whenever you have large amounts of type. When the eye has to follow a line of type that spreads across an 8½-inch-wide sheet, it can waiver and jump from line to line. If the same article is broken up into two or three columns, it allows the eye a shorter distance to stay on the line and not get sidetracked.

## Leading and kerning

The term *leading* refers to the space between the lines of type. Layout programs have an automatic setting for adjusting the leading, but you can also adjust it manually. Adjusting it manually comes in handy when you're trying to get just one more line to fit in a particular article. By adjusting the leading to a smaller size, you can scrunch up the lines and allow that extra line to fit in. Type size and leading is usually written 10/12. The type size appears on top of the slash and the leading size appears on the bottom. Figure 15-4 shows you what kinds of spacing leading and kerning control.

**Figure 15-4:**
Leading and kerning control the spacing of your type.

The quick brown fox
jumped over the lazy
dog. Then the lazy black
cat crawled under the fence.

Leading →

The quick

Kerning

Try to be fairly consistent with leading and type size through the publication because irregular type and leading sizes look out of place. *Kerning* refers to space between characters (letters). Like leading, layout programs adjust the kerning between letters automatically, but you can manually override this as well.

After you write and set (lay out) your newsletter, check for widows and orphans. Redesign as necessary to eliminate them. It only takes a few minutes to eliminate these disorienting strays — and if you don't, any experienced designer will know you don't know your stuff!

## Flow and readability

Make sure that your publication flows (see Figure 15-5). If articles have to be continued on another page, don't make it hard for the person to find the continuation. If at all possible, keep articles together — it makes reading less frustrating for the reader. If your newsletter is published on a tabloid-size sheet (11 x 17 inches), try to lay out the articles so as to keep page-turning from becoming a problem. Don't make the reader have to flip the document over because the next articles are upside down. Also try to minimize the amount of flipping back and forth between pages. You lose readers when you make the reading path too challenging.

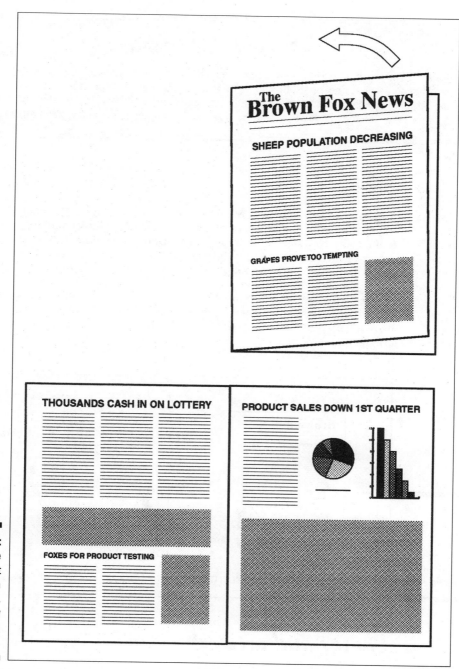

**Figure 15-5:**
Make sure the layout supports a natural, easy flow through the pages.

## Widows and orphans

*Widows* and *orphans* are short lines or words that become separated from other lines in a paragraph. They appear at the top or bottom of a page or a column. Widows appear at the bottom of the column, and orphans appear at the top of the column. It is best to avoid these, and they can be removed by adjusting the kerning or alignment or simply rewriting the text.

## Size

You can publish newsletters on virtually any size paper. The main determining factor is the amount of content you have (but think smaller if your budget is limited!). Newsletters can range from both sides of an 8½-x-11-inch sheet to a 11-x-17-inch sheet that is printed on both sides and folded in half. Or you can add more sheets and staple at the fold to make lengthier newsletters.

Figure 15-6 shows the two most common and easy formats for newsletters. Plan to use one or the other of these paper sizes and layout styles unless you have a very good reason to deviate from them (and extra money in your budget).

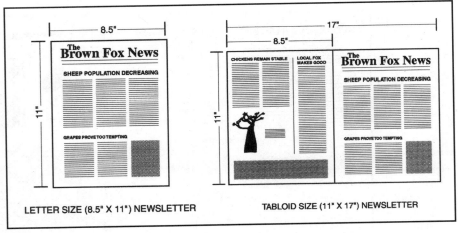

**Figure 15-6:** The two most practical formats for newsletters.

LETTER SIZE (8.5" X 11") NEWSLETTER

TABLOID SIZE (11" X 17") NEWSLETTER

## Photos and artwork

I cover the use of visuals in many places in this book, especially in my discussions of brochures and print ads (and you'll find some stock photos on your CD, as well). As with brochures, photos and artwork can be used to make an article more interesting and create an appropriate mood or feeling. *Text wrap* can also be effective in a publication like a newsletter — that's when the text wraps around a box containing artwork instead of stopping above it and continuing below.

For technical information about how to handle artwork, what your choices are when it comes to photocopying and printing, what screens are, how to handle color, and so on, please see Chapter 14. I cover all these details in my discussion of how to design brochures, and the knowledge is directly applicable to newsletter design and production.

# Why You Need a Newsletter

I really like newsletters as a marketing medium. I want you to create a newsletter if you don't have one already, or if you do, I want you to agree to improve it and make it more central to your sales and marketing. Why do I think you need a newsletter? Newsletters are

- Relatively cheap to produce (but that's just the beginning of why I like them).

- A great engagement device that gets people involved and interested.

- One of the best ways to express your personality and values as well as your offerings.

- Remarkably flexible — you can use them to convey information, promote your own offerings, share customer testimonials, provide interesting or amusing content, and so on.

- A relationship builder that helps retain good customers as well as attract good prospects.

And best of all, most of your competitors don't know how powerful a well-done newsletter can be. So you have a chance to outflank them on this one!

# Some Great Newsletter Designs

The first newsletter I'm going to show you is one that expresses the unique character of Collective Copies very well. This business is, as its name implies, a worker-owned collective, which gives it some distinguishing values and ensures a high level of commitment and concern from all employees. As a result, the business tends to build long-term relationships with customers based on superior service and a willingness to be flexible and helpful. The newsletter helps communicate the business's uniqueness and serves as an active communication channel between the business and its customers.

Figure 15-7 shows a page from one of Collective Copies' newsletters. The newsletter was given away in the store and also sent to a mailing list of regular customers, so plenty of customers had a chance to learn all about the organization's planning retreat and to see a copy of their mission statement. See what I mean about how newsletters can communicate so much about your unique personality and character?

**Figure 15-7:** This newsletter page gives plenty of insight into Collective Copies' character and values, and also displays a nice use of wrapped text around the central box.

# Planning Retreat

During the final weekend in February, with our business still growing, our customers coming to us with ever more novel requests, and technology roaring on into the 21st century, Collective members closed-up shop and headed for the quiet of Delta Organic Farms (see the side-bar) to do some serious thinking about our business over the next five years. What can you look forward to? One of the first things to come out of our efforts is a mission statement. We found it useful to clarify what we're about when we set about visualizing where we're going.

5 Years ago, we set goals that seemed pretty ambitious at the time. We met them all. With that in mind, we once again set the bar high with plans ranging from an improved computer network to just short of world domination. Not all of what we'll be doing will be visible from the

other side of the counter, but some of the things that will be include: additional staff, new document-feeders in the self-serve area, wider desktop publishing and scanning capabilities, added equipment for things like booklet-making, a second fax machine, expanded oversize copying, on-line networking, pickup and delivery, mailing services, new carpeting in the customer area and a really cool web site.

We're looking to offer educational workshops and materials to help customers who do it themselves do it right, and to organizations wanting to know more about collectives and our business structure.

Behind the scenes, we'll be scheming away to find more space, restructure the space we have and make our space more enjoyable with a 25 disc CD player. We'll be interviewing prospective collective members and training ourselves on the many new technologies available to us. We'll be upgrading our computer system and organizing our donations procedure. Work on our website is nearing completion and we hope to have it up this Spring!

*How could I possibly overthrow the government when I can't even keep my dog down?*

*– Dorothy Parker*

## Mission Statement

We are committed to achieving success in business by...

**Serving our customers to the very best of our ability and resources.**
In the service of this goal, we apply our knowledge, creativity and experience to communicating effectively, foster an atmosphere of mutual trust, kindness and respect, and continually educate ourselves and our customers.

**Fostering a fun, safe, free, creative, trusting and respectful working environment.**
We commit ourselves to taking the time to celebrate one anothers' successes, console our losses and promote personal growth.

**Minimizing our environmental impact.**
To this end, we will continue to seek out alternative fiber papers, recycle, minimize our waste and our use of waste-producing materials and methods, and explore promising alternatives to such materials as they become viable..

**Contributing to our community and supporting local business.**
We return 10% of our profits to the community that sustains us. We resolve to implement ways beyond this by which we might be of help to the community. We will promote, frequent and assist area businesses how and whenever possible.

**We strive to empower all workers and to be a model/resource for positive and profitable worker-ownership.**
We create secure, empowering and financially rewarding jobs for our own workers, and strive to facilitate the creation of similar opportunities for all

## Delta Organic Farm

We held our retreat at this nearby farm Bed & Breakfast and Conference Center and want to express our thanks and appreciation to owners, Jim and Penny. Our stay was pleasant, the conference room comfortable and sunny. Coffee, tea and fresh fruit apeared throughout each day as if spirited there by elves. And the food! We opted for vegetarian fare and the meals, prepared in the Delta kitchen from their own organic produce, eggs and even maple syrup, were out of this world. We give Delta our enthusiastic recommendation. Delta Organic Farm Bed & Breakfast & Conference Center, E. Hadley Rd., Amherst, MA. 253-1893

On your CD, you can find two full newsletters from Collective Copies (filenames CD1501 and CD1502), which exemplify good home-done publishing — clean, appealing design; good use of headers and columns to break up the text into bite-sized chunks; and lots of interesting content, from practical how-to tips to information about new services and interesting stories. And note that the glossary and quick tips sections might contain some useful information for you as you prepare to design your own newsletter.

Also note that these newsletters include an Erratica column, which is made up of amusing quotes from famous people. This is an example of the same strategy I described and gave you Wisdom Ad templates for in Chapter 12. Good involvement devices from the world of advertising can often be done more easily and inexpensively in newsletters.

Good PR principles also apply. You can use your newsletter as a kind of ultimate press release, as does Verité, a human rights group that inspects factories in dozens of countries to ensure safe and fair labor conditions. Its newsletters are more sophisticated than most, and they look and read like fine magazines. The organization gets a great many compliments and thank-yous for its newsletter. In addition, this newsletter is a source of revenue and helps support the group's charitable work. Many individuals and organizations pay an annual subscription fee to receive this quarterly publication. That just goes to show that if you put enough care and valuable content into a newsletter, it can have a very high perceived value out there in the wide world of customers and prospects.

Figure 15-8 shows a cover of one of Verité's newsletters. Note that it features a striking photograph and a bold, distinctive, graphic design that combine to make it visually intriguing and very professional in appearance. The organization's name and logo are displayed on the masthead along with the newsletter's name (Monitor) set in a distinctive type style. And while the cover obviously does not contain any of the content of the newsletter itself, it certainly makes clear what the newsletter is about. The subtitle, "exploring the dynamics of the global assembly line," sums up the scope of subject matter. The photo and its caption ("Garment Workers on their way to work in Bangladesh") helps set the scene. And the "In this issue . . . " feature teases readers with a preview of the contents of this issue.

The back cover of the Verité Monitor (which you can view on your CD, filename CD1503) provides a much more detailed "In this issue . . . " listing of contents by page number. It also does what every good marketer should do: Asks for the business it wants! Its "sponsorship and subscription" box asks readers to subscribe at various levels, from a 25-dollar individual subscription all the way to a 150-dollar corporate subscription. And there is also an option for funding the newsletter at higher levels as a sponsor or donor. Because these options are presented, every issue yields new subscriptions and donations.

Verité

# MONITOR

EXPLORING THE DYNAMICS
OF THE GLOBAL ASSEMBLY LINE

Garment Workers on their way
to work in Bangladesh
© CHANDAN/Map 1999

**In this issue...**
- **Too Expensive to Work?**
- **Hot Spot: Northern Mexico**
- **The Anti Sweatshop Movement: A Call for Unity**

Fall 1999
Issue 3

**Figure 15-8:**
This newsletter from Verité, a well-known human rights group, presents a sophisticated, magazine-like appearance.

You'll also find the interior pages of the *Monitor* on display on your CD (filename CD1503) if you want to peruse this well-written, excellently designed newsletter. It is perhaps more ambitious than any you are likely to produce—the issue on display here has 28 pages including front and back covers! But it is designed and written by employees of the organization, demonstrating what is possible if you take your newsletter seriously. (And if you do generate a nice newsletter, remember to send it to your media list! Verité gets some coverage from the press each time it mails this newsletter.)

# A Newsletter Case Study

Ira Bryck is the director of the UMass Family Business Center, a nonprofit organization that businesses join in order to participate in educational events such as presentations and discussion groups. Under Ira's guidance, the majority of the organization's marketing budget goes into a well-written, informative newsletter that includes summaries of the many events his group puts on.

Figure 15-9 displays the front page of one of his newsletters, and much of it is displayed on your CD (filename CD1504).

## A first-person account

Because Ira Bryck of the UMass Family Business Center is such an experienced and enthusiastic newsletter publisher, I thought you'd appreciate his insights and experiences. Here are some comments he provided me when I asked him how he produces his newsletter and what it accomplishes for his organization:

> When I first started this program, Mass Mutual, one of my sponsors, interviewed seven directors of family business centers with more experience than me, and each said the newsletter was a total waste of time. But I looked at their newsletters, and they really lacked any real content and their articles on companies were really shallow and self-serving.

> So I decided to do a much better newsletter. A lot of the presenters whose three-hour talks are boiled down to a thousand words by a professional writer tell me these articles are the best pieces they've ever seen on their work, and they want to use them for their own marketing.

> When I was in retail (I had a children's-wear store), we would put a great deal of energy into our window displays, and they were the silent salesmen. They gave people the ability to see who we were and see if it was a fit. I use the newsletter the same way. It shares what we do and demonstrates that we have a wealth of information. I've basically decided to make my "window dressing" extremely helpful and not just a tease. I mail this to thousands and thousands of people who have never been to a forum, and a healthy percentage of them end up joining as a result.

**Figure 15-9:**
A highly
informative
newsletter
that attracts
many leads
for its
publisher.

## THE UMASS FAMILY BUSINESS CENTER
# RelatedMatters
### NEWS AND VIEWS FROM THE CONFERENCE ROOM AND THE DINING ROOM.

## The Greniers Learn How to Develop a Picture-Perfect Family Business

*By Jayne Pearl*

*Innovative Program Award*

THREE THINGS GO INTO taking a professional photograph: lighting, posing and capturing the right expression, insists Marc Grenier, director of photography at The Greniers, a Holyoke-based family photography business run by four Grenier brothers. But they learned the hard way that it takes more than that to run a photography business. Success also requires keeping professional and personal needs in focus at the same time.

In 1982, cofounder R. Robert Grenier suffered a sudden, major heart attack. He revealed to his eldest son, Larry, that he would not be

*l to r: Marc, Larry, Bob, Dan, Chris Grenier
(out photographing a wedding: Helene)*

*continued on page 6*

**Summer 1999**

I put my address sticker on the opposite side of the box requesting more information. That way I know which newsletter I'm getting back. A lot of times I'll see people have mailed back a newsletter that I addressed to someone else. So I know that it's often passed along, too.

The newsletter often helps me develop new customers. A couple years ago, I got a local business into a discussion, and I sent them some stuff in the mail. When I called them back, the guy was very negative. He said I was pestering him — which is a more negative reaction than I usually get. So I said, "I'm really sorry, I don't mean to pester you, but let me just send you the newsletter." Anyway, he read this newsletter quarterly for sixteen issues, each one full of information that would have cost him $2,200 to get as a member. I decided to call back and they said, 'You know, it's funny, we've all been reading your newsletter for three years and talking about it, and we were just thinking of calling you and asking to join.'

I also get people telling me that they agreed to take my free offer of the newsletter just to get me off the phone, but after reading it, they realized that what I'm doing is really great and they want to participate.

It's also a great giveaway at talks that I give at Chambers and Rotaries and business groups. It's a lot better than a pencil! I tell my audience, if you're interested in information about family businesses, just give me your business card and I'll send you the newsletter. And I've got many people who just came to Rotary to eat the lunch and ended up getting involved after reading a few issues.

## Thinking about costs

As long as I was interviewing Ira about his newsletter, I decided to quiz him on the costs involved. His approach (because he really wants to make sure that his articles are good) is to hire a professional writer at 50 cents a word, or about $500 per article. Each newsletter is made up of four of his articles, plus contributed pieces from interesting people Ira bumps into who aren't necessarily right to be speakers at his events, but who can contribute a good article. People usually give him articles for free, and his corporate sponsors also give him articles (which he accepts as long as they are educational and noncommercial).

The newsletter cost about 50 cents to make and 21 cents to send via bulk mail. He sends it out for free — no subscription cost. He also hires a graphic designer to lay out the newsletter, so that adds a few hundred dollars to his costs. He sends out about 4,000 issues, which he has offset printed.

Ira gets double duty out of his newsletter by posting all the content on his organization's Web site. He points out that this has really helped make the site a valuable and popular one: "My Web site was recently recognized by Yahoo! as the most comprehensive family business Web site, partly because I post all my newsletters on it."

# The Simplest Newsletters

All this talk of offset printing, expensive freelance writers, and bulk mailings may put some marketers off. If you don't want to put as much time and money into a newsletter as that approach requires, consider doing a simpler one that is printed on single or stapled 8½-x-11-inch sheets and distributed by hand.

That's what Alfredo's Photo Gallery does. With a retail storefront featuring a wide range of photographic artwork, a virtual gallery on the Web, and professional services from aerial photography to sports photography, this small business has a big message to communicate. How to make sure customers and prospects are aware of all it has to offer? A simple two-page, self-published monthly newsletter, printed on the gallery's color laser printer and designed using standard desktop publishing software, serves the purpose well and costs almost nothing. (Figure 15-10 shows the first page of this newsletter, and you can see all of it in more detail on your CD, filename CD1505.)

# On the CD

Check out the following items on the CD-ROM:

- ✔ Collective Copies newsletters (CD1501 and CD1502)
- ✔ Verité Newsletter (CD1503)
- ✔ The UMass Family Business Center newsletter (CD1504)
- ✔ Alfredo's Photo Gallery News (CD1505)

## Alfredo's
# Photo Gallery News
### October 1999

### Pioneer Valley Photographic Artists

The new organization of world class photographers now has a membership of 40 with diversified portfolios of various types of photography. Projects now underway are a year 2000 calendar, permanent exhibition space at the Arts Alive Gallery at the BayState Medical Center in Springfield, Mass.; an exhibit at Arts Unlimited in Chicopee, Mass.; a cooperative calendar effort with the Pioneer Valley Planning Commission; a professional video of the organization; and initial work toward setting up a web site. It appears that the mission of the organization is well on the way to being met!

### Photographic Artist of the Month

Greenhouse Ruin by PVPA Member Ken Kipen

This month's recognition goes to Ken Kipen. Ken specializes in black & white photography using, primarily, a medium format camera system. He does all of his own processing, printing, matting and framing enabling him to control the results to his high quality standards. His work centers on landscape, things of beauty, and interesting subjects such as the "Greenhouse Ruin" shown above. He has a unique capability of capturing composition and lighting to give excellent results. Ken resides in Ashfield, Mass. and samples of his work are regularly on display at Alfredo's.

### Alfredo's Sports Corner
## Former UMass Stars Receive National (International) Recognition

Former UMass Stars Brian Scurry and Marcus Camby have been in the limelight recently. Briana Scurry with her dramatic goal blocking giving the US Women's Soccer Team the World Cup Championship in an event internationally televised. This exciting event is being called one of the most significant of the past 50 years in sports and has catapulted women's sports to a new level. Marcus Camby's excellent play in the NBA Finals was also given special recognition. Larry Bird called Marcus the MVP of the semi-finals between the New York Knicks and the Indiana Pacers!

An Affectionate Hug, Briana Scurry, UMass Coach Jim Rudy

Game 5 NBA Finals, Marcus Camby, David Robinson

### Monthly Supplier Quality Recognition

This month's recognition goes to the US **Postal Service**! They simply have done an excellent job in sending glass framed photographs for Alfredo's around the country. They have been delivered on time with no damaged shipments--100% good quality and service. A special thanks goes to postal workers in Amherst and South Hadley for their help and care.

**Figure 15-10:** Alfredo's Gallery News is an engaging, self-published newsletter that communicates effectively at minimal cost.

# Part IV
# Web Marketing Techniques

The embarrassment of Laptop Static Cling

## In this part . . .

More of your prospects and customers are online today than yesterday. You can find plenty of marketing opportunities on the Web for any and all businesses, although, to be honest, most businesses need not be trying to create "virtual" versions of themselves that only exist in hyperspace. Nonetheless, they can gain a great deal by representing themselves well on the Web. In these three chapters, I cover the essentials of representing any business on the Web and using the Web to generate leads and sales. Whether your strategy involves an appealing Web site, the use of advertising on other sites, or the use of an electronic newsletter, you find plenty of ideas and hands-on techniques in this part to help you execute the strategy quickly and successfully.

# Chapter 16

# Marketing through Web Sites

- - - - - - - - - - - - - - - - - - - - - - - - - - - - - - - - - - -

## In This Chapter

▶ Determining your Web site's purpose

▶ Running through the basics of Web page design

▶ Hooking up with search engines

▶ Putting your Web site online

- - - - - - - - - - - - - - - - - - - - - - - - - - - - - - - - - - -

The World Wide Web is obviously the hottest new marketing medium, and most businesses are at least experimenting with it. Whether you decide to go whole hog and launch an e-commerce business or you just dabble in it, you need to be aware of its many valuable contributions to marketing. Here are a few of the options that are working well for many businesses:

- ✔ Create interactive, interesting, and/or informational *virtual brochures* on Web sites for customers and prospects to visit. Sites often generate good leads.

- ✔ Go fishing for prospects by sending e-mails or buying banner ads.

- ✔ Build relationships with prospects by creating e-mail newsletters.

- ✔ Create a *virtual store* or *virtual catalog* where people can go to examine your wares and place orders.

- ✔ Create a site that fulfills service needs of your customers — for example, by giving them up-to-date information about their orders.

# Understanding the Importance of a Well-Defined Objective

No matter how you choose to use your Web site, you must have a clear marketing objective. That way, you can see what each Web marketing option is supposed to do for you and why it might appeal to prospects.

That's the basic rule of Internet marketing: _Always design your Web marketing with a specific, well-defined, marketing objective in mind._ The Web is simply a tool that you can use to perform many tasks. But using that tool is not an end in itself. You'll never make money by picking up a hammer and banging things with it. Nor will you help your business by spending time or money "creating a presence" on the Web. Know what you're accomplishing. Know why the Web is a good way to accomplish it. Then, and only then, are you ready to learn how to take advantage of this complex tool's many possibilities.

In this chapter and the next, I cover several of the most important options — Web pages, e-newsletters, and banner ads. But remember, don't do any of them just because everyone's on the Web these days or just because your competitors are. Know what you want to accomplish. Then use these tools to pursue your goal. And keep track of how well your Web marketing achieves your goal. If it's not working, cut your losses or find a way to improve it.

The Web's no different from any other marketing medium. It has to _pay its way by generating new customers and/or retaining good customers_ at a reasonable profit. At least, it does for us mere mortals. If you're lucky enough to raise millions of dollars to start a speculative Internet company and take it public, then perhaps you can risk operating on the Web at a loss, like many virtual companies do these days. But if you want the Web to help your marketing program make sales and profits, you'd better establish reasonable goals and stick to them. And don't do anything or spend anything on the Web that doesn't have a reasonable likelihood of returning your investment right away.

# Designing a Web Site

Let's start by looking at a great example of a business Web site that accomplishes the goal of reaching out to customers to inform and persuade them. It's basically a heck of a good virtual brochure, aimed at the regional market served by a copy shop called Collective Copies. Figure 16-1 shows the opening page of this Web site, which at time of writing was located at www.collectivecopies.com.

This is a good first page because it

- ✔ Presents the business in a neat, highly professional manner with good, clean, clear design (especially important for anyone in their business!).

- ✔ Tells you quite a bit about who Collective Copies is (it's the first copy shop in the United States to win a Premier Print Award, it's a worker-owned collective, it's proud of its work, it has good prices, it's open late, it likes dogs, and so on). This opening page reflects quite a bit of the business's character.

**Figure 16-1:**
First page of
Collective
Copies
Web site.

> ✔ Gives you easy access to useful information about the company's ser-
> vices and prices. Every page has the same button for downloading the
> latest price list, and they all feature the same set of icons on the left
> giving access to pages detailing its services and a way to contact the
> company directly by e-mail.

As a retail shop (or actually, a chain of shops), Collective Copies looks to its
Web site primarily to support its stores by bringing in new customers and
helping to retain old customers and cross-sell them additional services. The
site is effectively designed to accomplish these goals.

## Determining whether your site measures up

Designing a good site takes time. Most large companies hire someone from
America's own newly created Brahmin class, the professional Web designer.
But you don't have to. Your local access provider can help you establish the
necessary account, register a site name, and get ready to put up your site.
Then all you have to do is design one or more pages; code your design in

HTML, the Web's own programming language (or let a Web design software package like Microsoft FrontPage code it for you); and send the pages as a file to your access provider by e-mail. Easy, right? Maybe.

Web sites are like most marketing communications in that you can hire a free-lancer or agency to do it for you, or you can do it yourself. But if you're willing to learn a few new skills, putting up your own Web site can be a rewarding venture indeed. Why? Because when you (or one of your staff) know how to create and update pages, you can make your site highly flexible. Changes are almost free when you have in-house capabilities. Your site can evolve with your business and permit you to experiment with many marketing strategies and promotions. Having the skills to manage your site ultimately enables you to alter your site as often as you need to.

So assume that you buy the argument that at least a minimum of competence makes sense for you, and you actually do want to learn how to design Web pages. In the next few pages, I give you a quick crash course to help you become a competent Web designer.

## Picking your priority

Your Web site can do lots of good things for you: Get you noticed. Make you look good. Bring you new prospects. Make more sales. But to do *anything* well, the site needs to be designed specifically *for that purpose*. So the first step in site design is to grab a pen and a napkin, sit yourself down in a comfortable coffee shop, jot down ideas for what you want your site to do, and then circle the one that you feel is most important. Here, to make sure that you got it, is the primary planning process for designing your site (or for redesigning sites that you want to improve):

1. Take a little time away from your busy routine to think about what you'd like a Web site to accomplish.

2. List some possible goals or objectives for your site — the more, the better.

3. Choose one objective that you think should be the most important.

If you have difficulty with this sophisticated planning technique, give me a call. I'll send you a napkin. You just have to supply the pen and coffee.

Prioritizing your objectives is the place to start because your life will be ever so much more pleasant if you select a single top-priority purpose for your site before you do any designing or hire anyone to help you with it. I made the mistake of skipping this step when I developed a site to support one of my books on employee motivation. I thought that having a site for readers to visit to get more details would be nice. And I thought that having a site for the media to use where I could post press releases and such would be good as well. Also, I thought that the site could attract organizational buyers of my workshops and presentations on motivation. And then there was the no-brainer idea that I could sell my book on the Web.

Well, the site went up, and I really liked all the neat stuff that it offered. And I found that others liked it, too. I got hundreds of visitors a day, sometimes even thousands, and lots of people told me that they liked the stuff on my site and were using it in their work. But I was frustrated that nobody ever bought my book from the site. The purchase rate was about 1 in 1,000. That's pretty poor! And yet buying the book was easy because the site had a direct link to Amazon.com, which could do the order fulfillment efficiently and cheaply.

So why didn't anybody buy my book? Because I'd failed to focus on selling the product when I designed the site. I didn't realize that selling the product was the best thing to do with the site, and that I'd really be happy with my investment in it only if I had a steady stream of sales to show for it. And because I hadn't made sales my priority, I hadn't designed the site to sell the book. I hadn't told the expert site designer who helped me with it to empha-size book sales. In fact, I realized that *the Web site never asked people to pur-chase the book* or gave them a simple, obvious way to do so! You had to noodle through multiple pages before stumbling upon the option. Few people even knew that the site sold the book.

When I belatedly prioritized my goals and put sales at the top of the list, it was obvious what to do. We added an icon on each page offering the book for sale. (See the "BUY IT!" button above the picture of the book on the Web page shown in Figure 16-2.) And when we added that purchase button to the site, surprise, surprise, the book suddenly began to sell. Nothing like knowing what you want, is there?

Notice that the Collective Copies site on your CD and in Figure 16-1 is very good at explaining what the company does. The first-page link in the row of buttons on the opening page says "Services," and when you click on that button, you get the "What we can do" page shown in Figure 16-3. This page gives a clear, organized list of the company's services, including many things that people may not know to expect, such as desktop publishing, scanning, and binding. The page also shows a photo of one of the pieces of equipment that permits Collective Copies to offer many of those services: a very expen-sive, top-of-the-line digital publishing system from Xerox.

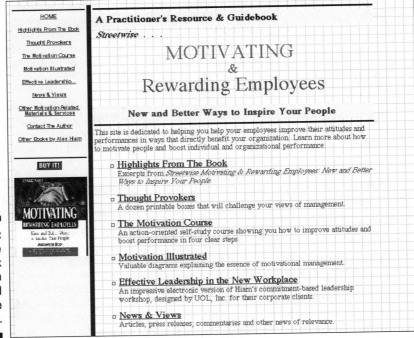

HOME

Highlights From The Book

Thought Provokers

The Motivation Course

Motivation Illustrated

Effective Leadership...

News & Views

Other Motivation-Related
Materials & Services

Contact The Author

Other Books by Alex Ham

BUY IT!

A Practitioner's Resource & Guidebook

*Streetwise . . .*

MOTIVATING
&
Rewarding Employees

New and Better Ways to Inspire Your People

This site is dedicated to helping you help your employees improve their attitudes and performances in ways that directly benefit your organization. Learn more about how to motivate people and boost individual and organizational performance:

□ **Highlights From The Book**
Excerpts from *Streetwise Motivating & Rewarding Employees: New and Better Ways to Inspire Your People.*

□ **Thought Provokers**
A dozen printable boxes that will challenge your views of management.

□ **The Motivation Course**
An action-oriented self-study course showing you how to improve attitudes and boost performance in four clear steps.

□ **Motivation Illustrated**
Valuable diagrams explaining the essence of motivational management.

□ **Effective Leadership in the New Workplace**
An impressive electronic version of Hiam's commitment-based leadership workshop, designed by UOL, Inc. for their corporate clients.

□ **News & Views**
Articles, press releases, commentaries and other news of relevance.

**Figure 16-2:** A Web Site for a book with an easy-to-find purchase option.

# *Naming the thing*

Now that you've figured out what you want your site to accomplish, you can pick and register a name for it. Check with your Internet service provider or any of a number of registration services that advertise on the Web for help in registering the name of your choice. And don't be disappointed if the first name you try is already taken. Just try a variant of it.

The best names meet two simple criteria:

✔ They are relevant to the site's purpose.

✔ They are easy to remember and spell.

So, for example, www.airtravel.com would be a great name for a site that brokers airplane tickets. It's relevant. It's easy. Nobody is likely to spell it wrong. People will tend to remember it because it's obvious and intuitive.

**Figure 16-3:**
A good
description
of services
on a Web
page.

If you're creating a site that supports your business, just use your business name or an obvious variant of it. That's obvious and intuitive, isn't it? For example, the Web address www.collectivecopies.com is a no-brainer for any customer who knows that the company is called Collective Copies. In fact, many people can find this site just by guessing its name. That's the first guess most people would type in if they wanted to find out whether that business has a Web site.

Note that some of the best-known sites don't have names that meet my two criteria of relevance and obviousness. Amazon.com doesn't relate to books, CDs, or toys. It sounds like something to do with travel in Brazil or preservation of rain forests. That's not really a problem for Amazon.com because it spent so much money on advertising and got so much press coverage that it taught us all to associate its name with its products. But you don't want to have to do that. Better to pick a name that is obvious and will cost far less to teach people about!

Oh, and one more thing: Avoid words that could be spelled more than one way. Often people give out Web addresses verbally, over the phone, in conversation, or on the radio in an interview or ad. You don't want to have to spell a name or explain that the user has to type an underline to separate two words.

For example, if you're a sail maker, you might choose the address `sail.com`. But this address is ambiguous because people might think that you were saying *sale* instead of *sail*. Better to lengthen it enough to make the name unambiguous. `Sailmakers.com` works better.

If you're marketing in a non-English-speaking country, consider creating more than one domain name — one in the local language and one in English. English seems to be emerging as the dominant language of the Web, at least for businesses. And your ISP can easily route visitors from more than one address to the same site.

## Planning your content

After you've defined your top priority for what you want your site to accomplish, you need to think about another key issue that is often overlooked. Before you even lay down the first line of code, think about what content you want your site to offer its visitors. People don't surf the Internet to read sales pitches and lengthy brag-a-logues about how great a company is. The number one reason people return to a site is content.

What information can your site give to prospective customers? There are three good strategies for answering this question. I recommend that you try them all.

### Ask the Web

Many top designers say that the best resource for getting ideas about what you'd like your site to say is the Internet itself. They often ask clients to spend a few hours surfing the Net and visiting the sites of businesses that are similar to their own. If you do this, keep a notepad handy and jot down things that catch your eye and things that turn you off. If your business has a lot of competitors, use the Internet to check out your competitors' sites, taking careful notes of what strategies they employ. Use this information to make your own site even better.

Other sites can provide good benchmarks for you as you develop your own content plans. You'll get good ideas for how to bundle and present content, and inspirations as to what sorts of information or other content might work on your site. Content development is a creative process, and the more input you get and the more options you look at, the more creative your content design will be.

### Ask your customers

When I used to do a lot of marketing consulting, I realized that the single most common piece of advice I gave clients was, "Go ask your customers." After all, it's the customers that matter. If they like a site, it's a success. If they don't, it's a failure. So ask them what sorts of reference information, help, downloadable files, or other things they might like to see on your site. And when you ask, try to give them as many options and starting points as possible so that you fuel their imagination and encourage detailed responses. For example, you may ask customers the following questions:

- ✔ Do they want to see detailed descriptions of your products?

- ✔ Do they want to be able to find previous product users or reviewers and get their perspectives?

- ✔ Do they want you to provide up-to-date information in a newsletter or e-magazine format?

- ✔ Do they wish there was someplace to go for step-by-step how-to advice?

- ✔ Would they like to use the site to get quick answers to questions and puzzles?

- ✔ Would they like your site to serve as a portal to other sites of specific types — are there sites or information sources they currently have trouble finding?

- ✔ Do they need to be able to track their orders on your site?

- ✔ Would they like to be able to access customer service or technical support via the site?

- ✔ Do they want to be able to make certain purchases on your site?

When you start asking detailed questions like these, your customers give you rich and useful input. Don't let them get away with simple "yes" or "no" answers. Probe by asking why until you get to the bottom of their thinking. Customers rarely know what they know, but when you go fishing with probing questions, you often learn interesting things that help you create a breakthrough site.

## Check your files

What information do you have that you can give away on your site? Most businesses have lots of raw content just gathering dust. Search your file cabinets and hard drives for how-to lists, old press releases, catalogs, brochures, and even old customer proposals or reports. You should be able to create lots of useful pages by editing these source materials.

How little information businesses really manage to communicate to their customers is a constant surprise to me. Most customers know very little about the companies they do business with. It's common, for instance, for buyers of one product to be unaware of all the other products a marketer sells. Many a cross-sell goes unsold for lack of this basic knowledge! Web sites are an easy, cheap way to work on this problem. Make sure that anyone visiting your site can learn all about your business — what it sells, to whom, why, and so forth. You have all this information at hand, but your customers probably don't.

## Organizing the content

The fourth step in Web page design is no more technical than the preceding three. (You still haven't had to code anything in HTML, have you? Maybe this is easier than it seems!) At this point, you have your priorities clear, and you've collected or specified a bunch of content that you'd like to put on the site. Now you're going to organize that content into piles and figure out what paths you want to offer visitors for moving between the piles.

I'm a literal-minded designer, so I actually lay out printouts of different chunks of content on the rug of my conference room as a way to rough out a Web page design. Real designers don't need to see it; they just imagine it and map it out in a flowchart. (By the way, *HTML 4 For Dummies,* 2nd Edition, by Ed Tittel and Stephen Nelson James [IDG Books Worldwide, Inc.] has good coverage on flowcharting Web sites.)

However you approach the design phase, the end result should be a rough flowchart of what you want your site to look like. Lay it out with lines from a box representing your opening page. Each line runs to another page. (Those lines can become links when you get to the next step.)

Ask yourself some simple questions as you do your layout:

- ✔ What will the customers see when they first log in?
- ✔ How easily will your visitors be able to contact you from each page?
- ✔ How far will they go before they get sick of burrowing into your site? (Four layers is usually quite enough!)

Remember that what separates the Internet from any other medium is the interactivity that the Web promotes. Use this interactivity to your best advantage. In Figure 16-4, you can see an example of a finished flowchart or site map. Note that it is designed to permit people to move about the site in their chosen patterns, thus maximizing the interactivity of the basic design.

The simple site flowcharted in Figure 16-4 has only two layers, but it still offers many opportunities for visitors. From the opening page, they may select one of four second-level pages. Each of these has a link back to the home page, and also links to all the other pages (as indicated by those little numbers in the boxes, which were used to avoid an absurdly complex spider-web of lines and arrows).

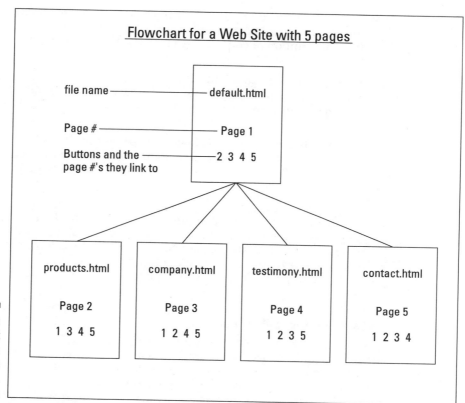

**Figure 16-4:**
Flowchart
for a Web
site with
five pages.

The simple flowchart in Figure 16-4 is a good starting point for any site plan. If you want to add more content to this design, you can add to either its width or its depth. In other words, you can add a fifth page at the second level. Or you can choose to create a third level below one or more of the second-level pages. If you add levels, you probably want to limit the links to pages within the same level. Otherwise, you give the visitor too many options on any single page, and the result may be confusing. As long as they can move around within each layer and can jump back to the opening page from any other page, they'll probably be content.

### Planning the pages of the flowchart

What might you do with the pages in the basic flowchart design in Figure 16-4? Here's one example of a set of specifications for each page in the flowchart:

✔ **Page 1:** This is the welcoming room of the site. The filename is default.html, and it's the first place the visitor sees. This might be a nice place to put a snappy logo and a well-thought-out company slogan. This page offers links to pages 2, 3, 4, and 5.

✔ **Page 2:** The second page may be devoted to the product line. Its content includes a few well-done photos of the product line accompanied by a brief description of your wares. This page links back to page 1 or onward to pages 3, 4, and 5.

✔ **Page 3:** This page could be a brief history of your company and any personal business philosophy that you may wish to describe through text or image. This page goes back to pages 1 and 2 and forward to pages 4 and 5.

✔ **Page 4:** The fourth page might contain some sort of testimonials from previous clients, articles written about your business, or some snappy sound bites. This page goes back to the first three pages and onward to page 5.

✔ **Page 5:** This page is where the contact information, price sheet, payment, and other pertinent information can be kept. Not only should this page have a direct link to your e-mail box, but it should eventually have some sort of automatic script which will allow the visitors to join a mailing list or order products. From this page, you can go to any of the preceding four pages. It's also a good place to put links to sites outside this site.

### Envisioning the look of your site

Flowcharting the site helps you develop a clear image of what you want the site to look and feel like. When you can visualize what you want your customers to see, you're ready to create it. If you're Web-savvy, you may be able to visualize your pages quite easily. But many people find this stage difficult. If you fall into this category, don't despair. Even the most Web-illiterate people can create good Web sites!

A sculptor decided that he'd like to have his work on the Web. He had recently gotten a computer after a decade-long hiatus from computers to find all the information he'd learned in college pretty out-of-date, but was eager to learn how to design and manage his own site. He went to an acquaintance named Josh Brown, who designs such sites professionally. Because Josh does some work for my business, too, I have his account of the sculptor's experiences. Here's how their conversation went:

**Sculptor:** Basically, a Web site is just text, pictures, and links to other pages, right?

**Web designer:** Basically. There's a bit more to it than that, but you can learn it as you go.

**Sculptor:** What's all this HTML I keep hearing about? I don't want to have to study a whole new language to get this done.

**Web designer:** It's the language that makes Web pages work. But don't worry; you can avoid having to learn too much of it.

The sculptor was not completely reassured but at least felt brave enough to proceed. He mapped out a simple concept for a site that operated pretty much like a walk through an art gallery. Each page held an image and description of one of his sculptures and led to the next page and sculpture. Now he has a Web site that presents his work to prospective collectors and dealers all around the world. Yes, he did learn a little about Web page design — at least enough to decide what content he wanted and how he wanted the flow to work on his site (see Figure 16-5).

Note that the site's structure is clean and simple, carrying viewers from image to image as if in a gallery. If you aren't into avant-garde sculpture, you may not go wild over sculptures made out of cigarette butts, beans, glass, and metal. But remember that some collectors may flip out over this work, *provided they learn of its existence.* Using the Web to create a virtual gallery in which viewers can stroll from one display to the next is clever, and this site's design is appropriate to its purpose of showing the work to the art world.

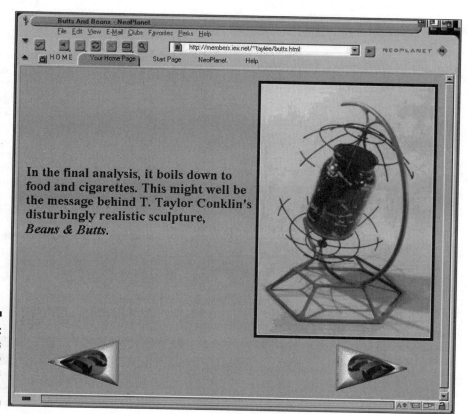

**Figure 16-5:** An artist's Web page features his work.

# Coding in HTML — or avoiding it

HTML code is the code that tells things where to be on your Web page. You can see the code to any page by going into the view column on your Web browser and clicking on SOURCE. All those strange words inside the <brackets> are code. Everything else? That's what the Web site visitor sees. The bracketed codes tell the computer *how* to display the rest of the content.

Back in the old days of the Internet, if you wanted a Web site, either you learned to write out the code by hand on a regular word processor (a laborious project) or you hired someone to do it for you. Now, thanks to the multitude of software packages that promise users codeless what-you-see-is-what-you-get (or WYSIWYG for short) Web design, anyone can design a Web site without having to attend night school. The idea is that you can do your designing of specific pages within one of these programs. (I recommend Microsoft's FrontPage for entry-level users, although you have plenty of other options, including free ones I cover later in this section.) The program inserts the right HTML codes to make your page look the way you select. You don't ever have to learn the codes.

Some of the simplest WYSIWYG programs are the browsers themselves. Netscape now comes automatically joined with a program called Composer that allows you to create your own page from scratch without lifting your hand off the mouse. If you're really feeling lazy, you can use Netscape to search out one of the many sites on the Web that offer templates, which are ready-made Web sites. You just add words and pictures.

To find templates, try these search engine keywords: **web page templates**. (Also useful: **HTML editors**, **free web publishing software**, and **web design software**.) Figure 16-6 shows you what sorts of goodies you can find by searching for **free web publishing software** in a search engine.

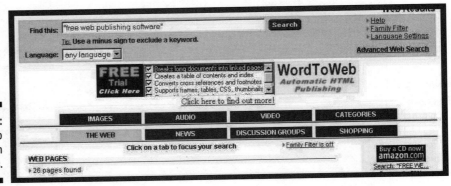

**Figure 16-6:** Finding Web design templates.

## Getting and using software

Tons of Web-site–spinning software is available on the Web itself, from basic (and free) shareware programs to more complicated programs offering bells and whistles such as frames, picture modification, and more advanced features of various use (or uselessness, according to some Web purists). Most of the larger programs cost money, but nearly all of them offer downloadable demo versions, good for anywhere for ten days to two months.

One that Web designer Josh Brown recommends is called Allaire's Homesite (30-day demo available through www.allaire.com at time of writing). Allaire's Homesite utilizes pull-down menus and tags as a graphical user interface, so you don't ever have to type any of the dreaded HTML code yourself. You can switch between a browser-style window and a text window by pressing the F12 key, letting you see what your page looks like before you save the file.

What you see in the text window is nothing like the actual page. It is simply a list of HTML codes telling the computer how to create the page. If you were a computer, you'd read that code and instantly create an image of a modern sculpture with descriptive text to the left of it.

And when you get into a template, go under the File menu to Edit Page. Then just put the cursor where you want and type away. You control things like placement, fonts, and style much in the way you would with any word processor. You can also add a photo with a few clicks (presuming that you have a digital file of your photo; if you don't know anything about that, talk to a photographer or take your prints or negatives to a Ritz Camera or other photography store because they now can digitize images for a small fee).

The following table shows some of the most popular commercial software packages designed to help you create and manage a Web page, and it also lists the address of the Web page describing each site (as of writing). I recommend that you visit these sites not only to see how each authoring program compares but also to see some pretty professional site designs.

| Program | Site |
|---|---|
| Microsoft FrontPage | www.microsoft.com/frontpage/ |
| HomeSite | www.allaire.com |
| Dreamweaver | www.macromedia.com |
| Adobe GoLive | www.adobe.com |

Programs such as these also help in debugging your site by identifying "orphan" pages that don't link properly to others. They also "weigh" the Web page, pictures and all, giving you an estimate of how many seconds it will take for other people to see your page on their computers. This estimate of load time is important because if your site takes too long to download, people will be less apt to visit you. Not more than once anyway.

## Measuring your load time

When people have to wait for a table, their interest in a restaurant declines. It's the same with a Web site. No matter how much cool information you give away or how many great products you sell at what incredible price, your site may not be appealing unless people can get into it in a hurry.

What's a hurry? One way to think about it is to compare your site's load time to the load times of some of the most popular e-commerce sites:

| Site | Average Load Time (Seconds) |
| --- | --- |
| Amazon.com | 2.6 |
| bn.com | 4.7 |
| Cdnow.com | 5.1 |
| jcpenney.com | 2.8 |
| Egghead.com | 5.7 |

I wonder if it's any coincidence that Amazon.com does a lot more business than competitor bn.com (the Barnes and Noble Web site) and happens to have a 45 percent shorter load time, too?

Anyway, you get the idea. If your load time isn't measured in a very small number of seconds, you are going to lose a lot of potential visitors. Those big, expensive sites are investing a lot in fast load times, and they're setting the pace for anyone who wishes to market on the Web.

## Refining your design

A good rule for designing sites is to keep it simple. Very simple. The Web is an immediate medium, meaning that people seek instant gratification on it. If they can't figure out what to do or don't find what they're looking for in a few seconds, they'll just click out of your site. So after you've got your basic design coded, review it to seek ways to make it simpler and more powerful. Make sure that it works for viewers in a hurry.

It has often been said that a picture is worth a thousand words. Nowhere is this statement more true than on the Internet. A site that is all text quickly becomes tedious to a visitor. On the other hand, a site that has too many images per page tends to be slower to download. Obviously, a site needs to strike a balance between images and text. Again, it all depends on what your business is and what you want your site to promote.

High-quality scanned photographs are fairly large files, so before you turn that great-looking photograph that you just scanned into a 1MG (100,000K) file onto your Web site, put it through a crash weight-reduction course. How? Again, the Web can provide software to help you. Try the search engine keywords **image optimization**. You're likely to find tools such as the one I found and captured in Figure 16-7.

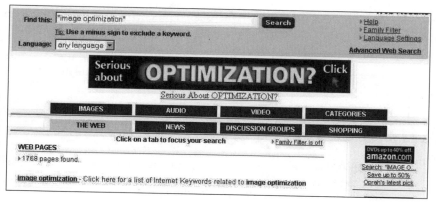

**Figure 16-7:** An image file optimization tool.

An *optimizer* is a piece of software that takes an image saved as a .jpg or a .gif file and "shrinks" it to a more Web-friendly size while still maintaining much of the original quality. Optimizing enables you to take images that are quite large and optimize them into more Web-friendly images while still maintaining good quality. How big is too big? It depends, really. How long do you want to wait for a picture to materialize when you're surfing a site? The slower your site's download time, the less repeat traffic you're likely to get.

In the case of the sculptor's Web site shown in Figure 16-5, the photographs were the focus of the site. Using a free image optimization program downloaded from the Internet, he was able to make each image around 30K, which kept wait time for each page to a minimum.

## Placing images on your site

It's hard to avoid playing around with photos if you need to show products, or even if you simply want to create an atmosphere for your site by using attractive stock photography. Sites benefit from the inclusion of art. But how to get your art into the right form for your site? Here are some tips:

- If you're scanning photographs, reduce file size by "cropping" the photo — that is, cutting out any unneeded background. Doing so shrinks both the file size and the physical size of the photo. (The Crop command is available under the Edit menu in graphic manipulation programs such as Adobe Photoshop, Paint Shop Pro, and many others.)

- Some Web surfers choose to set their browsers to "Do not display images." When building your own site, make sure that you include Alt tags in your photo tags. Doing so allows these browsers to display whatever words you've chosen in place of the nondisplaying image. Otherwise, they'll just see a blank space.

At this point, you can call the design phase over, at least for now. You'll certainly return to your Web design over and over, refining it, adding content, updating it, and so on. But with the steps you've walked through, you should have a decent site design that is basically ready to be uploaded to an Internet service provider. Now you have to get people to come and visit.

# Getting Seen by Search Engines

Congratulations. You can now design and publish your own site like a pro. You're ready to create your site, put it on the Web, and start answering the thousands of e-mails that are flooding in.

"Now I just wait for the world to beat a path to my site, right?"

Not quite yet, Internet citizen. By some estimates, more than 6 billion URLs are out there. (That's a Web page for every person on the planet, but who's counting?) The chance of having somebody "accidentally" stumble on your site is slim at best. You'll need to up the odds in a big way by getting your site noticed by search engines. This section shows you some tricks and tips to do just that.

The key to getting your site found by search engines lies in the meta-tags. Meta-tags are a few lines of information that few people will ever see, but these hidden codes can lead more than just a few people to your site. Meta-tags are like the air traffic controllers of the Internet — unseen, underappreciated, but totally vital to getting you where you need to go.

Just as an air traffic controller tells a pilot where to land the plane, meta-tags tell search engines how and where to list a site.

The HTML code divides a Web page into two basic parts, a <head> and a <body>. The body is what you want to tell the world, and the head is what you want to tell the search engines. Meta-tags go into the head section. Most WYSIWYG programs are able to walk you through making your meta-tags, but you may want to try making your own — it's pretty easy. Even if you use a program, it's better to understand the principle of the thing.

Assume for a moment that William Shakespeare is alive today and that his publishers have asked him to turn the play *Hamlet* into an interactive Web site to promote Denmark's castles and other historical sites. (Yes, the play's set in Denmark, in case you haven't been reading your copy of *Shakespeare For Dummies* recently.) The Bard could use meta-tags that look like this:

```
<head>
<TITLE> Hamlet, The Prince of Denmark. </TITLE>
<META name="Description" content="This is the interactive Web
        site where you can read the play Hamlet and be
        enticed to visit Denmark, a great place to spend
        your European holiday.">
<META name="Keywords" content="Hamlet, Denmark, Shakespeare,
        famous plays, plays about monarchs, tragedy,
        tragedies, to be or not to be, Copenhagen, travel
        in Denmark, European history, castles, gloomy
        monarchs, regicide, interactive drama, Danish Board
        of Tourism, lovely holidays, European holidays ">
</head>
```

Let's review the cyber-bard's work and, in doing so, study some valuable strategies for marketing your own site. Notice that the <head> contains three sections that I've covered so far. The first is <title>. Nearly every browser displays the title in a box above the page, so the title bar is a good place to reinforce the name of your site. Your title needs to describe your site in a few words. Many search engines catalog sites by using information from the title bar, so make yours count.

The meta-tag "description" explains the purpose of your site in plain English. The meta-tag "keywords" is just that: a list of keywords relevant to your site. Keywords must be separated by a comma, and many search engines will rank your site higher if your keywords are found within the first 200 words of your page's text. When deciding on your keywords, try to anticipate what words people who are interested in your site may enter into search engines.

A good way to learn about meta-tags is to get under the hood of another site's tags. Figure 16-8 shows the sculptor's Web site presented earlier in this chapter (it's on the Neoplanet browser), along with a notepad displaying the meta-tags through the Source command, located under the View menu.

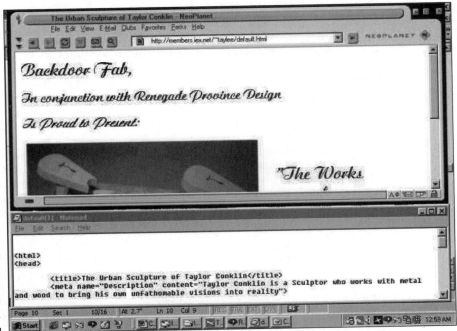

**Figure 16-8:**
Viewing the meta-tags on a site.

You may peek at a site's meta-tags and see something strange and different. In the past, some unscrupulous Web designers tried to stack the odds of being found in their favor simply by repeating the same keywords over and over, like this:

```
Discount, Discount, Discount, Discount, Discount,
Discount, Discount, Discount, Discount, Discount,
Discount, Discount, Discount, Discount, Discount,
Discount, Discount, Discount, Discount, Discount,
Discount, Discount, Discount, Discount . . .
```

However, as search engines become more intelligent, such engine-clogging tactics will fall by the wayside. Many search engines are limiting the number of meta-tag characters that they recognize and ignoring sites with "broken record" tags. So when designing your own meta-tags, be as honest and direct as possible. Or, as the Bard himself might say: "The meta-tag's the thing, wherein will catch the attention of the king."

# Uploading Your Site

You're now ready to upload your site to a server and wait for the traffic to roll by. Hundreds of services can host your site for you; GeoCities and Angelfire are two popular free ones. Such free site-hosting services usually attach some sort of advertisement to your site, either as a banner ad on top of your site or a separate pop-up window that appears whenever somebody surfs to your site. Although this exchange is fair, it may detract from your own site's message and attractiveness.

I recommend that you get your site hosted as part of a package deal with your Internet service provider, both for the preceding reason and to avoid having to put your visitors through the hassle of information superhighway traffic jams — free site-hosting services attract millions of Web sites, making the servers themselves more heavily trafficked (and thus slower). Free site hosts are cheap, but you get what you pay for.

If you use a local ISP to host your site, it will probably provide you with options such as the following:

- A local dialup line
- Three e-mail accounts
- Unlimited surfing time
- 5MB of Web-hosting space

One United States ISP is currently offering this package for $14.95 a month, to give you a general idea of the costs involved. Other, larger servers may cost three to four times as much but may also offer more options, space, or speed.

## Transferring files from your computer to an ISP

If you want to get more free help on the Internet, go to your favorite search engine and try these keywords: **FTP**, **WS_FTP**, **file transfer software**, and **Fetch**. You'll find helpful software and how-to information for use in transferring files to your Web site. Or if you're using a design program such as FrontPage, you'll find that it contains easy-to-use transfer routines. Then, if you get stuck and all else fails, you can try talking to someone at your ISP. To them, these things are routine.

I hope that you chose an Internet service provider with an easy-to-reach technical support person. This person should be able to walk you through the steps necessary to take your Web site from your computer and put it on the World Wide Web. An important question to ask is what filename to give the lead document of your Web site. The lead document is the first page of your site — imagine it as the "lobby" of your new Web presence. My server requires that the lead page to be called default.html.

Many WYSIWYG page design programs have an automatic publishing feature that uploads your site to the Net. Or you can use a separate transfer program downloaded from the Internet, such as WS_FTP, to transfer files from your computer to your server. Josh Brown recommends this program because he feels that it gives him more "fine point" control over his sites. WS_FTP is a neat little program because of its simple graphic interface. Opening the program gives you a control panel with a split-screen window. The files listed in the left window are on your computer. On the right are those of your server. All you need to do is to copy the documents and photos that make your Web page from left to right. Figure 16-9 shows what the screen looks like.

Here's how to do it:

1. **Log in to your server in the usual way.**

2. **Open your WS_FTP program.**

3. **Create your user profile.**

    Usually, this information is the same as whatever you use to log in and get your mail. (Check with your server.)

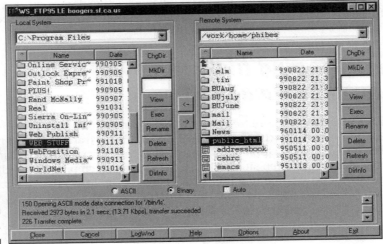

**Figure 16-9:**
Using a program to upload files to a site.

4. **Click on the Connect button.**

   If everything is working properly, you should be looking at your Internet account from the inside out — usually, a few folders that make up your account. These folders are where your information gets stored. You should see a folder in the right window called public_html.

5. **Open the public_html folder.**

   This is where all your Web files go.

6. **On the right hand of your screen, find the folder with all your Web files.**

   (If you didn't store all your Web files in one folder, you may want to go back and do so for simplicity.)

7. **Highlight the files, click on the arrow button, and watch as your files are magically transported to the server.**

You should now be able to open up your browser and surf to your site along with the rest of the world.

## Troubleshooting tips

Even the best Web designers find glitches in their sites. Common glitches include the following:

- ✔ Nonloading pictures
- ✔ "Page not found" errors

These glitches are usually easy to fix. For example, HTML is a case-sensitive language. If your Web page calls for an image called Picture.jpg and the file itself is called picture.jpg, the picture simply won't load. Avoid confusion by sticking to lowercase letters in your code and filenames.

If you get persistent, hard-to-track-down error messages, use one of the authoring programs discussed earlier in this chapter. Many of them have error-checking routines that identify improper HTML code.

Once you have your site set up, send the address to a few trusted friends or business associates and ask them to give your site the once-over. Remember that different browsers, computers, and monitors may alter your design. If these initial reviewers give it a thumbs-up, try it on a larger group that includes some friendly customers. If you still hear no problems or complaints, you're ready to start publicizing your site.

# Chapter 17

# More Web Marketing Strategies

*T*he previous chapter, where I review the principles and methods of good Web site design, brings you to the brink of Internet marketing success. For the majority of marketers, the Web site is the cornerstone of their Internet marketing program. But a site on its own does little good until it's publicized. You can't count on those meta-tags alone to do the work of bringing all the visitors you need. So in this chapter, you can look at a number of options for building traffic on your site.

This chapter also examines other options for Internet marketing, options that don't necessarily even require a site. But more on that later!

## Publicizing Your Site

The Internet is still in its infancy as a marketing medium. In many ways, this affords you, as a small business owner, a good degree of competitive edge against the bigger guys. They may have been around longer, but you can equalize that advantage on the Web. An Internet marketing campaign should be ongoing. In this chapter, we discuss ways to get your site publicized and, in doing so, create customers for your business.

One of the first things you need to do once your site is up and running is to make sure that you can be found through the major search engines. Search engines have their own programs that collect data from the meta-tags of the billions of Web pages on the Internet. Called *spiders,* these programs crawl the Web recording and cataloging information, so that when the searcher enters a query, the search engine can provide as many relevant links as possible. These programs crawl the Web 24/7, and in a perfect world you wouldn't even have to notify search engines about your site — the spider would find it and catalog it automatically. However, with millions of new pages being added every day, your chances of simply being discovered are only slightly greater than those of 100 computer-operating chimpanzees randomly writing your resume. The bottom line is this: If you want to attract traffic, you need to submit your site to the search engines.

There are basically two ways to let search engines know about your site. You can, if you like, go to each search engine itself and submit your newly created site's URL address to the sites themselves (see sidebar for list). This method is cheap, but it involves quite a bit of time-consuming data-entry, time that may better be spent in other pursuits (running your business, for instance). Many people prefer to use one of the many services that can submit your site to major search engines. How do they work?

One such service is called Add Me (www.addme.com). Add Me allows you to enter information into their own form — information such as your site address, description, and keywords (this should all be copied and pasted from your meta-tags). From there, Add Me automatically submits your site to the major search engines absolutely free. The catch? You need to put a small Add Me banner advertisement and link somewhere on your site.

Submit-It (www.submit-it.com/) is a paid service that offers a wider range of promotional services. For a fee, Submit-It not only submits your site to search engines on a monthly basis, but also promotes your site through banner advertisements, tracks visitors to your site, creates customer lists and helps you improve your site's ranking in the search engines.

# A Behavioral Approach to Web Design and Promotion

A Web site is just an address on a server with a bunch of stuff at it. It doesn't do a thing for your sales and marketing effort until you couple it with some appropriate human behavior.

People have to go to the site and do something there. What should they do? When? Why? Until you figure that out, and then make it clear to them, nobody will like your site and few will even visit it. So every Web site needs to be designed and promoted with human behaviors in mind.

# Designing a behavioral plan for your Web site

A *behavioral plan* is what I call the description of what you want people to do at your site. It starts with a clear picture of what should motivate them to visit. Then it describes what they'll do and what the site will do for them in return — the behavior and its benefit. Those elements are the basics of a good behavioral description of a Web site. To write it, you don't need to know HTML or any other programming language. Nor do you need to be a good graphic designer. You just have to think hard about people and what motivates them. Then design a site to support and reward the targeted behavior and create a communications campaign that lets people know what sort of behavior is appropriate to your site.

Table 17-1 shows an example of a behavioral plan, which I wrote to describe Encyclopaedia Britannica's Web site. The site is supposed to be supported by advertising revenue, so the goal of its developers was to create a site that lots of people would visit frequently. But why will they visit? Take a look at the behavioral plan in Table 17-1.

| Table 17-1 | Behavioral Plan for Visitors to Britannica.com |
|---|---|
| **Motivation:** | They have a question they can't answer |
| **Behavior:** | They go to site and search using keywords or topics, then study the extensive information available until they have satisfied their curiosity |
| **Rewards:** | They get their questions answered in great depth for free, and they get to feel like they are special because they are participating in a special behavior that is characteristic of highly successful, accomplished people's lives |

This behavioral plan is quite short and simple; yours can be, too — simple, clear, and above all, *likely*. When you sit down and describe a motive, resulting behavior, and reward for that behavior, each needs to look plausible. The plan should feel like something lots of people would want to do, over and over. If not, back to the drawing board.

On your CD, you can find a set of planning worksheets that walk you through the sometimes difficult task of identifying specific motives for visiting your site, then linking those motives to specific on-site behaviors and resulting rewards. I urge you to take a half hour or more to roll up your sleeves and really think through your site's behavioral plan. If you don't, you may miss many great opportunities to improve your site and to communicate its benefits to prospective users. See file CD1701.

The CD also contains a Site Communication Plan worksheet (CD1702), which flows naturally from the Behavioral Planning Worksheet activity. You'll find it far easier to design great marketing communications and bring appropriate traffic to your site if you use this tool, too. Figure 17-1 shows an example of how the two planning templates can be used to design marketing messages that link back directly to the need that you want your site to satisfy.

## Behavioral Web site promotion

After you've designed a site with a specific behavioral plan in mind, you're in a much better position than 99 percent of marketers to promote that site. Your behavioral plan gives you a clear idea of what to communicate to prospective visitors. You need to teach them to associate your site with the motivation and behavior it's designed to serve.

**Behavioral Planning Worksheet**

| **Motivation #1:** Need to find a rare book | |
|---|---|
| On-site **Behaviors** that flow from the Motivation. | **Rewards** for behaviors (what they get): |
| a. Search for book by title <br> b. _____ <br> c. _____ | Find and read book; receive discount on book; receive thank you note |

*flows into...*

**Communication Plan Worksheet**

| Ref | **Messages** (What to say?) | **Targets** (To whom?) | **Media** (How?) |
|---|---|---|---|
| 1a | When you can't find that special title you want anywhere else, search our site for it. It's here! | Regular book buyers. Heavy readers. Professors. | Ads in book review sections of magazines and newspapers. |

**Figure 17-1:** Planning for Web promotions.

For example, the Britannica.com site was launched with an advertising campaign that used print ads and TV spots that portray the behavior the site is designed to support. In each ad, a celebrity writer, musician, athlete, or other recognizable individual is shown posing a question and then visiting the site to find the answer. The ads are generally humorous because they put the celebrities in situations in which they are required to do something new and different. They are definitely in over their heads until they get help from Britannica.com.

This ad campaign to launch Encyclopaedia Britannica's Web site is focused clearly on a behavioral goal. It communicates the context and motive for visiting the site so that people know what to do with the site. Any Web marketer with a site can use the same strategy, even if they lack the 37 million dollars Britannica spent on advertising. For instance, a business wishing to attract only a specialized group of visitors to its site might use publicity and small ads in trade magazines, combined with e-mail and/or fax and mail announcements, to publicize the site.

It is entirely possible to get the word out about a site for a few thousand dollars if that's all you have in your budget. But to spend even that amount wisely enough to get a good return in Web traffic, you need to understand and communicate the behavioral plan for your site. When and why should people come? What will they do there? What are the benefits or rewards? When you communicate these three points clearly, then you attract the right people at the right time and build your site's value.

# Tracking Return Rate

Imagine you were offered your choice of two Web sites for your business, each guaranteed to bring in 100,000 visitors a month for the next three months. There is just one difference in their traffic patterns. The first site only brings in new visitors. Nobody revisits it. The second site brings in a mix of new and repeat traffic. Which would you rather have?

I agree. The repeat visitors are valuable. They not only indicate that your site is seen as valuable; they also give you the opportunity to build relationships with your visitors — relationships that you can no doubt find many ways to turn into profitable business. So the return rate is important to any Web site. Yet very few businesses track their site's return rate. Odd, isn't it? But the Web is still a novelty and marketing practices have not yet been perfected.

Chris Howard, the Webmaster at Webmasters Only, which bills itself as The Complete Resource Guide for Webmasters and Developers, advises people that, "Before you go and spend thousands of dollars and precious time promoting your Web site, be sure your current visitors are returning to your site. Otherwise, it's not even worth the hassle of promoting your site in the first place. Your site will never be successful if your visitors are coming once and leaving with no intention of ever returning again. If at least 30 percent of your daily traffic is from return visitors, then your site has an excellent return rate." (By the way, you can subscribe to his free newsletter, or check out other Webmaster-related resources and a Webmaster forum, at `www.webmastersonly.com`.)

Don't know how to track your return rates? If your ISP doesn't give you a good measure of rate of return, you can probably find a free service on the Web. For example, at time of writing, Stat Track (www.stattrack.com) offers the service for free. I recommend signing up for reporting services such as this so that you can get a clearer idea of who is visiting, how often, and what they are looking at when they visit your site. This is an important form of feedback that can help you identify strengths and weaknesses of your site and make it easy to test changes.

So how do you make sure that your return rate is higher than Howard's 30 percent threshold? He offers the following tips for boosting rate of return:

- Create a sense of community by encouraging interaction among visitors, for example, through the use of bulletin boards, discussion forums, and chat rooms (the latter only works well if you have high traffic).

- Stimulate interest through the use of contests for visitors. Pick something that is participatory (visitors submit something of their own), and give prizes or announce winners fairly frequently, for example, every Friday. Post submissions if possible to encourage people to spend time examining them. (For example, a florist may invite people to submit photos of flower arrangements, and pick the best arrangement every two weeks.)

- Provide new content regularly, for example, on a What's New section or page, or in a regularly updated News and Views section, guest columns, or a Headline News section summarizing the news in your industry.

- Use links to create lots of easy paths back to your site. Often people fail to return to a site because they simply don't recall it. But if they run into a link, and remember your site was great, then they will probably come back. How do you create links? Asking other people with Web sites is the general strategy. Usually they'll want a reciprocal agreement, which is fine. Also, Howard suggests that you "Create a 'link to us' page that contains linking images that other site owners can use to add on their pages. You'd be surprised at how many people will link to your site." And remember that on most search engines if you type **link:*yoursite*.com**, you'll be able to see which sites link to yours.

- To Howard's list I have to add the single most important factor driving return traffic: *content!* If your site has plenty of useful information, activities or other content for visitors, then they will find it valuable and return often. For example, on the site I created for my last book, StreetwiseMotivation.com, we emphasized giving away plenty of useful content. As a result, we get a high return rate. Many visitors come back over and over to find content of use to them in their work. And, probably because of the high content-driven return rates, we get quite a few inquiries from the site, some of which lead to book sales or even to larger sales of workshops and the like. So when in doubt, simply add more useful content to your site.

# Buying Banner Ads

You may have a great Web page, but how many people actually visit it? Depends on a lot of factors, of course, but one thing is for sure. You'll never get 55 million visitors in one week. Yet perhaps you'd like to put your marketing message in front of that many people.

Enter banner ads. That 55 million figure is the number of visitors to the ten most-visited Web properties in a recent week. I found the number in the Interactive section of *Advertising Age*, the weekly publication from Crain's that everybody who can afford it in the advertising field subscribes to. (Don't want to pay for a subscription? Much of their information is given away at their Web site, which as of writing is at adage.com. And see adage.com/dataplace for lots of statistics such as the one I quoted above.)

So let's just say I really wanted to put a message in front of more than 50 million people next week. One simple way to do it is to buy banner ads on a selection of frequently-visited sites, such as those Ad Age tracks in its top ten list. For instance, at time of writing I could get a crack at 23,765,783 weekly visitors by placing banner ads on America Online sites (they were ranked #1 in audience size). I could pick up as many as 21,569,775 more by advertising on Yahoo!, which ranked second. Or maybe I'd like to target a banner ad at, for instance, book readers. So how about the 3,801,695 people who visited Amazon.com last week? With enough banner ads on that site, I could certainly expect to get onto the monitors of more than a million people next week.

All I have to do is shell out some money and the audience is mine. Or is it? Depends on who actually *notices* the darn banner ads. Most are ignored.

## Maximizing the reach of banner ads

Yes, it's sad but true. Most banner ads are ignored. Nobody bothers to click on them, so they simply fail to reach most of the potential audience. This pattern means that the most important factor in designing a banner ad for your business is whether it will be noticed or not.

Or put it this way. Imagine that you go ahead and spend around 100,000 dollars to place some banner ads on some top Web properties. Now assume that those properties are reaching, say, 3 million people in the course of a week. Is that a good deal or not? Depends largely on the effective reach of those ads. Do they get any attention or not? Table 17-2 shows three possible scenarios, each one within the range of banner ad performance. Yet only one of them is really a good deal for the marketer.

| Table 17-2 | Banner Ad Cost Analysis | | |
|---|---|---|---|
| | Reach (%) | Number Reached | Cost/Exposure |
| Scenario 1 | 0.01 | 30,000 | $3.33 |
| Scenario 2 | 0.1 | 300,000 | $0.33 |
| Scenario 3 | 4.0 | 1,200,000 | $0.08 |

As the table demonstrates, it can cost a lot or a little to reach people with a banner ad. Usually, it costs way too much because most banner ads simply don't capture much attention. But some banners do far better than average. The best banner ads generally reach 2.5–5 percent of their audience (Actually, it's called *unique audience* on the Web to make it clear that you're talking about visits from different people, not just repeated click-throughs by the same person.) So if you want to make banner advertising work for you, you really need to make a study of those top-pulling banner ads and figure out how to make yours that appealing, too.

How do you find the best banners so you can figure out what works from them? Again, I suggest *Advertising Age* or its Web site, adage.com. Both profile the top banner ads on the Internet every week and recently have been showing the actual banner ads along with their reach statistics so you can see for yourself how they were designed.

And, even more important, how do you *design* a great banner ad that breaks through the 1 percent barrier and has a crack at 3–5 percent reach? If you examine enough high-performing banner ads, you begin to notice certain patterns. These patterns give you good indications of the elements your banner ought to have in order to achieve high reach:

- ✔ **Offer something clearly useful for free.** (Example: "Your Internet Connection Is Not Optimized. Download InternetBOOST '99 Now!" achieved a fabulous 5 percent reach.)

- ✔ **Offer a really nice prize or premium item.** (Example: "WIN FLOWERS for a year! FTD.COM" achieved an enviable 4.4 percent reach.)

- ✔ **Amuse and engage people.** (Example: "WHERE DOES HOMER SIMPSON WORK? _Bar _Bank _Nuclear Power Plant _Sewer" drew a healthy 4.5 percent reach for Uproar.)

✔ **Simplify a complex process.** (Example: "Find: A Loan for Me. [click for] Refinancing Second Mortgage Debt Consolidation" drew 4 percent of its unique audience for GetSmart with a banner that looked just like a tool bar.)

✔ **Give access to valuable information.** (Example: "The news that your doctor reads. The latest health news CLICK HERE WebMD" achieved a profitable 3.4 percent reach.)

✔ **Put an appealing site address in their faces.** (Example: "SURETRADE.COM" used nothing but huge block letters to expose people to its address, and it consistently pulled 3–4 percent for the site owners, Fleet Financial. The promise of stock trading on the Web was so obvious from the name alone that the designers figured people interested in e-trade options would check it out. They were right.)

✔ **Promote an upcoming event.** (Example: "Watch the latest BRITNEY SPEARS video!" rated a 2.7 percent reach.)

✔ **Keep it simple. Very simple.** (All these examples use clean, bold designs with few words and a single, obvious appeal. Make sure that you don't try to stuff too much into a banner ad, or it will break records for lowest reach instead of highest.)

Use one of these approaches, or perhaps an even better one if you can think of it, and you have a good chance at breakthrough performance.

## Finding out who sells banner ads

You can buy banner ads direct, by visiting popular sites and poking around or examining their site maps until you find the section that tells you all about how to advertise. Just like any property in any medium that takes paying ads, you can go directly to a Web site, and the company ought to have warm bodies eager to help you make a purchase. Alternatively, you can work through an ad agency, which may charge you more but hopefully can also make your banners more effective by selecting the right placements and designing catchier ads.

But don't be afraid to experiment with a minimal purchase on a few sites just to get your feet wet. Remember, the only way to get good at marketing in a new medium is to practice. Doing it on a small scale first means you can afford to learn from your mistakes!

## Exploring new frontiers in online advertising

Also consider using a specialized advertising broker, one of the newly emerging companies that places your banner ads for you for a small fee, often with added values such as:

- ✔ Finding sites that are rich in your targeted viewers

- ✔ Keeping track of who clicks on banner ads and what happens and providing summary reports

- ✔ Capturing information about people who click on the banners for use in other marketing efforts

- ✔ Helping you design and place good banners

I think *targeting* is the most exciting option offered by these specialized online agencies. Targeting means placing your banner ad where it's most likely to be seen by the people you want to see it and not by others you don't care about.

If you sell some kind of service to small businesses, then you want to expose small business owners to your banner ads. The ads are wasted on anyone else. Targeting can give your ad an audience that is richer in small business owners.

NetZero is one seller of banner ad space that helps advertisers target their advertising. Some of its targeting options include:

- ✔ Audience interests (sports, stocks, entertainment, home living, health, and so on)

- ✔ Demographics (gender, age, marital status, education, income, occupation, and so on)

- ✔ Geographics (state, city, zip code, phone in the U.S.)

NetZero also offers an aggressive option called the Ad Missile, which puts your banner ad on your competitor's Web sites. Guess marketing on the Web is getting down and dirty! (See www.netzero.com for details.)

Engage AudienceNet is another option for effective targeting. According to an Engage spokesperson, "Engage AudienceNet is the first profile-driven network" on the Web. What does that mean? Well, it means that you can choose to advertise to people, as opposed to on sites. The service follows those people you want around and makes sure that your banner ad pops up on whatever sites they do. Kind of Big Brotherish, but effective. As the Engage spokesperson further explained, "You can define your target audience with precision, purchase online media on the audiences you want to reach, and then reach them as they travel across sites and networks."

Engage AudienceNet's customers are using this capability to target audiences such as those profiled in Table 17-3.

| Table 17-3 | Sample Target Audience Profiles |
|---|---|
| *Audience Profile Category* | *Description* |
| Active and Athletic Adults | Active recreation is the antidote to their high-stress lives. They are adventurous and challenge is important to them. They are concerned with health and appearance. They enjoy activities such as hiking, climbing, mountain biking, wilderness travel, tennis, and running. |
| Business Professionals | Entrepreneurs who use the Web actively in running their businesses. Often use the Web to make purchases or obtain business and financial news. May be starting a new business or working on advancing their careers. |
| Online Shoppers and Browsers | They research and buy computers, software, gadgets, music, and books online. They search for discounts and browse for information on important and expensive purchases (cars, homes, vacations). They tend to respond well to online promotions. |

Target groups (or segments) such as these can be defined based simply on how they behave on the Web. And they can be targeted using the Engage service (at time of writing, information was easy to find at mediasales@engage.com).

The Web offers a brave new world for the advertising industry, and they are having a ball exploring it. I've just scratched the surface, and many new options will develop in the coming years as well. A recent conference (the annual Online Advertising event of the World Research Group in New York or at info@worldrg.com) featured sessions with titles like "Calculating the New Trends of Profitability and Mindshare in Digital Media Convergence for your Online Campaign" and "Evaluating Traffic-to-Site Advertising Strategies and Tactics for On- and Offline Media Placement." In other words, the Web has grown up to the point that the experts no longer speak our language (if they ever did). And there are lots of new frontiers to explore.

If you really want to immerse yourself in Web marketing options, go to one of these online advertising conferences. And don't be embarrassed to ask people to translate their advice into lay terms so you can see if there is any steak behind their sizzle!

# Electronic Newsletters

Electronic newsletters are an amazingly easy relationship-building tool. They take full advantage of the flexibility, cheapness, and reach of the Internet, but don't require sophisticated programming or technical knowledge. Basically, you can simply write some text, send it out by e-mail, and you are in the electronic newsletter business.

Contrast that to the time and costs associated with developing, designing, printing, and mailing a traditional newsletter, and you can see just how fun and easy the Internet can make marketing communications. A virtual, or electronic, newsletter can do everything a printed newsletter does and more. It can inform and impress your subscribers, whether they are current customers or a broader selection of people or businesses interested in your work. It can position you as the expert, encouraging people to come to you when they need help. And it can help build and maintain your business relationships in a natural, genuine way that the subscribers will feel grateful for (assuming you deliver good content!).

In addition, electronic newsletters tend to be a good vehicle for building or expanding your network. Because it's so inexpensive to communicate by e-mail, you will find it easy to pick up subscribers from far afield, including people who aren't on your in-house list and whom you wouldn't normally bump into in the non-Internet world. So electronic newsletters are a great outreach tool, a kind of goodwill ambassador that can go forth and spread good feelings about you and your business that you can often convert to sales later on.

## Building your subscription base

*Use personal relationships and word of mouth to grow subscriptions naturally.* Start with the e-mail addresses you already know, the people you already communicate with. Send them a copy of your first issue, and a brief explanation saying you've just launched a newsletter and want to let people know about it so that those who want to can add their names to the subscriber list. Also encourage them to forward your message to the people they know so as to spread the news about your new newsletter.

In theory, you can reach everyone on the Internet by networking just from the people you currently communicate with. Unless you ask for referrals, however, you'll never have a chance to put this theory into action.

*Publicize the newsletter to appropriate newsgroups and on your own Web site, if you have one.* Make sure that your offer of a free newsletter subscription is visible and professional-looking on the first page of your own site. And approach professional organizations in your field to see if they'd like to publicize the free newsletter on their sites too. They may well see it as a benefit to members.

*Convert people from other lists.* Many businesses have customer lists, mailing lists, membership lists, or other lists of people who might very well enjoy your electronic newsletter. You just need to let them know all about it.

How do you convert members or subscribers to a new electronic newsletter? You can, of course, send e-mails if you have their e-mail addresses. But often you don't. So another good way is to send a one-page fax or mailing (fax tends to have higher response) announcing the newsletter and inviting a faxed (or mailed) subscription form.

Create a simple, action-oriented message such as the one used by the American Society of Advertising Executives. It was a one-page fax with a big, bold headline reading, "Last chance! ASAE E-newsletters are coming! Are you ready?" It went on to tell members that if they received the fax, the organization did not have their e-mail address. And the fax described the planned newsletter and gave recipients three options for submitting their e-mail address. They could send in an e-mail, log on to the organization's site and fill out an online subscription form, or complete and fax back a brief form on the bottom third of the fax sheet.

As with all direct-response communications, response rate is higher when you give people several ways to respond. Different people find different response methods preferable, so choice makes it easy for all.

The bottom line of ASAE's faxed request for subscribers to its newsletter said, "Fax back to (phone number) by December 3, 1999." Why? Because, as with all direct response communications, the use of a deadline helps stimulate immediate action by creating a sense of urgency. When you send out communications to convert or enlist subscribers to your electronic newsletter, remember you need to take advantage of any events — such as the publication of your next issue or upcoming coverage of an important and timely topic — to create a feeling of urgency.

Otherwise, your prospective subscribers may say to themselves, "Well, that looks good, but I'm awfully busy right now. Maybe I'll get around to subscribing later." Or maybe not. The ASAE fax minimized this common response by presenting the transition to electronic newsletters as imminent.

## Reviewing a successful e-newsletter

Gary Vikesland of online business `employer-employee.com` does a monthly newsletter which he sends out as a text file or in e-mail. "People who come to the Web site can subscribe to the newsletter," he explains. "Also, they can go to www.listbot.com, a free service for people to use that they put their e-mail in, then they get generated an e-mail from there to confirm they are on the list. Then I get their names. Currently I have about 550 managers, HR people, and owners of companies on my mailing list, and it's been growing pretty fast — about 10 to 20 percent every month."

Gary's newsletter covers techniques for handling problems in the workplace, especially problems with your employees. And this makes sense because his Web-based business generates revenues by providing consultations via e-mail. He gets lots of managers, and also many employees, who are eager to pay him for advice on how to solve problems such as an employee who comes in late too often or a boss who seems to discriminate against you.

To see Gary's newsletter, check out the file CD1703 on your CD. And Figure 17-2 shows you what the first screen of it looks like. As you can see from the figure, it's really quite simple compared to most marketing communications — and certainly far simpler to create than a Web site!

Because of the simplicity of the e-newsletter medium, it's probably the quick-est and cheapest way to communicate with customers and prospects. Cheaper than sending them a letter, faxing, or renting a billboard. Nothing beats it for ease and efficiency. Gary estimates that he spends no more than three or four hours a month writing and sending his newsletter, yet it has been very effective at generating business and driving visitors to his site. (Because he uses listbot, Gary doesn't have to manage his own mailing list. That's the only part that can take up serious time and effort.)

**Figure 17-2:**
The first screen's worth of an electronic newsletter.

November's Workplace Tips from Employer-Employee.com

- Employee Motivation 101: The Basic Principles.

- Do You Work for a Company that is Conflict Prone?

- Telephone Consultation.

Employee Motivation 101: The Basic Principles

If I could give managers just one motivation tip, it would be simply not to rob their employees of motivation. A new employee usually arrives at work ready to perform duties with energy, meet new challenges with creativity, and cooperate with coworkers. A few years later that same employee is watching the clock, taking as many sick days as allowed, avoiding new challenges by sticking to routine, and disagreeing with coworkers. Does that scenario sound familiar to you? If it does, your company is probably robbing employees of their motivation.

The first principle of employee motivation is to set up your company's work environment without motivation robbing practices. How many

Because Gary is so familiar with his topic, the actual writing of the newsletter articles is not much of a chore. He explains his process and the results as follows:

"I generate monthly workplace tips and go to listbot and they have a nice setup where you transfer your information to their site and hit Send, and they send it out to the list for free. I used to do it more manually, but that got uncontrollable. Now it is done automatically, and I don't have to do anything with it. For instance, if someone moves and the e-mail bumps back, listbot takes them off automatically. And they collect demographics so you can get information about who is on your list."

# Employing the Lowly E-Mail Message

Perhaps the most powerful form of Web marketing is also the easiest by far: the simple e-mail. You can use e-mail to communicate with clients and prospects. In fact, like most marketers, you probably do by now. And most people in business at least have e-mail addresses, so this format is the most ubiquitous Web channel. Use it!

## Building your e-mail list

To begin with, make sure that you collect the e-mail addresses of your customers. Many companies with otherwise highly sophisticated databases have yet to integrate this information into them. I recommend adding a line for e-mail address to any form designed to be filled in by customers or salespeople. If you don't ask for the information, you can't find it. Also make sure that you ask for identities and e-mail addresses of visitors to your Web site.

And make it easy and rewarding for people to e-mail you, for example, by offering a free sample or some information or participation in a contest for those who e-mail in a request. Since you capture the originating address whenever you receive an e-mail, this can become a good source of e-mails for your database.

If you go to trade shows, you probably collect business cards. But do they have e-mail addresses? Perhaps not. Train yourself or the people who staff your booth to ask. Train your salespeople — or your distributors — to ask. If you have retail locations, design countertop sales promotions (a prize drawing, for example) in which people participate by filling in a form that requests their e-mail address. Also encourage people to sign up for sales promotions, events, meetings, and so forth by e-mail. Whatever you can do to build your e-mail communications with customers and prospects is worthwhile because e-mail is a free, easy, personal medium that's great for frequent one-to-one messages.

# Knowing when to use e-mail

Basically, e-mail makes it easy to be in frequent touch with customers and prospects. And because they can read (or delete) your messages on their own schedule, it's not as intrusive as a phone call. Yet it feels more immediate and intimate than a letter. As a result, you can use e-mail to maintain personal relationships with lots of customers. Anyone in sales or general marketing needs to *make a point of building up their volume of e-mail with customers and prospects.*

You can also use e-mail to make general announcements, for example to announce a new product or service, a new employee, a hot tip for customers, or the opening of a new facility. Figure 17-3 shows an example of a broadly distributed announcement inviting people to a new store opening. This store's managers decided that a good way to start a buzz about their new enterprise would be to send out a mass mailing, using various mailing lists that they'd compiled through additional business ventures they'd been involved in, old clients, and people who had requested to be on prior mailing lists. However, instead of sending out a mailing announcing their new site and shop (not a bad idea in itself, but not terribly exciting), they sent out the announcement you can read in to hundreds of friends and potential customers.

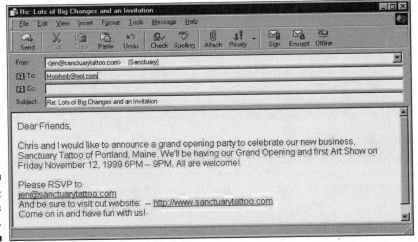

**Figure 17-3:**
A mass
e-mailing.

The message in Figure 17-3 includes directions to the store at the bottom of the letter, and repeats the store's Web site address again for good measure. And the company modified its Web site so that the lead page announced the grand opening party and repeated the general information (directions, and so on) included in the mailing. Response rate was close to 10 percent, and many of the attendees brought friends, some of whom became customers themselves. The e-mail also generated a lot of hits (visits to the store's site) in the days following the mailing, indicating that others on the mailing list at least took the time to visit the business's site.

But be careful to send such mass e-mailings only to people who know you and will appreciate your attention!

## Legitimate mass mailings versus spam

If you have an e-mail account, you get spam. Spam, in a nutshell, is unwanted, unasked-for e-mail, usually sent to you by someone you don't know. The more business you do on the Net, the more spam you get — it's just a fact of life on the Web. In general, people dislike getting unwanted e-mail advertisements, and if you use mass-mailed spam unwisely, your reputation can suffer. However, there are legitimate uses for mass mailings, and discovering how to use mass mailings is a critical part of marketing yourself on the Internet.

What's the difference between a legitimate mass mailing and spam? Spam comes from lists that the recipient never asked to be on. Often, when you put your e-mail address on a mailing list, the owner of that list will turn around and sell your address, along with thousands of others, to other businesses. If the recipient didn't ask to be on your list, then it's spam. Sending out announcements to friends, family, and associates is generally fine, but remember to put your e-mail addresses on the BCC line (blind carbon copy) and not the CC line (carbon copy). This practice prevents every recipient of your mailing list from getting the e-mail addresses of every other recipient, and may keep you from being accused of poor "Netiquette."

# On Your CD

- ✔ Behavioral Planning Worksheets (CD1701)
- ✔ Site Communication Plan worksheet (CD1702)
- ✔ Electronic Newsletter (CD1703)

# Chapter 18

# A Simple Web Site Template

## In This Chapter

▶ Editing HTML templates for a simple Web site

▶ Paying attention to good Web page design

▶ Following a plan for your Web site

*I*f you want to get up and running with a simple business Web site quickly and easily, you can use the template on your CD and the instructions in this chapter to do so. If you aren't interested in making a Web site right now, well, here's a chapter you can skip without doing any harm to your marketing program!

This chapter gets you through the job of creating the HTML files needed for a Web site. That's the hard part. But you have to do four other things to make it work: Find an Internet service provider (ISP), set up an account, register a domain name for your site, and arrange for the ISP to host the site. Doing so puts you on the World Wide Web with a place where people can go to see and read your files. After you have that place, all you have to do is upload the files that you create in this chapter.

I'm not going to tell you how to establish your site's address because any local ISP can do that for you. Most will even help you select and register a name. (By the way, there's no need to get fancy. I recommend using your own business name or a minor variation of it that makes it more unique.) Ask around, check the phone book, or surf the Web to locate an ISP. For a minor monthly fee, it can set you up with a basic account and provide a place for your files to reside.

Before getting to work on your site, copy the templates from the CD (CD1801 through CD1805) into one folder on your computer. Put any images you may be using in your site in the same folder — don't worry if you don't have all the images you want now.

# Creating Your HTML Files

The Web site templates on your CD are filled with text and art for a fictitious business that I call the One Stop Home Center of Peoria. Review the files for the five pages of this site to see how it combines text and visuals in simple ways to provide basic information about a business to prospective customers. There's nothing fancy about this site. But it is a professional, helpful, Web-based brochure about the business, and it certainly presents a positive image as well as draws customers to the business.

Of course, you will not be using the same text or visuals — just the underlying code. You will substitute your own company's name, text, and visuals. This chapter focuses on how you input your information to take advantage of the code in this template.

So far, I've described the site as a template. In truth, it's made up of five different files, each with its own set of HTML code, each a separate (but linked) template (see files CD1801 through CD1805). You are going to look at each one in turn as you adapt it to your needs. Take a good look at the first template, one.html.

## Using the one.html page template

Using this template, you should be able to build a site for your own small business with just a bit of alteration. When you're ready to make your site, do the following:

Open up the document called one.html in your browser. Open up the source file. This takes you into the code that makes the document. The first piece of information that you want to change is the title.

The result looks like this:

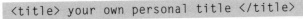

```
<title> your own personal title </title>
```

Note that you do not need to change anything inside the <brackets>. That's HTML code. Don't mess with it until you know what you're doing. Just change the plain text.

Keep in mind that this title is the first part of your page that anybody sees — many search engines also use the title when indexing your page. Use the title tag wisely; it's a small but important part of your marketing strategy.

The next two are the *meta-tags*. You may want to refer to the coverage of meta-tags in Chapter 16 if you need ideas on making the best use of meta-tags. If you're ready to go for it right now, simply replace everything after the tag `"content ="` with your own information.

The resulting tag looks like this:

```
<META name="Description" content="a short description of your
          site">
```

The last meta-tag is the keywords tag. Remove my keywords and put in as many of these words or phrases, separated by commas, as you feel are relevant to your site. The resulting tag looks like this:

```
<META name="Keywords" content="words, phrases, relevant to
          your site, separated by commas">
```

***Note:*** *Don't forget the final quotation mark!* The designer who created these templates for us forgot at first, and it caused the wood background to disappear. Finding this one omission took him three hours of frustrating searching, and boy was he unhappy. I had to avoid him until he cooled off. Also, please be sure to leave in the `</head>` tag.

Congratulations! You are now finished with the `<head>` portion of your site.

## How do you want it to look?

The next tag determines text color, link color, visited linked color, and of course the body background image. Mine looks like this:

```
<body background="wood.jpg" text="Blue" link="Green"
          vlink="Lime">
```

You can try alternative colors if you prefer. When choosing a background image, make sure that the image doesn't make your text unreadable. I think that the background I chose gives the site a nice, woodsy feel that's appropriate to a construction materials supplier. You can try something more appropriate to your business or just omit the background. You don't need to use a background image; if you don't choose to use one, your background color will be set at default white.

Also included in this tag are

- ✔ `<text=>` determines text color
- ✔ `<link=>` determines link color
- ✔ `<vlink=>` determines color of already visited links

If you're unsure of how to modify these tags, simply leave them unmodified. Better safe than sorry!

The next tag is <center>. This tag simply tells everything underneath it to be centered in the middle of the page. Leave this out and everything is pushed to the right.

The next tag inserts the image you see on the top of the page, and it looks like this:

```
<img src="logo.gif" border=0 alt="Logo">
```

<img src=> tells the browser what image should be inserted, usually a .jpg or a .gif. To insert your own image, simply replace my image name (logo.gif) with the filename of the image you want to use as your logo. If you don't want a logo gracing the top of your page, simply remove the tag entirely.

If you want to use some kind of logo to represent your business, this is a good place to put it. Scan your business's logo as you would any other image, or create one by using Paint Shop Pro, PhotoShop, or another image-creation program. (If you don't know what these instructions mean, go to a local copy shop with computer capabilities or a local graphic artist for help.)

The tag <alt=> is often neglected, which is a shame — this tag tells the browser to put whatever word you choose (in this case, *logo*) in place of the picture in the event that the viewer decides not to view images on his or her browser. (Some people choose to browse this way to save time. Without the alt tag, they see only a blank space.)

It's worth noting that the words in my logo were generated with the Paint program, and not through the HTML tags. Therefore, changing things such as font size, color, or style will not affect the logo.

Now look at some more tags in your template file:

```
<table>
<td>
<img src="barn.jpg" border=5 alt=""One Stop"" hspace=20
        vspace=5>
</td>
<td>
<font face="Bookman Old Style" color="Blue"><h2>Welcome to
        One Stop Home Center, your one stop shop for
        lumber & hardware.Our Hours are 8 - 7 Weekdays and
        9-3 on Saturday. Click on a button below to find
        out if we have what you need.
</h2></font></td>
</table>
```

The next tag is the `<table>` tag. Tables are the real workhorse of this site, keeping the pictures and text aligned with one another on each page and keeping the link table lined up (more on that in the next section, "Next, the links").

The `<table>` tag enables you to put images and text in columns, rows, or any combination thereof. Throughout this site, I use the `<table>` tag to put the picture on one side and the text on the other. Without this tag, the text will go above or below the image.

Now look inside the first `<td>` tag — there is no text in that tag, only an image called barn.jpg. You can replace it with another image of your choice.

The `<alt>` tag you've already seen, but the last two you haven't seen yet. The tags `<hspace=>` and `<vspace=>` determine the horizontal and vertical space surrounding the image. Use these tags if your images seem too crowded together. After you've inserted your image(s), you can play around with those two values until you find just the right effect.

Another component to be aware of inside this tag is `<border=>` — the number after the equals sign indicates how many pixels of black to put around the image. This is another "look" you can experiment with to get the effect you want.

The `</td>` comes next, telling the browser that nothing else goes in that box. If you write any text before this tag, it will go underneath the image. Instead, I put my text inside the next `<td>` tag.

The next tag is `<td>`, telling a browser that everything that follows goes into the next box, to the right of the image.

The following tag deals with the font. Remove this tag, and the fonts automatically revert to the default. By using this tag, I get blue words in a different font. Remove this tag and see how it looks — you may prefer it. It's just a matter of style.

The `<h2>` tag tells the browser how big to make the text. The numbers go from 1 to 5 — the larger the number, the smaller the text. After the `<h2>` tag comes the text that will appear next to the image.

Assuming that you've already replaced the template image with your own, you now need to do the same with the text. If you have more or less text than the template does, you can make it fit by experimenting with different text sizes.

```
</h2></font></td>
```

These three tags are just closing tags. You can ignore them, but please don't remove them.

## Next, the links

The link table is the last major component of your site, and the only one with links. It isn't as complicated as you may think, so take a look at it.

```
<table>
<table border="5" cellspacing="3" cellpadding="3"
     bgcolor="White">
<TR>
 <TD><A HREF="lumber.html"><h2>Lumber</font></A></TD>
 <TD><A HREF="tools.html"><h2>Tools</font></A></TD>
 <TD><A HREF="specials.html"><h2>Specials</font></A></TD>
 <TD><A HREF="location.html"><h2>Location</font></A></TD>
       <TD><A HREF="one.html"><h2>Home</font></A></TD>
</TR>
</table></TD>
```

I've created a small, easily reproduced table of dynamic links. This table is replicated exactly through the site. Changing the numeric values inside of the first tag, `table border="5" cellspacing="3" cellpadding="3"`, causes the text to get closer or farther apart — again, a matter of style with which you can experiment.

The tag `bgcolor="White"` assigns a background color only for this table. If I had left that tag out, the background of the table would revert to the default — in this case, the wood panel. Also a matter of style.

The purpose of this table is to enable visitors to navigate through your site, letting them go to any page from any page. Because this site has five pages, there are five dynamic links. In every page, one link doesn't seem to go anywhere. That's because it links to the same page.

The five HTML documents that make up the site are lumber.html, tools.html, specials.html, location.html, and one.html

(You can and probably should change the names as you create your own versions. Pick simple, descriptive names that will be easy for you to keep straight. I explain how to input the new file names in a moment.)

The tag `<A HREF="any.html">` is probably the most important HTML tag in any page because this tag creates links to other pages and Web sites. In the case of this site, all the links are internal — they don't lead anywhere outside the site itself. With only a few minor adjustments, these links could lead anywhere on the World Wide Web. Any text or image put between the `<A HREF="any.html">` and the `</A>` tags will be a link that leads to whatever HTML document is specified in the tag.

For example, if I wanted to create a link in my site to allow visitors to go directly to, say, CNN.com, I'd make a link that looks like this:

```
<A HREF=http://www.cnn.com>Click here to go to CNN </A>
```

That's all it takes to create a link. Your site can contain as many or as few links as you like.

# Design Considerations

What you want to do now is decide how many pages you want for your site and what you want on these pages. Take another look at the five pages that make up the "One Stop" site (files CD1801 through CD1805).

- The page "lumber" describes the store's lumber selection.
- The page "tools" describes the store's tool selection.
- The page "specials" describes the store's monthly sale items.
- The page "location" contains a map and some contact information.
- The page "one" is the introduction page.

Unless you're building a site for a lumber and hardware store, you probably want to change both the page titles and HTML document names to reflect your own business. To do this, do the following.

1. Change the name of the soon-to-be-created HTML document to which this link refers to something more suitable.

2. Change the link-activating text to reflect the page to which it is linked.

Repeat that process with all five documents referred to in the navigation table. If you want fewer pages on your site, delete a line (everything between <TD> and </TD>). For more pages, copy and paste a line, making the necessary changes.

A company that manufactures stereo speakers created a site using the same basic template. This is what the navigation table looked like for that site:

```
<table border="10" cellspacing="3" cellpadding="3"
          bgcolor="Black">
<TR>
 <TD><H3><A HREF="Sound.htm">Sound</A></TD>
 <TD><H3><A HREF="Simple.htm">Simplicity</A> </TD>
 <TD><H3><A HREF="set.html">Set Up</A></TD>
 <TD> <H3><A HREF="Genius.html">Genius</A></TD>
     <TD> <H3><A HREF="get.html">Get It!</A></TD>
     <TD> <H3><A HREF="home.html">Home</A></TD>
</TR>
</table></TD>
```

The only differences between this link table and the "One-Stop" table are cosmetic: slightly larger borders, different color backgrounds, and the fact that one has six links and the other five.

# Having a Game Plan

Whenever you build a Web site by using this template, first decide on the number of pages and their contents. Then make the first page (based on the one.html template, CD1801) and name the ones to follow.

If you take a quick look at the code behind the five HTML documents that make up our "One Stop" Web site (refer to files CD1801 through CD1805), you can see that they're pretty much the same. The major differences from page to page concern alignment. The template's designer has alternated sides, keeping the text in the left column on some pages, to the right on others for visual interest. This is pretty easy to do. Just remember that the <td> tags inside of the table tags read from left to right.

After you make your first page the way you like it, you can make any other pages from either the template or from scratch. If you use the templates on the CD, don't forget to change the names inside the <title> tags. Otherwise, your viewers will become confused.

Well, that's all there really is to using the template files on your CD to create your own Web site. Play around with them and then look at them. See what you think. Fiddle some more. If you want to get fancier, pick up some authoring software (see previous chapters), try *HTML 4 For Dummies* by Ed Tittel and Stephen Nelson James (IDG Books Worldwide, Inc.), or consider hiring a Web page designer to help. But the point of this chapter is that you don't really need to do anything fancy or difficult to get a basic virtual brochure up and running. Plan to spend a day or two and less than 50 dollars per month, and you can plug in your business.

# On the CD

- one.html (CD1801)
- lumber.html (CD1802)
- tools.html (CD1803)
- specials.html (CD1804)
- location.html (CD1805)

# Part V
# The Part of Tens

The 5th Wave       By Rich Tennant

"Get names!"

## In this part . . .

The heart of marketing is your creativity. Whatever you do, however you do it, just getting the technical side down is not enough. You need new and better ideas to succeed in marketing. It's that simple! So in this part I share some information, techniques, and ideas to help you take a more creative approach. First, I help you work on freeing up your own creativity and marketing imagination. And then I share a collection of neat ideas from other marketers that may serve as stimulants to your imagination.

# Chapter 19

# Ten Great Marketing Stories

*1* always like to look for inspiring marketing examples. A lot of people in a lot of organizations are trying to come up with good ways to market their products or services every day. So it stands to reason that some of them have pretty good ideas. And you can discover so much from other people's good ideas!

In this chapter, I review an assortment of neat marketing practices from the files of great marketing benchmarks that I maintain. (I should add that some of these stories come from Professor Charles D. Schewe, my coauthor on *The Portable MBA in Marketing,* who's a big believer in the value of marketing stories and has collected them for many years.)

## *Using Television Effectively*

The first example I want to show you is inspiring because it proves that you can use television — generally thought of as an expensive medium — for profitable local marketing. Have a look at file CD1901 on your CD. Designed by Balboni Associates and produced by Penfield Productions Ltd. (of Agawam, Massachusetts), the 30-second, black-and-white ad is for Haberman Insurance, a local agency. After you view it, come right back here for a brief discussion of its strongest points.

I bet you noticed how many ways they managed to get the Haberman name into that ad. It's everywhere — on the picket fence, on the seatbelt, and so forth. You actually find yourself looking for it out of curiosity to see where it may crop up next. This ad does a good job of achieving that most basic of marketing goals: creating name recognition. Awareness of your brand name is the foundation of all subsequent sales and marketing, yet many ads fail to emphasize the brand sufficiently. Not this one!

Also notice how clearly and strongly the ad focuses on creating a positive image to associate with that brand name. It ends with the line, "Look, you're trying to build a good life. Protect it with good insurance. Get it from good people" — a simple message, strongly communicated, with a clean, compelling look in black and white to evoke nostalgic recollections of life in the secure past for those parents whom the ad targets.

# Maximizing Returns by Focusing Your Marketing

This example represents a remarkably minimalist approach to marketing. But it works, so who can argue with success? I interviewed Molly Cantor, a successful potter who runs her own studio where she produces an assortment of attractive handmade mugs, plates, bowls, teapots, and so on. Unlike many small-scale studios, hers distributes product all over the United States. Stores in many states buy her work, and she's usually fully booked with orders as much as one year ahead.

How does she manage to be so effectively "on the map" as a supplier to upscale gift stores? She simply attends one trade show each year, where she rents a booth, shows her work, and collects orders. She recalls, "When I started, I applied to a show. That's the first thing I did, even before I had my own studio."

# Remembering What Your Customers Like

The gist of this great marketing idea is to keep a record of likes and dislikes in a customer's file or database entry. That way, you and your company can cater to each customer's preferences. Ritz-Carlton hotels, my inspiration for this idea, maintain a computerized database of past preferences so that returning guests receive customized service. For example, if you ordered a Kendall-Jackson Chardonnay from room service in one of their hotels last year, you may get a complimentary glass of the same wine the next time you check into any of their hotels around the world — a simple, inexpensive customer perk, but one that never fails to wow customers.

# Rewarding Large Purchasers

In a recent Christmas shopping season, retailer Toys R Us gave away a free Tickle Me Elmo doll to any customer who made a purchase of more than $100. Too many of the deals marketers use are not linked to size of purchase and thus tend to reward many small customers. But in most businesses, the fewer big customers are the most valuable. Why not target your promotions to them? Here's one way to think about it:

1. **Calculate your average purchase size.**

2. **Multiply it by 1.5.**

3. **Offer an incentive (discount, free product, special gift or reward, or extra service) to anyone who buys more than that amount.**

# Sending Interesting Mailings

Any mailing to customer or prospect lists will have a dramatically higher response rate if it's bulky — a box or envelope with something bumpy inside. People stop to wonder what's in bulky mailings. They open them. They give those odd mailings their attention, which gives you the opening you need to communicate with them.

Computer supplier CDW sent out a checked red-and-white pizza box that said "The right ingredients . . ." on the cover. When prospects opened it, they found out what those ingredients were in a list of the company's services and a copy of the latest catalog. They also found an amusing Velcro dart board in the shape of a pizza to hang on their wall. Yes, the game board was imprinted with CDW's logo and contact information.

Such three-dimensional mailings are rare because people assume that they cost too much. But ad agency Darby O'Brien finds that they usually cost far less than people think — and that they're cheaper on a per-response basis than a traditional mailing because of the higher response rates.

# Making It Easy for Customers to Access You

At Motorola, key customers receive pager numbers that link them to top executives at any hour of the day. Other companies use products such as the SoloCall SmartCenter, a box that can route customer calls to a choice of your beeper, your cell phone, your fax, an associate's phone, or your customer service center so that they're certain to reach someone on their first try, even if that person isn't you. The idea is to make sure that customers can get in touch immediately, whenever they feel the urge. No leaving phone messages. No busy signals or voice mail. No waiting, ever!

# Sharing the Customer's Pain

Service problems aren't very real for the average employee. They are the customer's problem, not the employee's. To bring service issues to life, try scheduling a weekly "Hour of Horror." Get everybody into the action if you can afford to call an all-employees meeting. Use the time to share reports of customer complaints, lost customers, and other service nightmares. Ask for suggestions about how to fix specific problems or avoid similar problems in the future.

# Letting Prospects Take You for a Test Drive

Do you think that your product is superior? Let prospects find out by offering them a free trial. Apple used this technique successfully with its "test drive a Macintosh" promotion, and it's a traditional technique among high-end rug dealers. They know that if prospects put a beautiful Oriental rug in their living room for just a few days, the odds of their buying it increase dramatically.

# Doing Something Outrageous Enough to Get Everyone Talking

One children's bookstore calls itself Wild Rumpus and lets roosters and cats roam loose through the aisles. Birds, lizards, and tarantulas peer out of cages, and a family of rats is housed beneath a glass floor. There's also a special purple children's entrance featuring a 4-foot-high doorway. Anyone who visits this store tells everyone else to go there, too.

With a little creativity, any business or salesperson can take advantage of the outrageousness strategy. One building materials distributor used to make sales calls with his favorite prop, a cinder block on an elaborate velvet cushion. He entered the prospect's office bearing his cinder block like the crown jewels of England. Placing it gingerly on the desk, he would launch into his sales pitch before the prospect had fully recovered from his amazement.

# Working for Your Customer

Companies that sell to other businesses seldom understand their customers as well as they should. Weyerhaeuser is an exception to this rule. It lends many of its employees to customer companies, where they work for a week as volunteers. They return with lots of insight and leave behind a reservoir of goodwill and friendship. And they often return with value-adding ideas to make customers happier.

# On the CD

Check out the following file on the CD-ROM:

- ✔ Ad for Haberman Insurance (CD1901)

# Chapter 20

# Ten Ways to Be a More Creative Marketer

• • • • • • • • • • • • • • • • • • • • • • • • • • • • • • • • • • • • • • • • • •

*1*'ve used the term *marketing imagination* throughout this marketing kit, and it's probably the most important factor in marketing success or failure. Your ability to imagine new approaches is vital to your success as a marketer. The salesperson who invents a new opener or comes up with a new strategy for generating leads is the one who sells the most. The distributor who finds creative new ways to serve customers over the Web gains on its competition. The small business that seeks new ways to promote its products or services makes a bigger impact at lower cost. And the advertiser who creates an imaginative message captures consumer attention and makes more sales.

In contrast, any marketer who fails to be creative, who tries to just use last year's formula or borrow directly from others, is destined for failure. Marketing demands more creativity than any other business activity. So it only seems fair for me to help you be more creative in your approach to marketing. In this chapter, I give you ten techniques to help you engage your creative imagination and come up with breakthrough sales and marketing ideas.

These creativity methods are drawn from my work in corporate training. My firm puts on a number of creativity trainings and sometimes facilitates creative problem-solving retreats. In addition, it develops and publishes a variety of resources for trainers and managers in the area of creativity. So it seems appropriate to share the best of these many resources with you. I don't want you to feel "stuck" and unable to come up with fresh ideas. If you ever get to that point (most people do fairly often), dip into this chapter and re-ignite that marketing imagination!

# Revel in the Irreverent

Seek out and enjoy unconventional and crazy approaches. Any examples of how people can flaunt the rules of convention are inspirational. Even if they have nothing to do with marketing, irreverent attitudes can inspire your marketing imagination.

When I get stuck on a marketing communication and can't seem to come up with a fresh idea, I like to put the movie *Crazy People* on my VCR and watch a few scenes. It's a comedy about an advertising copywriter who goes over the edge and gets sent to a mental hospital, where he and his fellow patients create such crazy and wonderful ads that his agency ends up begging them for more. It's silly and makes me laugh. And after 15 minutes of that silliness, my mind is much freer so I'm able to think more creatively about my own advertisements or other marketing communications.

I recommend any comedy, whether it has something to do with business or not. Humor is based on unusual viewpoints, and it helps you loosen up and find your own creative perspectives.

I also recommend keeping an eye out for "crackpots" and others who do things strangely on the fringes of your industry. For every successful business there are a dozen marginal ones who operate outside the normal rules and rarely amount to anything. But sometimes they have the weirdest ideas, and when those weird ideas are combined with a sound understanding of how the industry works, they might just lead to breakthrough insights. So don't forget to pay attention to the crazy people in your own industry. Sometimes they are better at inspiring your marketing imagination than more successful but conventional role models.

# Force Yourself to Develop Alternatives

This is the essence of creativity — the quest for new and better alternatives. The marketing imagination is never content. It always seeks new approaches. I remember one two-day product development session I helped facilitate for Kellogg's, the breakfast cereal company. They hoped to come up with one good new product as a result of the session. But which would the winning idea be? Hard to know. Best make sure there are plenty of alternatives. So we generated more than 900 new product concepts in our retreat.

Was it hard to come up with that many good ideas? Yes and no. The first five were pretty easy but, in hindsight, not worth a second look. The next 20 were much harder, but there were hints of inspiration in that list. But nothing to write home about. We had to keep going.

Once we got past the first hundred, we were on a roll and could have kept inventing new concepts forever if we'd had the time. In the long run, the few new product concepts that made it out to test market were in the high hundreds — we'd already come up with hundreds before them. That means we may not have come up with *any* useable concepts unless we'd been as persistent as we were.

Perhaps it also means we could have come up with even *better* ideas if we'd developed twice as many. . . .

# Don't Overplan

Most experts tell you to write a careful plan. Marketing plans and business plans in general can help you anticipate the future and make sure that you're ready for it. But they can also destroy creativity. Plans hurt creativity in two main ways:

- If you have to write everything down up front, you won't have the opportunity to come up with creative approaches later on. The weight of the planning exercise deadens creativity. To decide all the year's marketing activities in just one week of planning is pretty hard. It's certainly not fun. People who have to do that are not going to spend much time being creative. They're going to approach marketing in a mechanical way, looking up costs and writing things down one after the other until they've fulfilled their obligation.

- If you have to follow a detailed plan, then the plan does the thinking for you and you miss the opportunity to learn, experiment, and invent as you go. Rigid plans and microplanning that structures every decision and action are the enemies of creativity. They keep people from reacting and creating.

To make planning creative, leave room in your plan for improvisation. Sure, you face budget limits and you need to follow broad strategies that you expect to work. But also leave room for modifying the plan. I like to revisit my plans every month or two, and if I get a better idea, I simply rewrite my plan around it. It's only paper. Throw it out if it's getting in your way and write a new plan!

Also, make sure that your plans are not too detailed. For example, it's one thing to specify in a plan that you'll budget so much for publicity, most of which should be focused on generating press about your business activities. That's fine — it leaves plenty of room to invent clever ways of getting publicity. But it's quite another to plan exactly how that publicity budget should be spent. If you specify one press release a month to the in-house press list of 250 names, you've just guaranteed that nothing imaginative will happen all year. Don't overplan!

# Identify Your Personal Barriers and Enablers

A creativity barrier is anything that gets in the way of your creativity. And there are plenty of things that do just that. Being more aware of them helps you learn to avoid your barriers or minimize their impact. Here are some of the most common barriers:

- ✔ **Pressure to conform:** Thinking and behaving differently from others is taboo in many organizations and industries. This approach means that people are more conservative than they need to be.

- ✔ **Perfectionism:** If you worry too much about how well you perform, you'll be afraid to try anything really new. Sometimes I remind myself that when it comes to creative innovations, "If it's worth doing, it's worth doing poorly!"

- ✔ **Overconfidence:** It's easy to assume that you are doing the right thing without stopping to question yourself. Overconfidence keeps you from examining your assumptions or developing and considering alternatives.

When you know you're affected by a creativity barrier such as one of these, you can guard against it. Awareness is the key.

Creativity enablers are factors that help us be more creative. They work in the opposite direction of barriers, helping us overcome barriers and leading us to creative insights. Here are some of the more common enablers:

- ✔ **Open-mindedness:** An open, accepting approach to other ideas and methods is a great enabler. If you're open-minded, you often receive inspiration from others that you may otherwise miss.

- ✔ **Role models:** Creative innovators are great enablers. Try to find and spend time with such people. They'll get your creative motor running in no time!

- ✔ **Persistence:** Perhaps the most powerful enabler of all, persistence keeps you trying even when your initial efforts at creativity fail. Often the only major difference between highly creative people and those who aren't creative is that the creative people don't give up as quickly. Do you?

A lot of creativity trainings use this barriers/enablers model to help people identify factors they need to focus on in order to boost their personal creativity.

# Incubate!

*Incubation* is just what the term suggests. You sit on a problem or idea, keeping it warm, until it hatches a solution. But first, you have to lay that egg. In other words, start by focusing hard and furiously on the subject of concern. Research it thoroughly, bang your head against it over and over, all week long. Wear yourself out. Then relax. Time to sit on the egg you've just laid. Take a little time off. Or work on something else. Just stop to have a quick look at the problem or to turn it over in your mind every now and then.

After you've let it incubate for a while, you may begin to hear from it. It will start to call your attention back to it, as new ideas and approaches come to mind. Then, and only then, is it ready to be hatched. When you revisit it and give it your undivided attention again, you may find that you've got more and better ideas than before.

Because incubation works so well, try to schedule your marketing development efforts to permit incubation. For example, rather than plan to spend three consecutive days writing a new brochure, why not schedule two days to study it and begin work on it, followed by three days off the project, and then one final day to complete your work? The result will be more imaginative and better because of the incubation period, yet it won't really have required any more of your work time.

# Break It Down

I call this "breakdown brainstorming" in my book, *The Manager's Pocket Guide to Creativity,* and I've used it to good effect on many difficult tasks. The idea is to put some creative effort into thinking about the task itself instead of moving directly to solutions.

For instance, say you're working on a Web page and you want to do something creative and special. But what? You're stuck. So break down the task into as many subproblems or subtasks as you can imagine. Your list may include issues such as "attract people to our site," "make our site more entertaining," "create an opening page for the site that really wows people," and "find a game people can play on our site." Now you've broken the broad problem of designing a creative site into many smaller problems, some of which may fire your imagination more easily than the original problem could.

# Compete

The idea behind this strategy is that when you have two or more individuals or groups working on the same creative task in parallel, you're more likely to come up with a creative breakthrough. So why not create a contest for yourself and a few other associates or friends? Pick a good reward — sometimes a joke reward is best. Give each person or group the same amount of time and the same starting information. Then compete to see who comes up with the best ideas!

# Record More of Your Own Ideas

You often have ideas that you discard or forget. If you get in the habit of recording more of your ideas, you may find that some of them are more valuable than you thought. Also, the marketing imagination becomes more active when it gets attention. By simply making notes or recordings of your ideas, you stimulate their production and soon generate many more.

I record ideas in several ways. I keep a large daily planning book, with room in it to write down not only my appointments but also my ideas. Then I flip back through the pages when I'm stuck and pick out a good idea to follow through on. I also keep idea boxes where I can toss my own notes or interesting articles I clip out that stimulate my thinking. I have an idea box for each of my major projects. In addition, I keep a miniature tape recorder in my briefcase and often dictate ideas into it. Then I get the tapes transcribed so that I can read them later.

You need to come up with your own system for recording ideas. Whatever works best for you is the right one, so try several.

# Look Hard at Your Assumptions

Many smaller businesses assume that television advertising is too expensive for them. That's a silly assumption. You can buy local television advertising very cheaply in most markets, and there are even relatively inexpensive national cable ad slots. I'm not saying that everyone ought to be advertising on television. But some businesses could and don't realize it because of their assumptions.

All marketers make assumptions and, in general, most of them are questionable. It's common to assume that your business is not newsworthy, for example, and therefore never to explore the potential of publicity. And many people assume that they can't manage word-of-mouth, and so do nothing to try to build referrals. Watch out for such assumptions! They keep you from considering many creative alternatives.

# Talk to Ten Successful People

I recently ran into a friend who's an artist. She complained that she felt it was necessary to reach a broader market with her work but didn't know how to do it. She asked me if any of my books held the solution. I hate to pass up a chance to make a sale, but I had to tell her no. The specific solution to marketing her work is not found in *any* book. It has to come from her. It has to be something unique and creative. So where can she find the ideas she needs?

I suggested that she contact ten other artists and ask them how they market their work. Each one probably has a slightly different approach. By listening to each of their stories, she may begin to see more possibilities than she does right now.

It's a wonderful discipline to go out and interview ten people and ask them how they do their sales and marketing. Put on your journalist's hat, take along a pad and pencil, and collect information about how other people do it. You're sure to come across something new and different that gives you a good idea for your own business.

# Appendix

# About the CD

• • • • • • • • • • • • • • • • • • • • • • • • • • • • • • • • • • • • • • • • •

*H*ere's some of what you can find on the *Marketing Kit For Dummies* CD-ROM:

- ✔ Dozens of sample newsletters, ads, brochures, and other marketing materials.
- ✔ Templates that you can use to create your own marketing materials.
- ✔ Adobe Acrobat Reader for Mac and Windows, a freeware version that allows you to read the PDF documents on this CD.

## System Requirements

Make sure your computer meets the minimum system requirements listed below. If your computer doesn't match up to most of these requirements, you may have problems in using the contents of the CD.

- ✔ A PC with a 486 or faster processor, or a Mac OS computer with a 68040 or faster processor.
- ✔ Microsoft Windows 95 or later, or Mac OS system software 7.55 or later.
- ✔ At least 16MB of total RAM installed on your computer. For best performance, we recommend at least 32MB of RAM installed.
- ✔ At least 50MB of hard drive space available to install all the software from this CD. (You'll need less space if you don't install every program.)
- ✔ A CD-ROM drive — double-speed (2x) or faster.
- ✔ A sound card for PCs. (Mac OS computers have built-in sound support.)
- ✔ A monitor capable of displaying at least 256 colors or grayscale.
- ✔ A modem with a speed of at least 14,400 bps.

If you need more information on the basics, check out *PCs For Dummies,* 7th Edition, by Dan Gookin; *Macs For Dummies,* 6th Edition, by David Pogue; *iMac For Dummies,* by David Pogue; *Windows 95 For Dummies,* 2nd Edition, or *Windows 98 For Dummies,* both by Andy Rathbone (all published by IDG Books Worldwide, Inc.).

# Using the CD with Microsoft Windows

1. **Insert the CD into your computer's CD-ROM drive.**

   Give your computer a moment to take a look at the CD.

2. **Open your browser.** If you do not have a browser, we have included Microsoft Internet Explorer on this CD.

   Select File⇨Open (Internet Explorer) or File⇨Open Page (Netscape).

3. **Double-click the file called License.txt.**

   This file contains the end-user license that you agree to by using the CD. When you are done reading the license, close the program, most likely NotePad, that displayed the file.

4. **Double-click the file called Readme.txt.**

   This file contains instructions about installing the software from this CD. It might be helpful to leave this text file open while you are using the CD.

5. **In the dialog box that appears, type D:\START.HTM and click on OK.**

6. **Replace the letter D: with the correct letter for your CD-ROM drive, if it is not "D."**

   This action will display the file that will walk you through the content of the CD.

7. **To navigate within the interface, simply click on any topic of interest to take you to an explanation of the files on the CD and how to use or install them.**

8. **To install the software from the CD, simply click on the software name.**

   You'll see two options — the option to run or open the file from the current location or the option to save the file to your hard drive. Choose to run or open the file from its current location and the installation procedure will continue. After you are done with the interface, simply close your browser as usual.

To run some of the programs, you may need to keep the CD inside your CD-ROM drive. This is a Good Thing. Otherwise, the installed program would have required you to install a very large chunk of the program to your hard drive space, which would have kept you from installing other software.

# Using the CD with Mac OS

To install the items from the CD to your hard drive, follow these steps.

1. **Insert the CD into your computer's CD-ROM drive.**

   In a moment, an icon representing the CD you just inserted appears on your Mac desktop. Chances are, the icon looks like a CD-ROM.

2. **Double-click the CD icon to show the CD's contents.**

3. **Double-click the Read Me First icon.**

   This text file contains information about the CD's programs and any last-minute instructions you need to know about installing the programs on the CD that we don't cover in this appendix.

4. **Open your browser.**

   If you don't have a browser, we have included Microsoft Internet Explorer on the CD.

5. **Select File⇨Open and select the CD titled "Marketing Kit." Double-click the Links.htm file to see an explanation of all files and folders included on the CD.**

6. **Some programs come with installer programs — with those you simply open the program's folder on the CD and double-click the icon with the words "Install" or "Installer."**

   After you have installed the programs that you want, you can eject the CD. Carefully place it back in the plastic jacket of the book for safekeeping.

# What You'll Find on the CD

The CD-ROM contains business software as well as example files, templates, and forms that relate to specific chapters in the book.

## Business software

What follows are descriptions of the software applications available on the CD:

| | |
|---|---|
| Acrobat Reader 4.0 from Adobe Systems | *For Mac and Windows. Evaluation version.* This program lets you view and print Portable Document Format (PDF) files. You can get more information by visiting the Adobe Systems Web site at www.adobe.com. |
| Internet Explorer Microsoft | *Version 5.0 for Windows and Version 4.5 for Mac.* Commercial product. This browser from Microsoft enables you to view Web pages and perform a host of other Internet functions, including e-mail and newsgroups. |

| | |
|---|---|
| BBEdit Lite 4.6 | *For Mac.* This is the freeware version of the popular HTML editor. We also include a demo version of the more full-featured BBEdit 5.1.1. |
| Start Right Marketing | *For Windows. Trial version.* Start Marketing Right is multimedia software that teaches you the fundamentals of marketing. This is a demonstation version of the program. Vendor: Do It Right Software; www.doitright.com. |
| Maximizer 5.5 | *For Windows.* This a trial version of powerful contact manager software that allows you to manage your schedule and keep track of customers, prospects, and vendors. Vendor: Multiactive Software; www.multiactive.com. |
| ecBuilder | *For Windows.* This trial version of ecBuilder lets you create a commerce-capable Web site quickly and easily. Vendor: Multiactive Software; www.multiactive.com. |
| Act! 2000 For Windows | This trial version of ACT! 2000 is an application that helps you create to-do lists, schedules, and contacts databases. Vendor: SalesLogix Corporation; www.saleslogix.com. |
| Graphic Converter | *For Macintosh. Shareware software.* GraphicConverter is a powerful shareware application for Macintosh computers that allows you to open and converts pictures in many different file formats. Vendor: Lemke Software; www.lemkesoft.com. |
| Hotdog Professional 5.5 Webmaster Suite | *For Windows. Trial version.* HotDog Professional provides a flexible, text based HTML authoring environment. Vendor: Sausage Software; www.sausage.com. |

# Chapter files

What follows is a list of all of the documents on the CD.

| | |
|---|---|
| CD0101 | Five-Minute Marketing Plan |
| CD0102 | Sample Car Ad |
| CD0201 | Prospect Analysis Sheet |
| CD0202 | Question Preplanning Form |
| CD0301 | Professional Marketing Associates' "Make the Connection" Telemarketing Scripts |
| CD0302 | Closing Scripts |
| CD0401 | Attitudes of Success Profile |

| | |
|---|---|
| CD0402 | Learning Plan Worksheet |
| CD0501 | Modern Memoirs brochure |
| CD0502, CD0503, and CD0504 | Request letters/e-mails |
| CD0505 | Catalog page from HRD Press |
| CD0601 | The Marketing Research Process |
| CD0602 | Seven Questions to Ask When Reviewing a Survey |
| CD0603 | Customer Debriefing Form |
| CD0604 | 7 X 7 Customer Satisfaction Survey |
| CD0605 | Customer Service Audit |
| CD0606 | Professional Marketing Associates Survey |
| CD0701 | Difficult Customer Diagnostic |
| CD0702 and CD0703 | Interpretation Keys for the Difficult Customer Diagnostic |
| CD0704 and CD0705 | How to Adapt Your Sales Style for a Difficult Customer |
| CD0706 | The Gut (Newsletter expressing a strong style profile |
| CD0801 | The Marketing Audit |
| CD0802 | Marketing Agenda Worksheets |
| CD0803 | Marketing agenda templates |
| CD0804 | DiPeri's Marketing Plan Template (a Microsoft Word document template) |
| CD0901 | Advertising Objective Worksheet (an Excel spreadsheet) |
| CD0902 | Advertising Budget (an Excel spreadsheet) |
| CD1001 | Coupon profitability analysis form (an Excel spreadsheet) |
| CD1101 | Broyhill Furniture's "One Size" Press Release |
| CD1102 | Egreetings.com "Business Travelers" Press Release |
| CD1103 | Egreetings.com "Free Spanish Language Greetings" Press Release |
| CD1104 | Media Contact Sheet Template |
| CD1105 | Publicity Don'ts |
| CD1201 | Evaluation Form 1 |
| CD1202 | Two Dimensions of Your Appeal |
| CD1203 | Evaluation Form 2 |
| CD1301, CD1302, and CD1303 | The Al's Daily Grind campaign |
| CD1304 through CD1306 | Mood ad templates |
| CD1307 through CD1309 | Wisdom ad templates |
| CD 1310 | The Henion Bakery's sign |
| CD1401 | HRD Brochure |

| | |
|---|---|
| CD1402 | Pleiades Brochure |
| CD1403 | UMass Family Business Center Brochure |
| CD1404 | Modern Memoirs Booklet |
| CD1405 | Sample Business Cards |
| CD1406 | Sample Newsletter |
| CD1501 and CD1502 | Collective Copies newsletters |
| CD1503 | Verité Newsletter |
| CD1504 | The UMass Family Business Center newsletter |
| CD1505 | Alfredo's Photo Gallery News |
| CD1701 | Behavioral Planning Worksheets |
| CD1702 | Site Communication Plan worksheet |
| CD1703 | Electronic Newsletter |
| CD1801 | one.html |
| CD1802 | lumber.html |
| CD1803 | tools.html |
| CD1804 | specials.html |
| CD1805 | location.html |
| CD1901 | Ad for Haberman Insurance |

# If You've Got Problems (Of the CD Kind)

I tried my best to compile programs that work on most computers with the minimum system requirements. Alas, your computer may differ, and some programs may not work properly for some reason.

The two likeliest problems are that you don't have enough memory (RAM) for the programs you want to use, or you have other programs running that are affecting installation or running of a program. If you get error messages like `Not enough memory` or `Setup cannot continue`, try one or more of these methods and then try using the software again:

- ✔ Turn off any anti-virus software that you have on your computer. Installers sometimes mimic virus activity and may make your computer incorrectly believe that it is being infected by a virus.

- ✔ Close all running programs. The more programs you're running, the less memory is available to other programs. Installers also typically update files and programs. So if you keep other programs running, installation may not work properly.

If you still have trouble with installing the items from the CD, please call the IDG Books Worldwide Customer Service phone number: 800-762-2974 (outside the United States: 317-572-3342).

# Index

# Hungry Minds, Inc., End-User License Agreement

**READ THIS.** You should carefully read these terms and conditions before opening the software packet(s) included with this book ("Book"). This is a license agreement ("Agreement") between you and Hungry Minds, Inc. ("HMI"). By opening the accompanying software packet(s), you acknowledge that you have read and accept the following terms and conditions. If you do not agree and do not want to be bound by such terms and conditions, promptly return the Book and the unopened software packet(s) to the place you obtained them for a full refund.

1. **License Grant.** HMI grants to you (either an individual or entity) a nonexclusive license to use one copy of the enclosed software program(s) (collectively, the "Software") solely for your own personal or business purposes on a single computer (whether a standard computer or a workstation component of a multi-user network). The Software is in use on a computer when it is loaded into temporary memory (RAM) or installed into permanent memory (hard disk, CD-ROM, or other storage device). HMI reserves all rights not expressly granted herein.

2. **Ownership.** HMI is the owner of all right, title, and interest, including copyright, in and to the compilation of the Software recorded on the disk(s) or CD-ROM ("Software Media"). Copyright to the individual programs recorded on the Software Media is owned by the author or other authorized copyright owner of each program. Ownership of the Software and all proprietary rights relating thereto remain with HMI and its licensers.

3. **Restrictions On Use and Transfer.**

   (a) You may only (i) make one copy of the Software for backup or archival purposes, or (ii) transfer the Software to a single hard disk, provided that you keep the original for backup or archival purposes. You may not (i) rent or lease the Software, (ii) copy or reproduce the Software through a LAN or other network system or through any computer subscriber system or bulletin-board system, or (iii) modify, adapt, or create derivative works based on the Software.

   (b) You may not reverse engineer, decompile, or disassemble the Software. You may transfer the Software and user documentation on a permanent basis, provided that the transferee agrees to accept the terms and conditions of this Agreement and you retain no copies. If the Software is an update or has been updated, any transfer must include the most recent update and all prior versions.

4. **Restrictions on Use of Individual Programs.** You must follow the individual requirements and restrictions detailed for each individual program in the "About the CD" appendix of this Book. These limitations are also contained in the individual license agreements recorded on the Software Media. These limitations may include a requirement that after using the program for a specified period of time, the user must pay a registration fee or discontinue use. By opening the Software packet(s), you will be agreeing to abide by the licenses and restrictions for these individual programs that are detailed in the "About the CD" appendix and on the Software Media. None of the material on this Software Media or listed in this Book may ever be redistributed, in original or modified form, for commercial purposes.

5.  **Limited Warranty.**

    (a) HMI warrants that the Software and Software Media are free from defects in materials and workmanship under normal use for a period of sixty (60) days from the date of purchase of this Book. If HMI receives notification within the warranty period of defects in materials or workmanship, HMI will replace the defective Software Media.

    (b) HMI AND THE AUTHOR OF THE BOOK DISCLAIM ALL OTHER WARRANTIES, EXPRESS OR IMPLIED, INCLUDING WITHOUT LIMITATION IMPLIED WARRANTIES OF MERCHANTABILITY AND FITNESS FOR A PARTICULAR PURPOSE, WITH RESPECT TO THE SOFTWARE, THE PROGRAMS, THE SOURCE CODE CONTAINED THEREIN, AND/OR THE TECHNIQUES DESCRIBED IN THIS BOOK. HMI DOES NOT WARRANT THAT THE FUNCTIONS CONTAINED IN THE SOFTWARE WILL MEET YOUR REQUIREMENTS OR THAT THE OPERATION OF THE SOFTWARE WILL BE ERROR FREE.

    (c) This limited warranty gives you specific legal rights, and you may have other rights that vary from jurisdiction to jurisdiction.

6.  **Remedies.**

    (a) HMI's entire liability and your exclusive remedy for defects in materials and workmanship shall be limited to replacement of the Software Media, which may be returned to HMI with a copy of your receipt at the following address: Software Media Fulfillment Department, Attn.: *Marketing Kit For Dummies,* Hungry Minds, Inc., 10475 Crosspoint Blvd., Indianapolis, IN 46256, or call 1-800-762-2974. Please allow four to six weeks for delivery. This Limited Warranty is void if failure of the Software Media has resulted from accident, abuse, or misapplication. Any replacement Software Media will be warranted for the remainder of the original warranty period or thirty (30) days, whichever is longer.

    (b) In no event shall HMI or the author be liable for any damages whatsoever (including without limitation damages for loss of business profits, business interruption, loss of business information, or any other pecuniary loss) arising from the use of or inability to use the Book or the Software, even if HMI has been advised of the possibility of such damages.

    (c) Because some jurisdictions do not allow the exclusion or limitation of liability for consequential or incidental damages, the above limitation or exclusion may not apply to you.

7.  **U.S. Government Restricted Rights.** Use, duplication, or disclosure of the Software for or on behalf of the United States of America, its agencies and/or instrumentalities (the "U.S. Government") is subject to restrictions as stated in paragraph (c)(1)(ii) of the Rights in Technical Data and Computer Software clause of DFARS 252.227-7013, in subparagraphs (a) through (d) of the Commercial Computer–Restricted Rights clause at FAR 52.227-19, and in similar clauses in the NASA FAR supplement, when applicable.

8.  **General.** This Agreement constitutes the entire understanding of the parties and revokes and supersedes all prior agreements, oral or written, between them and may not be modified or amended except in a writing signed by both parties hereto that specifically refers to this Agreement. This Agreement shall take precedence over any other documents that may be in conflict herewith. If any one or more provisions contained in this Agreement are held by any court or tribunal to be invalid, illegal, or otherwise unenforceable, each and every other provision shall remain in full force and effect.

# Installation Instructions

The *Marketing Kit For Dummies* CD offers valuable information that you won't want to miss. To install the items from the CD to your hard drive, follow these steps (which are for computers using Windows):

1. **Insert the CD into your computer's CD-ROM drive.**

   Give your computer a moment to take a look at the CD.

2. **Open your browser.** Click on File⇨Open (Internet Explorer) or on File⇨Open Page (Netscape).

3. **Double click the file called License.txt.**

   This file contains the end-user license that you agree to by using the CD. When you are done reading the license, close the program, most likely NotePad, that displayed the file.

4. **Double click the file called Readme.txt.**

   This file contains instructions about installing the software from this CD. It might be helpful to leave this text file open while you are using the CD.

5. **In the dialog box that appears, type** `D:\START.HTM` **and click on OK.**

6. **Replace the letter D: with the correct letter for your CD-ROM drive, if it is not "D".**

   This action will display the file that will walk you through the content of the CD.

7. **To navigate within the interface, simply click on any topic of interest to take you to an explanation of the files on the CD and how to use or install them.** You will see Install buttons that will install the software for you. When you select that option, instead of installing directly from the CD, select Open this file when the Download File dialog box pops up. After you are done with the interface, simply close your browser as usual.

If you use a Macintosh computer, you can also use the documents on this CD. Simply insert the CD into your computer's CD-ROM drive, double-click the CD icon when it appears on the desktop, and read the Read Me file.

For more information, please see the "About the CD" appendix in this book.